KINGS OF STONE

The Hittite Enigma

R Jay Driskill

RED PIRATE MEDIA

KINGS OF STONE: THE HITTITE ENIGMA

Copyright © 2025 by R Jay Driskill

Published by Red Pirate Media, New York, NY

All rights reserved. Printed in the United States of America. No part of this book may be used or reproduced in any manner whatsoever without written permission except in the case of brief quotations embodied in critical articles or reviews.

For information contact: Red Pirate Media http://www.rjaydriskill.com

All Chapter Photos Courtesy of The Met

Map: "Ancient Near East 1400BC" by Enyavar is licensed under CC BY-SA 4.0.

Library of Congress Control Number: 2025916619

ISBN: 978-1-968989-00-2 Ebook

ISBN: 978-1-968989-01-9 Paperback

ISBN: 978-1-968989-02-6 Hardback

ISBN: 978-1-968989-03-3 Audiobook

First Edition: September 2025

10 9 8 7 6 5 4 3 2 1

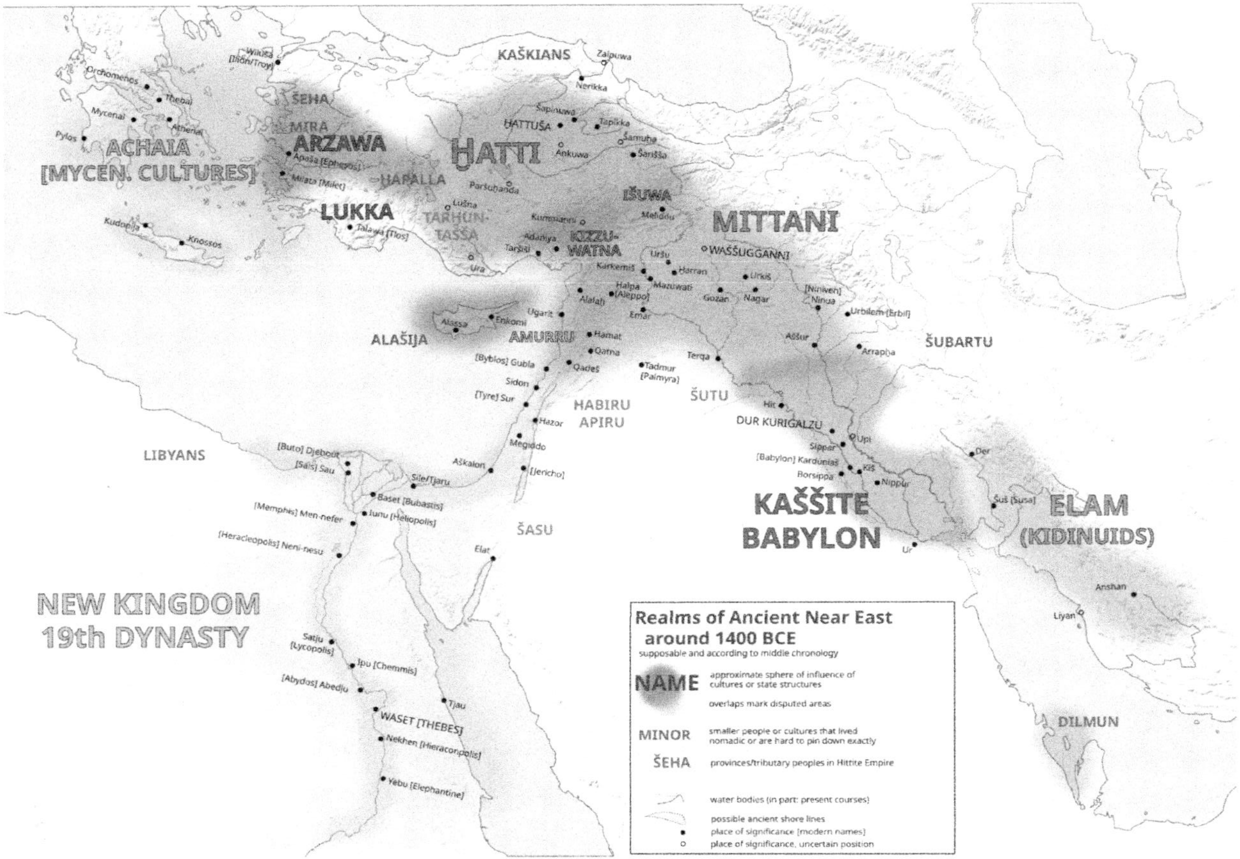

Realms of Ancient Near East
around 1400 BCE
supposable and according to middle chronology
NAME
approximate sphere of influence of cultures or state structures
overlaps mark disputed areas
MINOR
smaller people or cultures that lived nomadic or are hard to pin down exactly
ŠEHA
provinces/tributary peoples in Hittite Empire
water bodies (in part: present courses)
possible ancient shore lines
place of significance [modern names]
place of significance, uncertain position
ACHAIA
[MYCEN. CULTURES]
ARZAWA
MIRA
ŠEHA
LUKKA
HAPALLA
HATTI
TARHUN-
TAŠŠA
KIZZU-
WATNA
IŠUWA
MITTANI
KAŠKIANS
ALAŠIJA
AMURRU
HABIRU
APIRU
ŠUTU
ŠUBARTU
ŠASU
LIBYANS
KAŠŠITE
BABYLON
ELAM
(KIDINUIDS)
DILMUN
NEW KINGDOM
19th DYNASTY
Wiluša [Ilion/Troy]
Orchomenos
Thebai
Mycenai
Athenai
Pylos
Kudonija
Knossos
Apaša [Ephesos]
Milata [Milet]
Talawa [Tlos]
Zalpuwa
Nerikka
Šapinuwa
HATTUŠA
Tapikka
Šamuha
Ankuwa
Šarišša
Paršuhanda
Lušna
Ura
Kummanni
Adaniya
Taršiš
Melidu
WAŠŠUGGANNI
Uršu
Harran
Karkemiš
Mazuwati
Urkiš
Gozan
Nagar
Halpa [Aleppo]
Alalah
Emar
Ugarit
Enkomi
Alassa
Hamat
Qatna
Qadeš
[Byblos] Gubla
Sidon
[Tyre] Sur
Hazor
Megiddo
[Jericho]
Aškalon
Tadmur [Palmyra]
Terqa
[Niniveh] Ninua
Urbilem [Erbil]
Aššur
Arrapha
Hit
DUR KURIGALZU
Upi
Sippar
[Babylon] Karduniaš
Kiš
Borsippa
Nippur
Ur
Der
Šuš [Susa]
Anshan
Liyan
[Buto] Djebout
[Saïs] Sau
Sile/Tjaru
Baset [Bubastis]
[Memphis] Men-nefer
Iunu [Heliopolis]
[Heracleopolis] Neni-nesu
Elat
Satju [Lycopolis]
Ipu [Chemmis]
[Abydos] Abedju
Tjau
WASET [THEBES]
Nekhen [Hieraconpolis]
Yebu [Elephantine]

CONTENTS

Also by R Jay Driskill	VII
Epigraph	IX
Preface	1
Introduction: Rediscovering a Lost Empire	4
1. The Indo-European Arrival	17
2. The Emergence of Hittite Kingdoms	31
3. Toward Political Unification	44
4. Ḫattušili I and the Foundation of Empire	59
5. The Sack of Babylon and Its Consequences	71
6. Political Fragmentation and Recovery	84
7. Tudḫaliya I/II and Imperial Restoration	97
8. Šuppiluliuma I: The Great Conqueror	111
9. International Relations and the Great Power System	123
10. Muršili II and the Consolidation of Empire	135
11. Muwatalli II and the Egyptian Confrontation	150
12. Ḫattušili III and the Egyptian Peace	161
13. Tudḫaliya IV and the Beginning of Decline	173
14. Hittite Society and Administration	186

15.	Economy and Material Culture	199
16.	The Thousand Gods of Hatti	212
17.	Languages, Literature, and Learning	226
18.	The End of the Hittite Empire	243
19.	The Neo-Hittite Kingdoms	255
20.	Rediscovery and Modern Scholarship	269
21.	The Hittite Achievement in Historical Perspective	283
Appendix A: Chronological Data		297
Appendix B: Translation Excerpts		302
Bibliography		312
About the Author		327

Also by R Jay Driskill

Sunset in Bronze Series:

Stone Kings: The Hittite Enigma
Raiders of the Bronze Age Collapse: The Sea Peoples in Legend, History, and Archaeology
Ghosts of Arzawa: Beyond the Trojan War Myth
Song of a Lost City: Troy in Myth, Fiction, and Fact

"Whom the Gods would destroy, they first make mad."

Euripedes

PREFACE

It was a quite unexpected result, when my first exposure to Hittite cuneiform tablets at the University of Chicago's Oriental Institute launched me into years of dedicated study of Late Bronze Age Anatolia. The Hittites—once a forgotten empire whose very existence scholars doubted—have gradually emerged from historical obscurity to take their rightful place among the great civilizations of the ancient Near East. This book represents my attempt to synthesize the remarkable archaeological and philological discoveries of the past century into a comprehensive history accessible to both scholars and general readers.

The Hittite Empire, which flourished in Anatolia (modern Turkey) from approximately 1650 to 1180 BCE, stood as a formidable counterweight to Egypt, Babylonia, and Assyria. At its height, under rulers like Suppiluliuma I and Ḫattušili III, Hittite influence extended from the Aegean Sea to the Euphrates River. Their military innovations, diplomatic achievements, and legal traditions profoundly shaped the ancient world. Yet until the decipherment of their language in the early 20th century, they remained largely a biblical footnote—mysterious people mentioned fleetingly in the Old Testament.

My fascination with the Hittites began with their paradoxical nature: a people simultaneously central to ancient Near Eastern politics yet peripheral to our historical consciousness; innovators who adapted and synthesized cultural elements from their neighbors while maintaining distinct traditions; empire-builders who left behind thousands of clay tablets but whose capital at Hattuša fell into such complete ruin that their very existence was questioned until modern archaeological discoveries.

This book traces the arc of Hittite civilization from its origins in the early second millennium BCE through its imperial phase and ultimate collapse around 1180 BCE in the tumultuous "Sea Peoples" period. I have endeavored to integrate the latest archaeological findings with translations of key texts to present a multidimensional view of Hittite society, religion, diplomacy, and everyday life.

ACKNOWLEDGMENTS

This work would not have been possible without the generous support of numerous institutions and individuals. The German Archaeological Institute's ongoing excavations at Hattuša have been an invaluable resource, and I thank Directors Hans Schmidt and Andreas Schachner for access to their research.

My intellectual debt to pioneering Hittitologists cannot be overstated. The groundbreaking work of Hans Gustav Güterbock, Harry Hoffner, and Theo van den Hout at the Chicago Hittite Dictionary Project shaped my understanding of Hittite language and culture. Trevor Bryce's historical studies and Itamar Singer's insights into Hittite religion have been constant companions throughout this project.

Special thanks go to the staff of the Anatolian Civilizations Museum in Ankara and the Museum of Ancient Oriental Civilizations in Istanbul for facilitating my study of artifacts in their collections. The Turkish General Directorate of Monuments and Museums has been exceptionally supportive of foreign scholars in Turkey.

Any errors or omissions remain entirely my responsibility.

NOTE ON TRANSLITERATION AND DATING CONVENTIONS

Hittite texts present unique challenges for modern scholars. The Hittites employed a cuneiform writing system borrowed from Mesopotamia but adapted it to write their Indo-European language. Throughout this book, I follow the standard conventions for transliterating Hittite: italicized lowercase letters represent phonetic values, while uppercase letters indicate Sumerian and Akkadian logograms.

Personal names present difficulties. I have opted for the most accurate renderings of royal names (e.g., Ḫattušili rather than Hattusili)), while noting alternative forms where scholarly consensus is lacking. Place names generally appear in their Hittite forms as well, with modern equivalents provided at first mention.

For dating, I employ the "Middle Chronology," placing the fall of Babylon to the Hittites at approximately 1595 BCE. All dates should be understood as approximate, particularly for the earlier periods. Where scholarly disagreement exists regarding significant dates, I note the range of possibilities.

The Hittite scribes themselves dated events by regnal years rather than by an absolute chronology. When quoting Hittite texts directly, I preserve their original dating system while providing BCE equivalents in brackets.

INTRODUCTION: REDISCOVERING A LOST EMPIRE

The Hittites emerge from the fog of prehistory as one of antiquity's most enigmatic peoples. For nearly three millennia, their existence was known primarily through scattered references in the Hebrew Bible and occasional mentions in Egyptian texts. Unlike the civilizations of Egypt or Mesopotamia, which maintained a continuous presence in historical consciousness, the Hittites vanished so completely that scholars once questioned whether they had existed at all. Their rediscovery and the gradual reconstruction of their history represents one of archaeology's most remarkable achievements—a testament to the power of interdisciplinary scholarship to resurrect lost worlds.

This book aims to present the current state of Hittite studies, integrating textual analysis with archaeological evidence to construct a comprehensive picture of this Bronze Age superpower. The Hittite civilization, centered in what is now central Turkey, dominated much of Anatolia and northern Syria from approximately 1650 to 1180 BCE. At their height, they rivaled Egypt for control of the Near East, forging the world's first recorded peace treaty after the famous Battle of Kadesh. Yet despite these accomplishments, they remain less familiar to the general public than their contemporaries in Egypt, Babylon, or Assyria.

In the chapters that follow, I trace the rise, flourishing, and ultimate collapse of the Hittite state, examining its political institutions, religious practices, artistic achievements, and everyday life. Special attention is given to the extensive diplomatic correspondence that reveals a sophisticated system of international relations in the Late Bronze Age. By placing the Hittites within their broader Mediterranean and Near Eastern context, I hope to demonstrate their crucial role in the development of ancient civilizations and their lasting impact on subsequent cultures.

The Mystery of the Hittites in Biblical and Ancient Sources

The Hebrew Bible mentions the Hittites over forty times, portraying them as one of the indigenous peoples of Canaan. In Genesis 23, Abraham purchases the cave of Machpelah from Ephron the Hittite as a burial place for his wife Sarah. Later biblical passages describe Hittites serving in King David's army, most famously Uriah, whose wife Bathsheba became David's consort after Uriah's death. The biblical Hittites appear as a relatively minor group inhabiting the hill country of Palestine, quite different from the imperial power revealed by modern archaeology.

This discrepancy puzzled 19th-century scholars. Biblical references suggested a Canaanite tribe of limited significance, yet Egyptian monuments recorded battles against a formidable "Kheta" empire centered far to the north in Anatolia. The annals of Pharaoh Thutmose III (c. 1479-1425 BCE) mention tribute from the "great Kheta," while the famous Battle of Kadesh, immortalized in Ramesses II's monumental inscriptions around 1274 BCE, pitted Egypt against a powerful Hittite coalition. Assyrian records similarly referred to a land of "Khatti" in central Anatolia.

Classical Greek and Roman sources, however, preserved no memory of a Hittite empire. When Herodotus traveled through Anatolia in the 5th century BCE, he attributed ancient monuments to various peoples but never mentioned Hittites. The Neo-Assyrian empire's records from the 9th-7th centuries BCE refer to "Hatti-land," but by then this was merely a geographical term rather than a reference to the Hittite state, which had collapsed centuries earlier. The disconnect between biblical Hittites and these fragmentary references from other sources created a historical puzzle that would remain unsolved until the late 19th century.

Early travelers to the Near East occasionally noted curious hieroglyphic inscriptions in northern Syria and central Anatolia that resembled neither Egyptian nor Mesopotamian writing systems. In 1812, the Swiss explorer Johann Ludwig Burckhardt documented monuments at Hamath (modern Hama in Syria) bearing these strange symbols. Similar inscriptions were discovered throughout the 19th century across Turkey and northern Syria, but scholars could not determine who had created them or what they said.

The Irish missionary William Wright, working in Syria in the 1870s, was among the first to connect these mysterious inscriptions with the biblical Hittites. In his 1884 book "The Empire of the Hittites," Wright proposed these monuments represented the remains of a once-powerful empire centered in Anatolia that had extended its influence into northern Syria—potentially matching the "Kheta" of Egyptian texts and the biblical Hittites. British archaeologist Archibald Henry Sayce developed this hypothesis further, suggesting that the peculiar hieroglyphic script represented the Hittite language.

While these early scholars correctly identified the general connection, they lacked sufficient evidence to reconstruct Hittite history with any precision. The breakthrough would come not from these hieroglyphic inscriptions (now known as Luwian hieroglyphs, primarily used in the southern provinces and successor states), but from the discovery of thousands of clay tablets written in cuneiform—the wedge-shaped writing system of Mesopotamia—at the site of Boğazköy in central Turkey.

Archaeological Breakthrough: Boğazköy and the Decipherment of Hittite

The ruins at Boğazköy (modern Boğazkale) had attracted scholarly attention since the early 19th century. In 1834, the French architect and archaeologist Charles

Texier discovered the site, documenting impressive stone reliefs at the nearby rock sanctuary of Yazılıkaya. Local villagers had long known about the extensive ruins, but their significance remained unclear until systematic excavations began.

The crucial breakthrough came in 1893-94 when Ernest Chantre, a French archaeologist, uncovered cuneiform tablets at Boğazköy written in multiple languages. The real watershed moment, however, arrived in 1906 when Hugo Winckler, a German Assyriologist, began excavations in collaboration with the Ottoman archaeologist Theodore Makridi. Their work revealed a vast archive of over 10,000 clay tablets and fragments in the ruins of what proved to be the ancient Hittite capital, Hattuša.

Scribes primarily wrote the tablets in cuneiform, the wedge-shaped writing system developed in Mesopotamia, but many were clearly not in Akkadian, the lingua franca of the Late Bronze Age Near East. Winckler recognized he had discovered the archives of the Hittite state, confirming that Boğazköy was indeed Hattuša, the capital mentioned in Egyptian and Assyrian sources.

The decipherment of the Hittite language represents one of philology's outstanding achievements. In 1915, the Czech linguist Bedřich Hrozný, then working in Vienna, made the crucial breakthrough. While examining tablets from Boğazköy, he noticed a sentence that read: "*nu NINDA-an ezzatteni watar-ma ekutteni.*" The words NINDA and watar appeared in contexts suggesting they meant "bread" and "water." Based on the Indo-European pattern of the surrounding words, Hrozný correctly translated the phrase as "Now you will eat bread and drink water."

This insight led to the astonishing realization that Hittite was an Indo-European language—the earliest attested member of this language family, which includes Sanskrit, Greek, Latin, and most modern European languages. Previously, no Indo-European language was known to have been written before around 1500 BCE, and none had been documented in Anatolia before the arrival of Greek-speaking peoples after 1200 BCE. The discovery that the Hittites spoke an

Indo-European language revolutionized understanding of ancient Anatolia and Indo-European prehistory.

Hrozný published his decipherment in 1915, but World War I delayed wider recognition of his achievement. By the 1930s, however, the basics of Hittite grammar and vocabulary were established, allowing scholars to begin translating the vast corpus of texts from Boğazköy. The German Archaeological Institute resumed excavations at the site in 1931 under Kurt Bittel, work that continues to the present day with only occasional interruptions.

The texts revealed the Hittites called themselves "people of the land of Hatti," though ironically, they had adopted this name from the non-Indo-European Hattians, whom they had conquered. Their own language was called "Nesili," after the city of Nesa (also known as Kanesh, modern Kültepe), an early center of Hittite power. The archives included historical annals, religious rituals, international treaties, legal codes, administrative documents, literary works, and correspondence—a comprehensive record of a complex Bronze Age state.

Alongside Boğazköy, excavations at other sites have enhanced our understanding of Hittite civilization. At Kültepe (ancient Kanesh) near modern Kayseri, excavations revealed an Assyrian trading colony from the early second millennium BCE, documenting the period immediately preceding the rise of the Hittite state. The site yielded over 23,000 cuneiform tablets, mostly commercial records of Assyrian merchants, but also including some of the earliest documents in the Hittite language. These texts illuminate the transitional period when Indo-European speaking groups were establishing political control in central Anatolia.

Other important Hittite sites include Alaca Höyük, with its monumental sphinx gate and royal tombs; Maşat Höyük (ancient Tapikka), which yielded provincial administrative archives; and Ortaköy (ancient Sapinuwa), a major administrative center that served briefly as an alternative capital. In the southeast, sites like Carchemish and Tell Atchana (ancient Alalakh) document Hittite imperial control in Syria, while Eflatun Pınar and Yalburt preserve monumental inscriptions from the Empire period.

The material culture revealed by these excavations—monumental architecture, sculpture, ceramics, metalwork—complements the textual evidence, offering insights into aspects of Hittite society not covered in the written record. Particularly impressive are the massive stone fortifications of Hattuša, with walls up to 8 meters thick and elaborate gateways adorned with sculptures of lions, sphinxes, and warriors. The nearby rock sanctuary of Yazılıkaya, with its reliefs depicting a procession of deities, represents one of the most important religious monuments of the ancient Near East.

Historiographical Overview and Methodological Approaches

The study of Hittite civilization has evolved significantly over the past century, reflecting broader developments in archaeological and historical methodology. Early work focused primarily on political history, using the royal annals and international treaties to reconstruct the sequence of kings and their military campaigns. Scholars like Emil Forrer, Albrecht Goetze, and Hans Gustav Güterbock established the basic chronological framework in the 1920s and 1930s.

The post-World War II period saw increasing attention to social and economic aspects of Hittite civilization. The work of Sedat Alp, Heinrich Otten, and Emmanuel Laroche expanded understanding of Hittite religion, while scholars like Harry Hoffner and Theo van den Hout examined legal and administrative texts to illuminate social structure and economic organization. The Chicago Hittite Dictionary project, initiated in 1975, has provided an invaluable lexicographical foundation for all aspects of Hittite studies.

In recent decades, interdisciplinary approaches have become increasingly important. Paleoclimatology has offered insights into how environmental factors affected Hittite agriculture and settlement patterns. Dendrochronology (tree-ring dating) and radiocarbon analysis have refined chronological frameworks. DNA studies of human remains from Hittite sites promise to illuminate questions of population movement and ethnicity that textual sources alone cannot answer.

The methodological challenges in Hittite studies remain substantial. The texts, while numerous, represent primarily elite perspectives—the viewpoints of kings, priests, and scribes. Archaeological evidence helps balance this bias, but rural settlements and common people's lives remain underrepresented. The chronology, particularly for the early periods, continues to be debated, with competing "high," "middle," and "low" chronologies differing by up to a century in their dating of key events.

A particularly fruitful approach has been the integration of Hittite studies into the broader context of Eastern Mediterranean and Near Eastern interconnections during the Late Bronze Age. The Hittite empire existed within a complex international system that included Egypt, Babylonia, Assyria, Mitanni, and Mycenaean Greece. Treaties, diplomatic correspondence, and trade goods document extensive interaction among these powers. The Amarna letters from Egypt, the Ugaritic archives from coastal Syria, and Mycenaean Linear B tablets all complement the Hittite sources, allowing reconstruction of this international system.

Trevor Bryce's historical studies have been particularly influential in synthesizing textual and archaeological evidence to create comprehensive political narratives. Itamar Singer's work on Hittite religion and cultural interactions illuminated the syncretistic nature of Hittite culture, which absorbed elements from Hattic, Hurrian, and Mesopotamian traditions. Jürgen Seeher's archaeological work at Hattuša has transformed understanding of the capital's urban development and fortifications.

Recent scholarship has increasingly emphasized the multiethnic, multilingual nature of the Hittite state. Rather than viewing the Hittites as a homogeneous ethnic group, scholars now recognize the kingdom as a political entity encompassing diverse populations speaking Hittite, Luwian, Palaic, Hattic, Hurrian, and other languages. This perspective helps explain the apparent contradictions in earlier sources and bridges the gap between the imperial Hittites of Anatolian records and the more localized groups mentioned in biblical texts.

Sources: Cuneiform Archives, Archaeological Evidence, Egyptian and Assyrian Records

The reconstruction of Hittite history depends on integrating multiple categories of evidence, each with its strengths and limitations. The primary sources fall into four major categories: the Hittite cuneiform archives, archaeological remains from Hittite sites, contemporaneous records from neighboring civilizations, and later traditions preserved in classical and biblical texts.

Cuneiform Archives

The cuneiform tablets from Boğazköy form the cornerstone of Hittite studies. Over 30,000 tablets and fragments have been recovered to date, making this one of the most extensive archives from the ancient Near East. The texts span approximately five centuries, from the Old Kingdom (c. 1650-1400 BCE) through the Empire period (c. 1400-1180 BCE), with the majority dating to the later periods.

The Hittite archives are remarkable for their diversity. Historical texts include the Annals of Ḫattušili I, Mursili II, and other kings, which record military campaigns and political developments. International treaties document relations with neighboring states, from the Treaty of Kuruštama with Egypt (c. 1400 BCE) to the famous Egyptian-Hittite Peace Treaty between Ḫattušili III and Ramesses II (c. 1259 BCE), copies of which were inscribed on silver tablets and mounted on temple walls in both capitals.

Legal texts include the Hittite Law Code, which exists in multiple versions showing its evolution over time. Administrative documents record palace operations, provincial governance, land grants, and economic activities. Religious texts comprise the largest category, including detailed instructions for festivals, rituals, prayers, and myths. Many of these religious texts preserve traditions from non-Hittite peoples within the empire, particularly Hattic and Hurrian traditions.

Literary works include translations of Mesopotamian classics like the Gilgamesh Epic, as well as native compositions like the "Song of Release" and the "Kingship in Heaven" cycle. Letters illuminate diplomatic relations and administrative matters, from correspondence between kings and foreign rulers to communications between the central government and provincial officials.

The Hittite scribes wrote primarily on clay tablets, using a simplified version of the Mesopotamian cuneiform script. Most tablets were sun-dried rather than kiln-fired, making them vulnerable to water damage and other forms of deterioration. Paradoxically, the final destruction of Hattuša around 1180 BCE actually preserved many tablets by baking them in the fires that consumed the city's buildings.

Smaller archives have been found at provincial centers like Maşat Höyük (ancient Tapikka) and Ortaköy (ancient Sapinuwa), offering insights into regional administration. The tablets from Kültepe (ancient Kanesh) primarily document the Old Assyrian trading colony of the early second millennium BCE but include some of the earliest attestations of the Hittite language.

One methodological challenge in working with these texts is their often fragmentary nature. Many tablets were damaged in antiquity or during excavation, requiring painstaking reconstruction. Dating texts precisely can be difficult, as scribes rarely included absolute dates. Linguistic challenges persist despite a century of scholarship; the meaning of many words remains uncertain, and grammatical peculiarities continue to be debated.

Archaeological Evidence

Archaeological excavations complement and extend the textual record, documenting aspects of Hittite civilization that written sources don't address. The monumental architecture of Hattuša—its massive fortifications, temples, palaces, and storehouses—demonstrates the state's organizational capacity and ideological priorities. The city's layout evolved over time, with an older Lower City and a newer Upper City reflecting different phases of urban planning.

Distinctive Hittite architectural features include massive stone foundations for mud-brick superstructures, postern tunnels through fortification walls, and monumental gateways adorned with sculpture. Religious structures range from formal temples in the Upper City to the open-air rock sanctuary at Yazılıkaya, where relief carvings depict processions of deities.

Material culture offers insights into technological capabilities, artistic traditions, and everyday life. Hittite ceramics evolved from the distinctive "Cappadocian ware" of the early second millennium to the standardized mass-produced wares of the Empire period. Metalwork shows sophisticated techniques in bronze, silver, and gold, from practical weapons and tools to elaborate ritual objects and jewelry.

Burial practices varied across regions and over time. Royal tombs at Alaca Höyük from the Early Bronze Age (predating the Hittite state proper) contained spectacular grave goods, including solar discs and animal figurines in bronze and precious metals. Later Hittite practice favored cremation, with ashes placed in ceramic urns, though inhumation continued in some areas.

Settlement patterns document the organization of the Hittite landscape. The capital Hattuša, was surrounded by smaller administrative centers, agricultural villages, and religious sites. Monumental dams and reservoirs demonstrate sophisticated water management, crucial in the semi-arid central Anatolian plateau. Roads connected major centers, with bridges and rock-cut passages facilitating movement through the rugged terrain.

Bioarchaeological evidence provides information on diet, health, and population demographics. Paleobotanical remains document agricultural practices, with wheat, barley, and legumes as staple crops. Archaeozoological studies show animal husbandry focused on sheep, goats, cattle, and pigs, with horses reserved primarily for military and elite use.

Egyptian and Assyrian Records

Contemporary records from neighboring civilizations offer external perspectives on the Hittites. Egyptian sources are particularly valuable, documenting interactions from the early 15th century BCE through the end of the Hittite Empire. The Annals of Thutmose III mention the "great Kheta" among the powers of Western Asia. The extensive documentation of the Battle of Kadesh (c. 1274 BCE) between Ramesses II and Muwatalli II includes both textual accounts and visual representations on temple walls at Karnak, Luxor, Abu Simbel, and other sites.

The Amarna letters, a diplomatic archive from the reign of Pharaoh Akhenaten (c. 1350 BCE), include correspondence with Hittite kings Suppiluliuma I and Mursili II. These letters document the complex diplomatic maneuvering that characterized international relations in the Late Bronze Age, including the famous request from an Egyptian queen (possibly Ankhesenamun, widow of Tutankhamun) for a Hittite prince to marry.

Assyrian records mention the Hittites as both allies and adversaries. The Old Assyrian trading colony at Kanesh provides crucial documentation for the period preceding the Hittite state. Later Neo-Assyrian inscriptions refer to campaigns against Neo-Hittite successor states in northern Syria, preserving memories of Hittite traditions centuries after the empire's collapse.

Babylonian chronicles occasionally mention Hittite affairs, most notably the raid on Babylon by Mursili I around 1595 BCE, which ended the First Dynasty of Babylon. Ugaritic texts from coastal Syria document interactions with the Hittite empire during its control of northern Syria in the 13th century BCE.

Later Traditions

The Hebrew Bible preserves memories of Hittite populations in Syria-Palestine, though these likely represent Neo-Hittite groups of the Iron Age rather than the Bronze Age empire. Classical Greek and Roman authors occasionally mention "Syrians" or "White Syrians" (Leucosyrians) in Anatolia who may preserve aspects of Hittite heritage, but direct historical memory of the empire had faded by the first millennium BCE.

Medieval and early modern travelers occasionally noted the impressive ruins and rock monuments of central Anatolia but couldn't identify their creators. Only with the archaeological discoveries of the late 19th and early 20th centuries did the Hittites emerge from historical obscurity to take their place among the great civilizations of the ancient Near East.

Synthesis and Integration

Integrating these diverse sources—textual, archaeological, comparative—allows for a nuanced reconstruction of Hittite history and society. Where texts describe military campaigns, archaeology can document their destructive impact on settlements. When royal inscriptions proclaim agricultural prosperity, paleobotanical evidence can confirm or challenge these claims. Foreign sources provide crucial external perspectives, balancing the Hittites' own presentation of events.

This multidisciplinary approach has transformed our understanding of the Hittites over the past century. From fragmentary biblical references and mysterious monuments, scholarship has reconstructed a complex civilization that dominated Anatolia for half a millennium and shaped the history of the entire Near East. The Hittite archives preserve not only their own traditions but also those of earlier Anatolian cultures that would otherwise be lost to history.

The following chapters examine specific aspects of Hittite civilization in detail: political history, social structure, religion, international relations, art and architecture, and the empire's ultimate collapse around 1180 BCE. Throughout, I emphasize both the Hittites' distinctive characteristics and their connections to the broader world of the Late Bronze Age Mediterranean and Near East. By placing the Hittites in their proper historical context, we gain not only a better understanding of this specific civilization but also insights into the complex interconnections that characterized the ancient world.

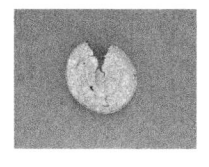

Chapter 1

THE INDO-EUROPEAN ARRIVAL

The Indo-European Question

The origins of the Hittites represent one of the most fascinating problems in ancient Near Eastern history. When Bedřich Hrozný deciphered the Hittite language in 1915, his most startling discovery was its unmistakable Indo-European character. This finding revolutionized our understanding not only of Anatolian history but also of Indo-European linguistics itself. As the earliest attested Indo-European language by several centuries, Hittite suddenly provided crucial evidence for reconstructing Proto-Indo-European and tracing the dispersal of its daughter languages.

The presence of an Indo-European language in central Anatolia by the early second millennium BCE raised fundamental questions: When and how did Indo-European speakers arrive in the region? What was their relationship with the indigenous populations they encountered? How did the distinctive Hittite culture emerge from this cultural contact? These questions continue to animate scholarly debate, with significant advances in recent decades through interdisciplinary research combining linguistics, archaeology, and archaeogenetics.

Proto-Hittite Migrations into Anatolia

Chronology and Routes of Entry

The timing of Indo-European migrations into Anatolia remains contested. The traditional view, advanced by scholars like Hans Gustav Güterbock and Albrecht Goetze in the mid-20th century, placed this migration around 2300-2000 BCE, coinciding with the transition from the Early to Middle Bronze Age. This chronology aligned with apparent disruptions in settlement patterns and material culture during this period, particularly in central Anatolia.

More recent linguistic research, however, suggests a considerably earlier timeframe. As Craig Melchert and others have demonstrated, the Anatolian languages (including Hittite, Luwian, Palaic, and later attestations like Lycian and Lydian) diverged from Proto-Indo-European at an early stage, before many innovations shared by other Indo-European branches. This linguistic evidence points to a separation perhaps as early as the fourth millennium BCE, making the Anatolian branch the first to diverge from Proto-Indo-European.

Archaeological evidence for this earlier chronology remains elusive, however. Archaeologist James Mellaart once proposed identifying the earliest Indo-European presence with the Demircihöyük culture of northwestern Anatolia (c. 3500-2500 BCE), but this connection remains speculative. More recently, David Anthony and Kristian Kristiansen have associated early Indo-European dispersals with the expansion of Yamnaya pastoralists from the Pontic-Caspian steppe after 3300 BCE, potentially including movements into Anatolia.

The routes by which Indo-European speakers entered Anatolia also remain uncertain. Three main possibilities have been proposed:

Recent archaeogenetic studies have shed new light on these questions. A 2019 study by Lazaridis et al. analyzed ancient DNA from Anatolian archaeological sites, finding evidence for steppe ancestry appearing in central Anatolia during the Early Bronze Age (c. 2800-2400 BCE). This timing broadly supports the traditional archaeological model, while being somewhat later than the linguistic evidence might suggest. However, the genetic contribution appears relatively modest, suggesting cultural and linguistic change may have occurred without wholesale population replacement.

Material Culture and Archaeological Signatures

Identifying archaeological signatures of early Indo-European speakers in Anatolia remains challenging. Unlike the Yamnaya expansion into Europe, which can be traced through distinctive burial practices and material culture, the material evidence in Anatolia shows more gradual transitions. This suggests a complex process of infiltration and acculturation rather than a single, dramatic invasion.

The Early Bronze Age III period (c. 2400-2000 BCE) does show significant changes in settlement patterns across central Anatolia, with many sites showing evidence of destruction or abandonment followed by rebuilding with modified architectural forms. At Alacahöyük, for instance, the famous "royal tombs" with their distinctive metalwork cease after this period, suggesting a significant cultural shift. Similar transitions are visible at sites like Kültepe, Alişar Höyük, and Acemhöyük.

Significant changes in ceramic traditions also appear during this period. The distinctive wheel-made "depas cups" and other forms associated with the "Anatolian Trade Network" of the mid-third millennium give way to new styles, including what Thissen has identified as "Central Anatolian Burnished Ware." These ceramic transitions, however, show regional variation and gradual adoption rather than sudden replacement, again suggesting a complex process of cultural interaction rather than simple replacement.

Changes in metallurgical traditions during this period may also reflect new populations or influences. The distinctive arsenical bronze traditions of Early Bronze Age Anatolia gradually give way to tin bronze technology, possibly reflecting new trade connections or technological knowledge. The appearance of distinctive toggle pins and other dress accessories might reflect changing clothing styles associated with new populations.

Perhaps most significantly, there appears to be a shift in settlement hierarchy and political organization during the late third millennium. The relatively egalitarian settlements of Early Bronze Age I-II give way to more hierarchical arrangements, with clearer evidence for elite residences and administrative structures. This transition might reflect the emergence of new forms of political organization associated with Indo-European social structures, though such connections remain speculative.

Interaction with Indigenous Hattian Populations

The Hattian Substrate

When Indo-European speakers arrived in central Anatolia, they encountered a well-established indigenous population now known as the Hattians. Our knowledge of Hattian culture comes primarily through the lens of later Hittite sources, as the Hattians themselves left no written records in their own language. Nevertheless, it is clear that Hattian cultural and religious traditions formed a crucial substrate for the emerging Hittite civilization.

Hittite archives preserve a small corpus of ritual texts that reveal the Hattian language, including phonetically recorded Hattian incantations with Hittite translations. These fragments reveal a non-Indo-European, non-Semitic language with no confirmed linguistic relatives, though some scholars have proposed connections to Northwest Caucasian languages. Key phonological features include distinctive consonant clusters and apparent vowel harmony, quite different from Indo-European patterns.

Hattian material culture is associated with the Early Bronze Age traditions of central Anatolia (c. 3000-2000 BCE). Archaeological sites like Alacahöyük, with its famous "royal tombs" containing sophisticated metalwork, represent the height of pre-Hittite civilization in the region. The distinctive zoomorphic vessels, solar discs, and standards found in these tombs reflect a rich symbolic tradition that would later influence Hittite religious iconography.

Settlement patterns suggest the Hattian cultural zone centered on north-central Anatolia, particularly the bend of the Kızılırmak River (classical Halys) where the Hittite capital of Hattuša would later be established. Major Hattian centers included Hattuša itself (known in Hattian as Hattus), Nerik, Zippalanda, and Arinna—all sites that would maintain religious significance throughout the Hittite period.

Cultural Synthesis and Adaptation

The interaction between Indo-European newcomers and indigenous Hattians appears to have been characterized more by integration and synthesis than by conflict and replacement. The archaeological record shows continuity in many aspects of material culture alongside gradual changes, suggesting a process of acculturation rather than conquest.

This pattern of cultural synthesis is clearly reflected in Hittite religion, where Hattian deities and rituals were incorporated wholesale into the emerging Hittite pantheon. The chief Hittite deities—the Storm God of Hatti and the Sun Goddess of Arinna—were Hattian in origin, their worship continuing with remarkable continuity despite the language shift. Hittite religious texts frequently specify that certain rituals should be performed "in the language of Hatti," indicating the prestige and perceived efficacy of Hattian religious traditions.

Hattian influence extended to royal ideology as well. The Hittite royal title, Tabarna/labarna, appears to be Hattian in origin. The practice of royal ancestors becoming deities after death, central to Hittite state religion, likely derives from Hattian traditions. Even the location of the Hittite capital at Hattuša represents continuity with earlier Hattian settlement, though the site appears to have been abandoned immediately before the Hittite reoccupation.

Material culture shows similar patterns of continuity and adaptation. Hittite artistic conventions, particularly in religious iconography, draw heavily on Hattian precedents. The double-headed eagle, which would become a prominent Hittite royal symbol, has antecedents in Early Bronze Age Anatolian art. Metallurgical techniques and stylistic preferences show evolution from Hattian traditions rather than wholesale replacement.

This pattern of cultural synthesis is not unique to Hittite-Hattian interactions but represents a broader pattern visible across Anatolia. In western Anatolia, Indo-European Luwian speakers similarly adopted and adapted indigenous Anatolian cultural elements. This process created distinctive regional cultures that, while sharing Indo-European linguistic features, developed along different trajectories based on their local substrates.

Elite Emulation and Population Genetics

The mechanism by which Indo-European languages came to dominate Anatolia despite apparent demographic continuity remains debated. One compelling model, supported by both archaeological and genetic evidence, involves elite dominance and language shift through social emulation rather than population replacement.

Under this model, relatively small groups of Indo-European speakers established themselves as political elites in Anatolian communities, perhaps leveraging military advantages (possibly including early use of horse-drawn vehicles) or new forms of social organization. Local populations gradually adopted the language of these elites through processes of social emulation and intermarriage, while maintaining many aspects of their traditional culture.

This model is consistent with the archaeogenetic evidence, which shows only modest genetic input from steppe-related populations in Bronze Age Anatolia. It also aligns with the archaeological evidence for continuity in material culture alongside changes in political organization. Similar processes of elite-driven language shift are well-documented in historical periods, providing plausible parallels.

The persistence of Hattian in religious contexts for centuries after it had ceased to be spoken in daily life reflects the common pattern of older languages maintaining ritual significance after vernacular use has ended. This phenomenon, visible in the use of Sumerian in Mesopotamia and Latin in medieval Europe, typically occurs when a language shift has been driven by prestige and social factors rather than wholesale population replacement.

Linguistic Evidence for Early Settlement Patterns

The Anatolian Branch of Indo-European

Linguistic evidence provides crucial insights into the early history of Indo-European speakers in Anatolia. The Anatolian languages—including Hittite, Luwian, Palaic, and later attestations such as Lycian, Lydian, and Carian—form the most divergent branch of the Indo-European family, lacking many features common to all other branches.

Key archaic features of Anatolian languages include:

These and other features suggest that the Anatolian branch separated from Proto-Indo-European before many innovations that characterize the remaining branches. This has led some linguists, including Edgar Sturtevant and Warren Cowgill, to propose an "Indo-Hittite" hypothesis, which treats Anatolian and

"Core Indo-European" (ancestral to all non-Anatolian branches) as sister groups descending from an earlier common ancestor.

Whether one accepts the Indo-Hittite model or views Anatolian as simply the first branch to separate from Proto-Indo-European, the linguistic evidence points to an early divergence, possibly as early as the late fourth millennium BCE. This chronology aligns better with the "Early Arrival" archaeological models than with traditional theories placing Indo-European entry into Anatolia around 2000 BCE.

Internal Diversity and Geographic Distribution

The internal diversity of Anatolian languages provides further clues about early settlement patterns. By the time of our earliest substantial written evidence (c. 1650 BCE), three distinct Anatolian languages are attested:

This distribution suggests an early diversification of Anatolian languages following their initial entry into the peninsula. The relationship between these languages indicates that Luwian and Hittite shared a period of common development after separating from Palaic, suggesting a historical scenario where Proto-Anatolian speakers first divided into northern (Pre-Palaic) and southern (Pre-Luwian-Hittite) groups, with the latter subsequently dividing into the ancestors of Luwian and Hittite.

Onomastic evidence (personal and place names) extends our understanding of this linguistic geography. Place names in -ssa/-ssos (like Hattuša, Taruntassa) appear to have a Luwian origin, while names in -ma/-man (like Ankuwa, Zippalanda) may reflect Hattian origins. The distribution of these toponymic elements helps map linguistic zones even in periods before written records.

Personal names show similar patterns. The Hittite royal family used both native Indo-European names (like Mursili, containing the element murs- "to be short") and names of Hattian origin (like Ḫattušili, "man of Hattuša"). This onomastic mixing reflects the cultural synthesis discussed earlier and provides evidence for bilingualism and cultural integration in the early Hittite period.

Loanwords and Contact Phenomena

Patterns of loanwords between Anatolian languages and their neighbors provide additional evidence for early contact situations. Hittite contains numerous loanwords from Hattian, particularly in religious and political terminology. Terms like Tabarna/labarna (royal title), halentuwa (palace), and numerous divine names entered Hittite from Hattian, reflecting the significant cultural influence discussed earlier.

Loanwords also flowed between the Anatolian languages themselves. Hittite borrowed extensively from Luwian, with loanwords increasing over time as Luwian speakers became more numerous within the Hittite kingdom. By the late Hittite period (13th century BCE), Luwian influence on written Hittite is substantial, reflecting what Theo van den Hout has called a situation of "Luwian drift" within the empire.

Mesopotamian influence appears early, with Sumerian and Akkadian loanwords entering Hittite through trade contacts and the adoption of cuneiform writing. Terms related to scribal practice, administration, and international diplomacy were particularly likely to be borrowed from Mesopotamian sources.

These patterns of linguistic borrowing confirm the picture of cultural synthesis visible in the archaeological record. Rather than simple replacement of indigenous cultures by Indo-European newcomers, we see a complex process of integration and mutual influence, with the emerging Hittite culture drawing on multiple sources.

The Kültepe Merchant Archives and Early Hittite Presence

The Old Assyrian Trading Network

Our most detailed written evidence for Anatolia immediately before the rise of the Hittite kingdom comes from an unexpected source: Assyrian merchants. Beginning around 1950 BCE and continuing for approximately two centuries, merchants from the city of Assur in northern Mesopotamia established a network of trading colonies (kārum) in central Anatolian cities. The largest and most important of these was at Kanesh (modern Kültepe), near present-day Kayseri.

The Kültepe archives, discovered beginning in 1948 by Turkish archaeologist Tahsin Özgüç, comprise over 23,000 clay tablets written in Old Assyrian, a dialect of Akkadian. These documents—primarily commercial records, contracts, and letters—provide an unprecedented window into the economic, social, and political organization of central Anatolia during this crucial period.

The Assyrian merchants operated through family firms, with senior partners remaining in Assur while junior family members and agents staffed the Anatolian colonies. They imported tin (essential for bronze production) and textiles from Mesopotamia, exchanging these for Anatolian silver and gold. Agreements with local Anatolian rulers, who provided protection in exchange for substantial customs duties, governed this trade.

The Old Assyrian trading system operated through a hierarchy of establishments. The main colony (kārum) at Kanesh administered smaller stations (wabartum) in surrounding towns. A sophisticated system of caravans and messengers kept the entire network communicating, with letters taking about six weeks to travel between Assur and Kanesh.

Anatolian Society Through Assyrian Eyes

Although written from an Assyrian perspective, the Kültepe texts provide crucial information about Anatolian society on the eve of Hittite state formation. Central Anatolia was divided into numerous small kingdoms; each centered on an urban center ruled by a king (rubā'um) and queen (rubātum). These polities engaged in frequent conflicts, forming shifting alliances and occasionally establishing temporary hegemonies.

The political geography revealed in these texts shows many cities that would later feature prominently in Hittite history. Kanesh itself was a major kingdom, while other significant centers included Purushanda (possibly modern Acemhöyük), Wahsusana, and Hattuša. The latter appears in the Kültepe texts as a minor center, destroyed during a regional conflict—an event also mentioned in later Hittite historical texts.

Socially, these Anatolian kingdoms appear to have been organized around extended royal families, with various relatives of the king holding administrative positions. Local assemblies (tuzinnum) also played a role in governance, particularly in commercial matters. The Assyrian merchants interacted primarily with urban elites, though their texts occasionally mention rural populations and agricultural activities.

Economically, the region was more developed than previously recognized. Besides agriculture and animal husbandry, local industries included textile production, metallurgy, and pottery manufacture. Internal trade networks predated and coexisted with the Assyrian system, with local merchants (alahhinnum) continuing to operate alongside their Assyrian counterparts.

Indo-European Presence in the Kültepe Texts

The Kültepe archives provide our earliest textual evidence for Indo-European speakers in central Anatolia. Although written in Akkadian, the texts contain numerous Anatolian personal names, allowing linguistic identification of the populations involved. Analysis by scholars like Gojko Barjamovic and Ilya Yakubovich has revealed three main groups:

This distribution broadly matches the linguistic geography known from later periods, suggesting that the basic pattern of Anatolian language distribution was already established by 1900 BCE. The concentration of Nesite names in and around Kanesh explains why the Hittites later called their language "Nesite"—it appears to have been the primary language of this important city.

Particularly significant is the appearance of distinctively Indo-European royal names in several kingdoms. The rulers of Kanesh during the period of level II (c. 1950-1836 BCE) include kings with names like Inar, Warshama, and Pithana—all plausibly Indo-European. This suggests that Indo-European speakers had already established themselves as political elites in parts of central Anatolia by this time.

The Rise of Pithana and Anitta

The Kültepe archives document the beginning of political consolidation that would ultimately lead to the Hittite kingdom. During level Ib (c. 1835-1700 BCE), the texts record the rise of two kings of Kanesh who expanded their control over neighboring territories: Pithana and his son Anitta.

According to both the contemporary Kültepe texts and a later Hittite document known as the "Anitta Text," Pithana conquered Kanesh but "did no harm to its inhabitants." His son Anitta then embarked on a series of campaigns that brought much of central Anatolia under his control. He defeated the king of Hattuša, cursing the site and sowing it with weeds—an act of ritual destruction meant to prevent its reoccupation.

Anitta's achievements represent the first documented attempt to create a unified kingdom in central Anatolia. He adopted the title "Great King" (rubā'um rabium), previously used by major powers like Assyria, and received diplomatic recognition from distant rulers. His kingdom, however, appears to have collapsed after his death, with central Anatolia returning to a system of competing small states.

The significance of Pithana and Anitta for later Hittite history is complex. Although the first documented kings of the Hittite Old Kingdom (beginning c. 1650 BCE) do not claim direct descent from Anitta, they clearly viewed him as an important predecessor. The preservation and copying of the "Anitta Text" in the Hittite capital—ironically built at Hattuša, the very site Anitta had cursed—indicates a desire to connect with this earlier tradition of central Anatolian kingship.

The "Dark Age" and Hittite State Formation

The period between the end of the Kültepe archives (c. 1700 BCE) and the emergence of the Hittite kingdom (c. 1650 BCE) remains poorly documented. Archaeological evidence suggests political fragmentation and conflict, with many sites showing destruction layers. This "dark age" may have resulted from several factors, including the collapse of the Old Assyrian trading system, climate deterioration evidenced in dendrochronological records, and possibly population movements from the east.

The emergence of the Hittite kingdom under Ḫattušili I (c. 1650 BCE) represents both continuity and innovation relative to the preceding period. Like Anitta, Ḫattušili sought to unify central Anatolia under a single authority. Unlike Anitta, however, he established his capital at Hattuša, deliberately rejecting his predecessor's curse. This choice may reflect practical considerations—Hattuša's naturally defensible position made it an ideal capital—but also symbolically connected the new kingdom to Hattian traditions.

Ḫattušili and his successor Mursili I expanded Hittite control beyond central Anatolia, campaigning in northern Syria and even raiding Babylon around 1595 BCE. These campaigns established patterns of imperial expansion that would characterize the Hittite kingdom throughout its history. They also connected the Hittites to the broader Near Eastern world, setting the stage for their emergence as a major international power.

Conclusion: The Emergence of Hittite Identity

The evidence reviewed above reveals the complex origins of Hittite civilization through a process of cultural synthesis. Rather than representing the simple replacement of indigenous cultures by Indo-European newcomers, the Hittite kingdom emerged through centuries of interaction between multiple populations: indigenous Hattians, Indo-European Nesites and Luwians, and influences from Mesopotamia and Syria.

This process of ethnogenesis—the formation of a new cultural identity from diverse sources—characterizes many ancient societies but is particularly well-documented for the Hittites. The resulting civilization maintained awareness of its composite nature, preserving Hattian religious traditions alongside Indo-European political institutions and adopting Mesopotamian scribal practices.

The Hittite case offers valuable insights into broader questions of cultural contact and language shift in prehistory. It demonstrates that linguistic replacement need not involve wholesale population replacement, with elite dominance and gradual language shift providing a plausible mechanism. It also shows how new political formations can emerge from the creative synthesis of diverse cultural traditions, producing innovative solutions to the challenges of state formation.

In the chapters that follow, we will examine how this synthetic Hittite civilization developed through the Old Kingdom period (c. 1650-1400 BCE) and into the Empire period (c. 1400-1180 BCE), becoming one of the great powers of the Late Bronze Age Near East.

Chapter 2

The Emergence of Hittite Kingdoms

Pithana and Anitta: The Precursors of Hittite Power

The emergence of the Hittite kingdom in central Anatolia did not occur in a political vacuum. Long before Ḫattušili I established what we recognize as the Hittite Old Kingdom around 1650 BCE, the groundwork for centralized authority had been laid by two remarkable rulers: Pithana and his son, Anitta. Their achievements, documented in both contemporary texts and later Hittite records, provide crucial insights into the political landscape that preceded and influenced the formation of the Hittite state.

The Textual Evidence

Our knowledge of Pithana and Anitta derives primarily from two textual sources. The first comprises contemporary documents from the merchant colony at Kültepe (ancient Kanesh), written in Old Assyrian during the level Ib period (c.

1835-1700 BCE). These include references to local rulers in business transactions and occasional mentions of political events. The second, more detailed source is the so-called "Anitta Text," a Hittite-language composition preserved in several copies from the Hittite capital of Hattuša, dating to the 16th-13th centuries BCE.

The "Anitta Text" presents itself as Anitta's own account of his achievements, beginning with the statement: "Thus (speaks) Anitta, son of Pithana, king of Kuššara." While clearly based on authentic historical traditions, the text as we have it is not a contemporary document but a later composition, possibly incorporating elements of genuine royal inscriptions. As the Hittitologist Harry Hoffner noted, "The Anitta Text represents the earliest attested example of historiography in an Indo-European language, predating even the earliest Greek historical writings by a millennium" (Hoffner 1997: 182).

The text's preservation and copying by later Hittite scribes indicates its significance in Hittite historical consciousness. It served to connect the Hittite kingdom with an earlier tradition of central Anatolian rulership, even as it described the destruction of what would later become their capital.

Pithana of Kuššara: The Foundation of a Dynasty

According to both the Kültepe archives and the "Anitta Text," Pithana originated from the city of Kuššara, a settlement that has not yet been conclusively identified archaeologically but was likely located in the anti-Taurus mountains east of Kanesh. The "Anitta Text" describes his conquest of Kanesh (Neša in Hittite) in straightforward terms:

"Pithana, king of Kuššara, came down against the city of Neša in the night by force of arms, and took it. He seized the king of Neša, but did no harm to the inhabitants of Neša; he made them mothers and fathers" (KBo 3.22 obv. 1-7).

This passage reveals several important aspects of Pithana's political approach. First, his conquest was strategic and swift, executed as a night attack that targeted the existing ruler while minimizing civilian casualties. Second, his treatment of the conquered population—making them "mothers and fathers"—suggests a policy of incorporation rather than subjugation. This idiom, which appears in later Hittite texts as well, indicates the establishment of a relationship of mutual obligation between ruler and subjects.

The archaeological evidence from Kanesh corroborates this account of relatively peaceful transition. Level Ib at Kültepe, which corresponds chronologically to Pithana's conquest, shows no evidence of widespread destruction. Instead, we see continuity in material culture alongside administrative changes that likely reflect the new political order.

Pithana's conquest of Kanesh represented a significant political development in central Anatolia. Kanesh was already a major economic center due to the presence of the Assyrian merchant colony (kārum), which connected central Anatolia to northern Mesopotamia through an extensive trading network. By making it his capital, Pithana gained control over important trade routes and access to the wealth generated by international commerce.

The Assyrian merchants, who had established their colony with the permission of local rulers, appear to have adapted pragmatically to the new political situation. Tablets from the kārum Kanesh level Ib mention both Pithana and Anitta, indicating that business continued under the new regime. One text refers to "the palace of Pithana," suggesting that he established a royal residence in or near the city.

While the "Anitta Text" focuses primarily on his son's achievements, the conquest of Kanesh established Pithana as the founder of what would become, under Anitta, the first documented kingdom to unite a substantial portion of central Anatolia. His decision to relocate his capital from Kuššara to Kanesh also set a precedent for later Hittite rulers, who similarly moved their capital for strategic purposes.

Anitta: Creator of the First Central Anatolian Kingdom

Upon succeeding his father, Anitta embarked on an ambitious program of territorial expansion that transformed the political landscape of central Anatolia. The "Anitta Text" details a series of military campaigns against neighboring cities, culminating in the defeat of Hattuša and its ruler Piyusti. Through these conquests, Anitta created what archaeologist Trevor Bryce has called "the first attested kingdom in central Anatolia" (Bryce 2005: 37).

Military Campaigns and Territorial Expansion

The "Anitta Text" presents Anitta's military activities as responses to aggression by neighboring rulers. Anitta first campaigned against Ullamma, whose king had "risen up" against him. After defeating Ullamma, Anitta faced a coalition led by Huzziya, king of Zalpuwa, who had previously stolen the divine statue of Neša, the Šiuš (Storm God). Anitta defeated Huzziya, captured Zalpuwa, and returned the deity to Neša, an act that legitimized his rule in religious terms.

Subsequent campaigns brought Anitta into conflict with Piyusti, king of Hattuša. After defeating him in battle, Anitta captured and destroyed the city:

"And in the night I took it by force. And in its place I sowed weeds. Whoever becomes king after me and resettles Hattuša, let the Storm God of Heaven strike him!" (KBo 3.22 obv. 48-50)

This dramatic curse against the future reoccupation of Hattuša acquires particular significance given that the city later became the capital of the Hittite kingdom. The archaeological evidence from Hattuša (modern Boğazköy) confirms a destruction at the end of the Old Assyrian Trading Colony period, with a subsequent gap in occupation before the site was rebuilt as the Hittite capital.

Anitta's final recorded conquest was the city of Šalatiwara, which had refused to send envoys to him. This campaign extended his control to the northern periphery of central Anatolia, completing the territorial unification described in the text.

Political Structures and Royal Ideology

Anitta's political achievements went beyond military conquest. The "Anitta Text" provides evidence for the development of institutions and ideologies that would characterize later Anatolian kingship. Following his victories, Anitta adopted the title "Great King" (rubā'um rabium in Akkadian sources), previously used by major powers like Assyria. This title, later standard among Hittite rulers, indicated his claim to superiority over other local rulers.

The text also documents Anitta's building activities in his capital:

"When I had built the temples of the gods, then I built my royal palace. I made gates of copper, and I named the gate of my palace the Gate of the Leopard" (KBo 3.22 rev. 49-52).

These construction projects served both practical and symbolic functions. The temples demonstrated Anitta's piety and secured divine favor, while the impressive palace with its copper gates materialized his royal authority. The naming of the palace gate as the "Gate of the Leopard" suggests the development of royal symbolism that connected the ruler with powerful natural forces.

Archaeological evidence from Kanesh level Ib provides some correlation with the textual description. Excavations have revealed substantial buildings that could represent Anitta's palace complex, though precise identification remains challenging. More compelling is the evidence for increased centralization during this period, with standardization in ceramic production and administrative practices suggesting stronger political control.

International Relations

Perhaps the most remarkable aspect of Anitta's reign is the evidence for his participation in the international diplomatic system of the early second millennium BCE. The "Anitta Text" mentions that "the man of Purušḫanda bowed down to me" and presented Anitta with an iron throne and scepter as tribute.

This reference to Purušḫanda, a major city in southern Anatolia known from Mesopotamian sources, indicates Anitta's recognition by established powers.

This diplomatic recognition is further evidenced by a remarkable artifact discovered at Kültepe: a dagger bearing an inscription identifying it as a gift from Zuzu, king of Alaḫḫa (possibly Alalakh in northern Syria), to "Great King Anitta." This object demonstrates that Anitta's political status was acknowledged beyond central Anatolia, placing him within the network of royal gift exchange that characterized international relations in the ancient Near East.

The archaeological context of the Kanesh level Ib period shows increasing connections with northern Syria and Mesopotamia, visible in imported luxury goods and the adoption of administrative practices. Under Anitta, Kanesh appears to have functioned not just as a commercial center but as a royal capital with diplomatic connections to distant powers.

The Assyrian Merchant Colonies and Native Anatolian Politics

The rise of Pithana and Anitta occurred within the context of the Old Assyrian trading system, which connected central Anatolia to northern Mesopotamia through a network of merchant colonies established in major Anatolian settlements. Understanding this commercial system is essential for contextualizing the political developments of the period.

The Structure of the Trading Network

Beginning around 1950 BCE, merchants from the city of Assur established permanent trading colonies (kārum) in Anatolian cities, with the largest and most important located at Kanesh. These colonies operated with the permission of local rulers, who benefited from taxation of trade and access to imported goods. The merchants, organized in family firms, imported tin and textiles to Anatolia and exported silver and gold back to Assyria, generating substantial profits.

The trading system was highly organized, with a central administrative body (the kārum) governing the activities of individual merchants. The extensive archives discovered at Kültepe—over 23,000 cuneiform tablets—document everything from major commercial transactions to personal correspondence, providing an unparalleled window into the economic and social life of the period.

The relationship between the Assyrian merchants and local Anatolian rulers was generally cooperative, as both parties benefited from the trade. Local rulers provided protection and legal frameworks for the merchants, while the commercial activity generated wealth for the entire region. This symbiotic relationship created conditions favorable for political centralization, as control over trading centers became increasingly valuable.

From Commercial Network to Political Consolidation

The rise of Pithana and Anitta coincided with significant changes in the Old Assyrian trading system during the transition from kārum Kanesh level II to level Ib (c. 1835 BCE). Archaeological evidence indicates a destruction at Kanesh at the end of level II, followed by rebuilding and reorganization in level Ib. While trade continued, the character of the commercial network appears to have changed, with greater involvement of local Anatolian elements.

Mogens Trolle Larsen, a leading authority on the Old Assyrian trading system, has suggested that these changes created opportunities for ambitious local rulers: "The political vacuum that may have existed after the destruction of Kanesh level II was filled by a new dynasty of kings who managed to create a territorial state centered on Kanesh" (Larsen 2015: 175). Pithana's conquest of Kanesh can be understood in this context as an attempt to gain control over a crucial commercial hub during a period of transition.

Under Anitta, the relationship between political power and commercial networks evolved further. The "Anitta Text" makes no direct mention of the Assyrian merchants, focusing instead on military conquests and relationships with other

Anatolian rulers. However, archaeological evidence from level Ib shows continued commercial activity alongside increasing political centralization. Standardized administrative practices and the concentration of wealth in the citadel area suggest that Anitta's kingdom incorporated the commercial networks into a more centralized political structure.

The eventual decline of the Old Assyrian trading system around 1700 BCE, marked by the abandonment of kārum Kanesh level Ib, coincided with the apparent collapse of Anitta's kingdom. This correlation suggests the interdependence of commercial networks and political structures in early second-millennium Anatolia. When long-distance trade declined, perhaps because of political changes in northern Mesopotamia, the economic foundation of centralized authority in central Anatolia was undermined.

Archaeological Evidence for Early State Formation

Archaeological evidence from central Anatolian sites can complement the textual sources for Pithana and Anitta, providing material correlates for the political developments described in the texts. This evidence, while sometimes ambiguous, offers important insights into the nature of early state formation in the region.

Kanesh/Kültepe: The Capital of an Emerging Kingdom

As the capital of Pithana and Anitta's kingdom, Kanesh (modern Kültepe) provides the most direct archaeological evidence for their rule. The site consists of a central mound (the ancient citadel) and a lower town where the Assyrian merchant colony was located. Excavations conducted since 1948 by Turkish archaeologists have revealed a complex urban center with evidence for social stratification, specialized production, and administrative activities.

The level Ib period, corresponding chronologically to Pithana and Anitta's rule, shows several significant developments. These archaeological patterns are consistent with the emergence of a more centralized political authority as described in the textual sources. Particularly significant is the evidence for what archaeologist Fikri Kulakoğlu has called "a new administrative system controlling production and distribution" during the level Ib period (Kulakoğlu 2011: 1025). This system, characterized by standardized weights and measures and centralized storage facilities, suggests the development of institutional structures that could support territorial expansion.

Hattuša: Destruction and Abandonment

The "Anitta Text" describes the conquest and cursing of Hattuša, and archaeological evidence from the site (modern Boğazköy) confirms a destruction at the end of the Old Assyrian Trading Colony period. Excavations have revealed a burned destruction layer dating to approximately 1750-1700 BCE, after which the site was temporarily abandoned.

During this early period, Hattuša's extent was limited to what would later become the Lower City of the Hittite capital; settlement concentrated around a spring. The material culture shows connections to the broader central Anatolian cultural sphere, with ceramics similar to those found at contemporary Kanesh. Although no textual evidence from this early period has been discovered at Hattuša itself, archaeological findings support the "Anitta Text"'s description of the city as a significant settlement that threatened Anitta's authority.

The temporary abandonment of Hattuša following Anitta's conquest created what archaeologist Peter Neve has called "a settlement hiatus of uncertain duration" (Neve 1996: 58). When the site was reoccupied and developed as the Hittite capital in the 17th century BCE, it represented a deliberate rejection of Anitta's curse by the early Hittite kings, who may have sought to appropriate the symbolic significance of the site while establishing their own distinct political identity.

Regional Settlement Patterns and State Formation

Beyond individual sites, broader settlement patterns in central Anatolia provide context for understanding the political developments under Pithana and Anitta. Survey data indicates significant changes in settlement organization during the early second millennium BCE, with a trend toward fewer but larger settlements and the emergence of clear site hierarchies.

This pattern of settlement nucleation is consistent with the development of territorial control described in the "Anitta Text." As Anitta expanded his authority through conquest, populations may have concentrated in protected centers, abandoning more vulnerable smaller settlements. The archaeological evidence suggests that this process was already underway before Pithana and Anitta but accelerated during their period of rule.

Particularly significant is the evidence for standardization across sites within Anitta's domain. Similar ceramic assemblages, architectural techniques, and administrative practices at sites mentioned in the "Anitta Text" suggest the emergence of a relatively integrated political entity. This material uniformity provides archaeological support for the textual claim that Anitta created a unified kingdom in central Anatolia.

Legendary Founders: Historical Memory and Political Legitimacy

While Pithana and Anitta were historical figures documented in contemporary sources, they also acquired legendary status in later Anatolian historical consciousness. The preservation and copying of the "Anitta Text" by Hittite scribes centuries after Anitta's death demonstrates his importance in Hittite conceptions of the past. Understanding how these figures functioned in historical memory provides insights into political legitimacy in ancient Anatolia.

The Anitta Text as Historical Memory

The "Anitta Text" as preserved in the Hittite archives is not simply a historical document but a carefully constructed narrative that served political purposes. Its preservation in multiple copies, some dating as late as the 13th century BCE, indicates its continued relevance throughout Hittite history. The text established Anitta as a paradigmatic ruler whose achievements—and limitations—defined the political landscape inherited by the Hittite kings.

Particularly significant is the text's emphasis on Anitta's relationship with the gods. His return of the Storm God statue to Neša and his construction of temples established him as a pious ruler who enjoyed divine favor. This religious dimension of kingship would become central to Hittite royal ideology, with later kings similarly emphasizing their role as servants of the gods.

At the same time, the "Anitta Text" establishes boundaries that later Hittite kings would transgress. The curse against reoccupying Hattuša created a dramatic tension in Hittite historical consciousness, as the Hittite kings deliberately established their capital at the forbidden site. This act of transgression may have distinguished the Hittite kingdom from Anitta's earlier polity, even as they appropriated aspects of his legacy.

Continuity and Discontinuity with the Hittite Kingdom

The relationship between Pithana and Anitta's kingdom and the later Hittite state remains a subject of scholarly debate. The first documented kings of the Hittite Old Kingdom, beginning with Ḫattušili I around 1650 BCE, do not claim direct descent from Anitta. Instead, they present themselves as originating from Kuššara, Pithana's original hometown, while establishing their capital at Hattuša in defiance of Anitta's curse.

This complex relationship suggests that the early Hittite kings sought to appropriate certain aspects of Pithana and Anitta's legacy while establishing their own distinct political identity. As Hittitologist Theo van den Hout has observed, "The early Hittite kings saw themselves as heirs to a tradition of kingship that included Anitta, even as they defined themselves in opposition to specific aspects of his legacy" (van den Hout 2011: 47).

Archaeological evidence indicates a gap of several decades between the collapse of Anitta's kingdom (around 1700 BCE) and the emergence of the Hittite state (around 1650 BCE). During this interval, central Anatolia appears to have returned to a system of competing small states, suggesting that Anitta's political achievements were not immediately sustainable. The Hittite kingdom thus represented not a direct continuation of Anitta's polity, but a new political formation that drew on earlier traditions while developing its own distinctive institutions.

Conclusion: The Legacy of Pitḫana and Anitta

Pitḫana and Anitta's achievements represent a crucial stage in the political development of central Anatolia. Through conquest and administrative innovation, they created the first documented kingdom to unite a substantial portion of the region, establishing patterns of rulership that would influence later political formations. Their kingdom, centered on Kanesh but extending through much of central Anatolia, demonstrated the possibility of territorial control beyond the traditional city-state model.

The evidence for their rule, drawn from both contemporary documents and later historical traditions, reveals a sophisticated political approach that combined military power with administrative innovation and religious legitimation. Particularly notable is Anitta's participation in international diplomacy, indicating that central Anatolia was already integrated into the broader Near Eastern political system by the early second millennium BCE.

While Anitta's kingdom proved ephemeral, collapsing after his death, its legacy endured in the political memory of later Anatolian rulers. The Hittite kingdom that emerged around 1650 BCE drew on this legacy even as it established its own distinctive political identity. By establishing their capital at Hattuša, the site

Anitta had cursed, the Hittite kings symbolically declared both their connection to and independence from this earlier tradition of central Anatolian kingship.

In the broader context of ancient Near Eastern history, Pithana and Anitta's kingdom represents an important case study in early state formation. Their rule coincided with similar processes of political consolidation in northern Mesopotamia and Syria, suggesting that the early second millennium BCE was a period of widespread political transformation. Understanding their achievements provides crucial context for the emergence of the more extensively documented Hittite kingdom that would dominate Anatolia for the next five centuries.

Chapter 3

TOWARD POLITICAL UNIFICATION

The Foundation of the Hittite State

Local Kingdoms and City-States in Anatolia

The political landscape of central Anatolia in the period between Anitta's death (c. 1700 BCE) and the emergence of the Hittite state (c. 1650 BCE) was characterized by fragmentation and competition among numerous small polities. This period, sometimes termed the "Proto-Hittite" phase, remains poorly documented, creating what historian Trevor Bryce has called "a dark age in central Anatolian history" (Bryce 2005: 35). Nevertheless, archaeological evidence and references in later texts provide glimpses into the complex political geography that the early Hittite kings would eventually unify.

Numerous small kingdoms, each centered on an urban hub controlling the surrounding agricultural territory, divided Central Anatolia during this period. These polities were typically named after their capital cities, reflecting the close identification between urban centers and political entities.

The most significant of these included Purušḫanda in the southwest, Šalatiwara in the southeast, Ḫattuša (the future Hittite capital) in the north-central region, and Kaneš/Neša in the east-central area.

Archaeological evidence from these centers reveals a pattern of increased fortification during the early second millennium BCE, suggesting intensified competition and conflict.

At Kaneš, for example, the lower city was abandoned after a destruction layer dated to approximately 1700 BCE, with settlement contracting to the more easily defensible citadel mound.

Similar patterns appear at other sites, including Alişar Höyük and Acemhöyük, indicating widespread political instability.

The political organization of these kingdoms appears to have combined elements of traditional city-state governance with more expansive territorial ambitions. The rulers, typically bearing the title *rubā'um* (prince) in the Old Assyrian texts from Kaneš, exercised authority through a combination of kinship networks, religious legitimation, and military power. Archaeological evidence suggests increasing social stratification during this period, with elite residences becoming more clearly differentiated from commoner housing.

"The collapse of Anitta's kingdom created a power vacuum in central Anatolia," notes archaeologist Ulf-Dietrich Schoop, "but it did not eliminate the underlying political and economic structures that had made regional integration possible" (Schoop 2018: 82). Instead, the foundations for larger-scale political organization remained, awaiting rulers with the military capacity and administrative vision to reconstruct a unified state.

These local kingdoms maintained complex relationships with one another, alternating between conflict and cooperation. Alliance networks, often reinforced through marriage ties, created temporary coalitions that could dominate regions before dissolving into renewed competition. The instability of these arrangements created opportunities for ambitious rulers to expand their influence, setting the stage for the eventual Hittite unification of the region.

Economic integration also connected these politically divided territories. Trade routes established during the Old Assyrian colony period continued to function, though at reduced volume after the collapse of the karum system around 1700 BCE.

Archaeological evidence indicates the continued movement of goods such as metals, textiles, and luxury items between regions, maintaining economic interdependence despite political fragmentation.

The mountainous geography of central Anatolia shaped these political developments in crucial ways. River valleys provided corridors for communication and trade, while mountain ranges created natural boundaries between territories. Control of key mountain passes thus became strategically vital, allowing rulers to regulate movement and extract resources from trade.

The distribution of natural resources, particularly metal deposits, further influenced political competition, with access to copper and silver providing economic advantages to certain polities.

This fragmented political landscape presented both challenges and opportunities for the emerging Hittite state. As Hittitologist Gary Beckman observes, "The early Hittite kings faced the difficult task of imposing unity on a region accustomed to political division, but they could also build on existing traditions of supra-local authority exemplified by figures like Anitta" (Beckman 2016: 112). Their success in this endeavor would transform the political geography of Anatolia for centuries to come.

Early Hittite Expansion and Consolidation

The transformation from this fragmented political landscape to a unified Hittite kingdom began around 1650 BCE with the reign of Ḫattušili I (also known as Labarna I in some sources). The circumstances of his rise to power remain obscure, with later Hittite historical traditions providing conflicting accounts. What is clear, however, is that he established his capital at Hattuša, the very site that Anitta had destroyed and cursed, marking a symbolic break with the earlier political order.

Ḫattušili claimed origin from Kussara, a city-state in southeastern Anatolia, suggesting that the Hittite dynasty emerged from the periphery rather than from the core regions of central Anatolia. This origin story appears in the later "Testament of Ḫattušili," which states: "I was a man of Kussara. In the lands of Hatti, enemies arose and made the land of Neša their frontier. But I, Ḫattušili, Great King, smote the enemy and seized the land of Neša" (CTH 6, translation after Sturtevant and Bechtel 1935: 177).

The military campaigns of Ḫattušili I, documented in both contemporary annals and later historical compilations, reveal a systematic program of conquest aimed at establishing control over central Anatolia. His initial campaigns focused on securing the core territories around Hattuša and Neša, followed by expeditions against more distant kingdoms such as Zalpa on the Black Sea coast and Purušḫanda in the southwest.

A combination of overwhelming force and strategic clemency characterized these campaigns. Cities that resisted were typically destroyed, their populations deported, and their lands redistributed to royal supporters. Those that submitted without resistance, however, were often incorporated into the kingdom with their local elites maintained in positions of authority, though now subordinate to Hittite officials. This pattern created a tiered administrative structure that balanced central control with local autonomy.

The "Proclamation of Anitta" (CTH 1), a foundational text of Hittite historical consciousness, describes how Ḫattušili established his authority: "When I conquered the city, I did not harm it. I took its king prisoner and brought him to Hattuša. I made him my servant, and I established my son as governor over the city" (translation after Hoffner 1997: 183). This combination of force and integration characterized the early Hittite approach to empire building.

Archaeological evidence confirms the expansion described in these texts. Destruction layers at sites throughout central Anatolia date to this period, often followed by rebuilding that incorporates Hittite architectural elements and material culture.

At Hattuša itself, extensive construction projects transformed the abandoned site into a monumental capital, with massive fortification walls, elaborate gateways, and imposing public buildings, demonstrating the new regime's power and ambition.

The consolidation of these conquests required not just military victory but administrative innovation. Under Ḫattušili and his immediate successors, particularly Mursili I (r. c. 1620-1590 BCE), the Hittite state developed increasingly sophisticated governance structures. The kingdom was divided into administrative districts, each overseen by a governor (typically a member of the royal family or high nobility) who represented central authority and ensured the flow of resources to the capital.

Scholars term the development of the "appanage system" a crucial innovation; this system assigned conquered territories to members of the royal family or high officials, who administered them as semi-autonomous fiefs while remaining subordinate to the king. As Hittitologist Theo van den Hout explains, "This system allowed the Hittite kings to maintain control over a geographically expansive territory with limited administrative resources, by co-opting local elites into the imperial structure" (van den Hout 2011: 72).

The most dramatic expansion of early Hittite power came under Mursili I, who led a daring expedition down the Euphrates River to sack Babylon around 1595 BCE, bringing the dynasty of Hammurabi to an end. This campaign, documented in both Hittite and Babylonian sources, represented an unprecedented projection of Anatolian power into Mesopotamia. The "Telipinu Proclamation," a later Hittite historical text, recounts: "Mursili was Great King, and his sons, brothers, in-laws, family members, and troops were united. He controlled enemy lands with his might, took away their lands, and defeated their armies. He destroyed the land of Aleppo and brought captives from Aleppo and its property to Hattuša. Afterward he destroyed Babylon and took the captives of Babylon and its property to Hattuša" (CTH 19, translation after Hoffner 1997: 182).

This remarkable military success, however, stretched Hittite resources to their limit. The logistical challenges of maintaining control over such distant territories proved insurmountable, and Mursili withdrew to Anatolia without establishing permanent Hittite control in Mesopotamia. More significantly, his assassination shortly after his return to Hattuša (c. 1590 BCE) triggered a succession crisis that threatened the stability of the young kingdom.

The period following Mursili's death saw a series of internal struggles that temporarily halted Hittite expansion. His successor Hantili I (r. c. 1590-1560 BCE), implicated in the assassination, faced rebellions and external attacks that forced a defensive posture. The "Telipinu Proclamation" describes this period in stark terms: "When Hantili was king, the land was peaceful. But then his offspring were destroyed by the hand of bloodshed, and his servants began to die" (CTH 19, translation after Hoffner 1997: 183).

Despite these setbacks, the fundamental structures of the Hittite state remained intact. By approximately 1525 BCE, under King Telipinu, internal stability was restored, and the foundations laid by Ḫattušili I and Mursili I allowed for renewed expansion. Telipinu's most significant contribution was the promulgation of a succession law that attempted to regulate royal succession, addressing one of the key vulnerabilities of the early Hittite state.

The "Telipinu Proclamation" explicitly links this reform to the goal of political stability: "Let only a prince of the first rank, a son, become king. If there is no first-rank prince, let a second-rank son become king. If there is no prince or second-rank son, let them take a husband for a first-rank daughter, and let him become king" (CTH 19, translation after Hoffner 1997: 185). This attempt to formalize succession rules reflects the increasing institutionalization of Hittite kingship during this period.

By the end of the Old Kingdom period (c. 1500 BCE), the Hittites had established control over most of central Anatolia and parts of northern Syria. While they would face continued challenges from neighboring powers, such as the Hurrian kingdom of Mitanni and the Kassite dynasty of Babylon, the foundations for the later imperial period had been securely laid. As historian Trevor Bryce concludes, "The achievements of the Old Kingdom kings, particularly Ḫattušili I and Mursili I, established the territorial, administrative, and ideological framework that would sustain Hittite power for the next four centuries" (Bryce 2005: 97).

Religious and Cultural Synthesis with Hattian Traditions

One of the most distinctive features of Hittite civilization was its remarkable religious syncretism, particularly its incorporation of indigenous Hattian religious traditions. When Indo-European speakers established political dominance in central Anatolia, they encountered a sophisticated religious culture maintained by the native Hattian population. Rather than suppressing these traditions, the Hittite elite adopted and adapted them, creating a syncretic religious system that combined Indo-European and Hattian elements.

This process is vividly illustrated in the Hittite pantheon, which incorporated deities from multiple cultural traditions. The storm god Tarhunta, clearly Indo-European in origin and comparable to the Greek Zeus or Vedic Indra, was identified with the Hattian storm god Taru and eventually took on many of his attributes and myths. Similarly, the sun goddess of Arinna, a central deity in the Hittite state cult, appears to have been originally a Hattian goddess whose worship was adopted and elevated by the Hittite rulers.

The Hittite religious texts explicitly acknowledge this cultural borrowing. A ritual text from the reign of Mursili II (c. 1321-1295 BCE) states: "When they celebrate the festival of the Storm-god of Nerik, they sing in Hattian, because the people of Nerik are Hattians, and their gods and their priests are Hattian" (CTH 672, translation after Singer 2002: 73). This recognition of cultural difference within a unified religious framework is characteristic of Hittite approaches to religious diversity.

Archaeological evidence confirms this pattern of religious syncretism. At Hittite cult centers such as Yazılıkaya near Hattuša, divine images combine iconographic elements from multiple traditions. The famous rock sanctuary depicts a procession of deities that includes both Indo-European and Hattian gods, represented in a consistent artistic style that fuses different cultural traditions. As art historian Billie Jean Collins observes, "The Yazılıkaya reliefs represent a visual theology that reconciles diverse religious traditions within a coherent cosmological framework" (Collins, 2007: 143).

The Hittite adoption of Hattian religious traditions extended beyond the pantheon to include ritual practices and sacred geography. The numerous festival texts preserved in the Hittite archives describe elaborate ceremonies that often specify the use of Hattian language for key ritual recitations, even as the administrative framework was recorded in Hittite. These festivals, some lasting for multiple days, maintained ancient patterns of worship while incorporating them into the state religion.

Sacred sites associated with Hattian worship became central to Hittite religious geography. The city of Nerik, mentioned in the ritual text quoted above, was considered so essential to proper religious observance that when it fell under enemy control, the Hittite kings established a temporary substitute location to continue its cultic functions. King Ḫattušili III (r. c. 1267-1237 BCE) made the recovery of Nerik a primary goal of his reign, emphasizing its religious significance: "The Storm-god of Nerik, my lord, ran to me and saved me. I rebuilt Nerik, which had been destroyed, and I restored its divine worship" (CTH 81, translation after Otten 1981: 22).

This religious synthesis served important political functions for the Hittite state. By adopting Hattian deities and ritual practices, the Indo-European speaking elite legitimized their rule over the indigenous population and positioned themselves as proper caretakers of the land's sacred traditions. Religious continuity helped to mitigate potential resistance to political change, facilitating the integration of diverse populations into a unified state.

The Hittite kings took particular care to maintain proper relationships with local deities throughout their territories. Royal prayers frequently list gods by their specific local manifestations, acknowledging the importance of place in divine identity. A prayer of Muwatalli II (r. c. 1295-1272 BCE) invokes "the Stormgod of Hatti, the Stormgod of Zippalanda, the Stormgod of Nerik, the Stormgod of Hurma," and dozens of other localized manifestations, recognizing each as a distinct divine presence requiring specific forms of worship (CTH 381, translation after Singer 1996: 166).

Beyond religion, Hittite culture showed similar patterns of synthesis in other domains. In architecture, Indo-European building traditions were combined with Anatolian construction techniques. The monumental architecture of Hattuša, with its massive stone walls and elaborate gateways, incorporated elements from multiple cultural traditions to create a distinctive Hittite style. As archaeologist Peter Neve notes, "Hittite architecture represents a creative synthesis of indigenous Anatolian building traditions with influences from Mesopotamia and the Levant, adapted to the specific conditions of the Anatolian plateau" (Neve 1993: 15).

Material culture shows similar patterns of cultural blending. Ceramic styles combined elements from different traditions, while metallurgical techniques drew on both local Anatolian traditions and imported technologies. Luxury goods often show influence from neighboring civilizations, particularly Egypt and Mesopotamia, indicating the Hittites' participation in international exchange networks and their willingness to incorporate foreign elements into their material culture.

Perhaps most significantly, the Hittite legal system demonstrated a pragmatic synthesis of Indo-European and indigenous Anatolian traditions. The Hittite law code, one of the earliest documented in the ancient Near East, combines elements recognizable from other Indo-European legal traditions with provisions that appear to reflect Anatolian customary law. Particularly notable is its relatively mild punishment scale compared to contemporary Mesopotamian codes, with an emphasis on compensation rather than retribution for many offenses.

As legal historian Gary Beckman observes, "The Hittite laws reflect a society in transition, balancing traditional Indo-European legal concepts with the practical requirements of governing a diverse population in an urbanized state" (Beckman 1999: 93). This legal pragmatism, like the religious syncretism discussed above, facilitated the integration of different population groups into a functioning political whole.

The cultural synthesis achieved by the Hittites was not without tensions and contradictions. Certain texts reveal anxiety about maintaining proper distinctions between different cultural traditions, particularly in religious contexts. A ritual instruction specifies: "When they perform the ritual of the Storm-god of Zippalanda, they must use vessels of Hattian manufacture, not those made in the Hurrian style" (CTH 625, translation after Miller 2004: 261). Such concerns indicate that cultural boundaries remained significant even as extensive borrowing occurred across them.

Nevertheless, the overall pattern of Hittite cultural development was one of creative synthesis rather than rigid separation. As historian Billie Jean Collins summarizes, "The Hittites' greatest achievement may have been their ability to forge a coherent cultural identity from diverse traditions, creating a civilization that was neither simply Indo-European nor Anatolian, but distinctively Hittite" (Collins 2007: 189). This synthetic approach would remain characteristic of Hittite civilization throughout its history, contributing to its resilience in the face of political and military challenges.

The Development of Hittite Royal Ideology

The foundation and expansion of the Hittite state was accompanied by the development of a sophisticated royal ideology that legitimized the authority of the ruling dynasty and defined the relationship between the king, the gods, and the land. This ideology, documented in royal inscriptions, prayers, treaties, and historical narratives, evolved over time but maintained certain core principles that distinguished Hittite kingship from other contemporary models of royal authority.

Central to Hittite royal ideology was the concept of the king as chief priest of the state religion. The Hittite term for king, *Tabarna* (or *labarna*, used interchangeably in the texts), carried religious and political connotations. The king's primary responsibility was maintaining proper relationships with the divine world through regular performance of rituals and festivals. A text from the reign of Mursili II states explicitly: "My Sun [the king] performs the regular festivals of spring, autumn, and winter. He celebrates all the festivals of all the gods in their proper sequence, and he gives to the gods what is their due" (CTH 375, translation after Singer 2002: 56).

This religious dimension of kingship was not merely symbolic but constituted a core governmental function. The extensive festival calendar documented in the Hittite archives required the king's personal participation in hundreds of ritual events throughout the year. When military or diplomatic obligations prevented the king's presence, substitute rituals were performed, or the ceremonies were postponed until the king could attend. As religion scholar Itamar Singer notes, "The king's ritual obligations were not peripheral to his role but constituted its essential foundation, defining his relationship to both the divine and human worlds" (Singer 2002: 24).

The concept of divine election reinforced the religious basis of royal authority. Hittite kings claimed to rule by the will of the gods, particularly the storm god Tarhunta and the sun goddess of Arinna, who were said to "run before" the king in battle and guide his decisions. Royal prayers frequently emphasize this relationship, as in this address by Muwatalli II to the storm god: "You, O Storm

God, my lord, raised me up and placed me in the lap of my mother. You protected me and raised me up and installed me as king over the land of Hatti" (CTH 381, translation after Singer 1996: 31).

This divine sanction was balanced by a strong emphasis on the king's accountability to the gods. Hittite historical texts frequently attribute political and military setbacks to religious transgressions, particularly failures to maintain proper ritual observances. The "Plague Prayers" of Mursili II provide a striking example of this conception, attributing a devastating epidemic to divine punishment for oath-breaking by previous kings: "The gods are bringing the matter of the plague before you [the king], because Hatti has sinned" (CTH 378, translation after Singer 2002: 58).

The king's role as military leader constituted another crucial dimension of Hittite royal ideology. Royal annals and historical narratives emphasize the king's personal courage and leadership in battle, often describing him leading charges against enemy forces and engaging in single combat with opposing rulers. While such accounts undoubtedly contain elements of propaganda, archaeological evidence confirms that Hittite kings did indeed participate directly in military campaigns, sometimes at considerable personal risk.

The "Deeds of Suppiluliuma," compiled by his son Mursili II, describes the great conqueror's military prowess in vivid terms: "My father went forth with the favor of the storm god, his lord. He destroyed the enemy lands one after another. He defeated the extensive land of Hurri. He took away their possessions and filled Hattuša with them" (CTH 40, translation after Güterbock 1956: 85). Such narratives established military success as a key indicator of divine favor and legitimate rule.

Complementing this martial aspect was the king's role as supreme judge and lawgiver. Royal edicts and legal texts emphasize the king's responsibility to ensure justice throughout his realm. The prologue to the Hittite laws states: "If anyone kills a man or woman in a quarrel, he shall bring him for burial and shall give four persons, either men or women respectively, and he shall look to his house for it"

(CTH 291, translation after Hoffner 1997: 17). This concern with establishing clear legal standards and ensuring their enforcement remained central to Hittite conceptions of good governance.

The king's judicial authority extended to international relations as well. Hittite treaties, among the earliest documented in world history, present the king as the guarantor of international order, authorized by the gods to establish and enforce agreements with other rulers.

The treaty between Suppiluliuma I and Shattiwaza of Mitanni states: "These words of the treaty and oath I have placed in the presence of the gods. Let the gods of the oath be witness to these words" (CTH 51, translation after Beckman 1999: 53). By invoking divine witnesses, the king positioned himself as acting within a divinely sanctioned legal framework.

A distinctive feature of Hittite royal ideology was its emphasis on the king's role within a broader familial and institutional context. Unlike some contemporary monarchies that emphasized the king's absolute and solitary authority, Hittite texts frequently mention the queen (referred to as *Tawananna*) as a figure of independent ritual and political significance. Royal inscriptions sometimes name both king and queen as joint actors, particularly in religious contexts, suggesting a conception of royal authority as at least partially shared within the ruling couple.

This familial dimension extended to the royal succession as well. The "Telipinu Proclamation," discussed earlier, establishes clear rules for succession that prioritize the extended royal family's stability over absolute paternal authority. By specifying that a son-in-law married to a royal daughter could legitimately become king in the absence of a direct male heir, the text suggests a conception of royal authority as vested in the dynasty rather than exclusively in the male line.

Hittite texts give similar emphasis to the institutional context of kingship. The *pankus* (assembly), composed of high officials and nobles, appears in early Hittite texts as a body with significant political authority, including involvement in succession disputes and judicial matters. While its power appears to have declined over time, its continued mention in texts suggests that Hittite kingship was conceptualized as operating within an institutional framework rather than as purely autocratic.

This emphasis on institutional constraints is particularly evident in the Hittite approach to conquered territories. Rather than imposing direct rule, Hittite kings typically established treaty relationships with subordinate rulers, allowing them to maintain local authority while acknowledging Hittite supremacy. These arrangements were formalized in detailed treaties that specified the obligations of both parties and invoked divine sanctions for violations. As historian Mario Liverani observes, "The Hittite imperial system represented a distinctive model of hegemony that balanced central control with local autonomy through institutionalized relationships" (Liverani 2001: 122).

The development of Hittite royal ideology reached its most sophisticated expression during the Empire period (c. 1400-1180 BCE), particularly under kings such as Suppiluliuma I, Mursili II, and Ḫattušili III. During this period, royal inscriptions became more elaborate and self-reflective, often including extended justifications for royal actions and detailed accounts of the king's relationship with the gods.

The "Apology of Ḫattušili III," which justifies his seizure of the throne from his nephew, represents a remarkable example of royal self-presentation, combining religious, legal, and personal elements in a complex narrative of divine favor and political legitimacy.

As Hittite power expanded beyond Anatolia into Syria and the upper Euphrates region, royal ideology adapted to encompass a more diverse realm. Kings began to employ multiple royal titles reflecting different cultural traditions, presenting themselves as "Great King" in the Mesopotamian tradition, "Labarna" in the Hittite context, and "Hero" in Hurrian terminology. This multiplicity of royal identities allowed Hittite kings to communicate effectively with different constituencies within their heterogeneous empire.

The resilience of Hittite royal ideology is demonstrated by its ability to weather severe political crises. Despite multiple succession disputes, foreign invasions, and internal rebellions, the basic framework of Hittite kingship remained remarkably stable over nearly five centuries.

As historian Trevor Bryce concludes, "The endurance of Hittite royal institutions through periods of extreme stress testifies to the effectiveness of their ideological foundations in maintaining the legitimacy of the ruling dynasty even in adverse circumstances" (Bryce 2005: 326).

This resilience stemmed in part from the flexibility of Hittite royal ideology, which could incorporate new elements while maintaining core principles. The increased emphasis on personal piety visible in late Hittite royal inscriptions, for instance, represents an evolution of traditional concepts rather than a radical break. Similarly, the growing prominence of the queen in imperial period texts builds on, rather than contradicts, earlier conceptions of shared royal authority.

The distinctive characteristics of Hittite royal ideology—its religious foundations, institutional context, familial dimension, and flexible adaptation to diverse cultural traditions—help explain the remarkable success of the Hittite state in unifying and governing a geographically challenging and culturally diverse region for nearly five centuries.

As archaeologist Jürgen Seeher observes, "The Hittite achievement in state formation represents one of the most successful political experiments of the ancient Near East, creating durable institutions that balanced central authority with local autonomy in ways that would not be replicated until the Persian Empire nearly a millennium later" (Seeher 2011: 178).

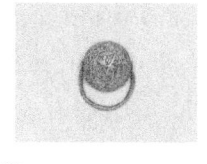

Chapter 4

HATTUŠILI I AND THE FOUNDATION OF EMPIRE

The Old Kingdom - Ḫattušili I and Muršili I

The foundation of Hittite imperial power can be traced to the establishment of Hattuša as the royal capital, a decision that defied the curse of Anitta yet proved strategically prescient. When Ḫattušili I (r. ca. 1650-1620 BCE) rebuilt this previously destroyed settlement as his seat of power, he initiated a transformation that would shape Anatolian geopolitics for centuries to come.

The Establishment of Hattuša as Capital

The selection of Hattuša as the Hittite capital represented a deliberate break with the political geography established by Anitta. Located approximately 150 kilometers northeast of modern Ankara, the site occupies a dramatic position on a steep rocky outcrop surrounded by deep valleys on three sides. This topography provided natural defensive advantages that would have appealed to the security-conscious early Hittite rulers.

"The site chosen by Ḫattušili I for his capital demonstrates remarkable strategic foresight," notes archaeologist Jürgen Seeher, who directed excavations at Hattuša for many years. "The defensible position, access to water sources, and central location within Anatolia all contributed to its suitability as an administrative center" (Seeher 2006: 37).

Archaeological evidence indicates that Ḫattušili I's rebuilding of Hattuša was not merely symbolic but represented a substantial investment of resources. The earliest Hittite construction phase at the site included massive fortification walls up to five meters thick, enclosing an area of approximately 18 hectares. Within this fortified zone, archaeologists have identified administrative buildings, workshops, and residential areas dating to this initial period of occupation.

The Anitta Text, our primary source for the earlier destruction of Hattuša, makes clear the symbolic significance of Ḫattušili's decision to rebuild the city:

"I conquered the city of Hattuša by night through military force. In its place I sowed weeds. Whoever becomes king after me and resettles Hattuša, let the Storm God of Heaven strike him down!" (KBo 3.22, trans. Hoffner 1997: 82)

By deliberately contravening this curse, Ḫattušili I was making a powerful statement about his own authority and divine favor. As historian Theo van den Hout observes, "The act of rebuilding what Anitta had destroyed and cursed can be read as a foundational moment in Hittite royal ideology, establishing the king's ability to overcome supernatural obstacles through his special relationship with the gods" (van den Hout 2011: 103).

The choice of name for the new capital is also significant. Rather than imposing a new Hittite designation, Ḫattušili retained the indigenous Hattic name "Hattuša," meaning "Silver City." This decision reflects the broader Hittite pattern of cultural appropriation and integration, acknowledging the pre-existing significance of the site while repurposing it for their own political project.

The architectural development of Hattuša under Ḫattušili I and his immediate successors established patterns that would characterize the city throughout its history. The Upper City contained the main administrative complex, including what archaeologists identify as the earliest phase of the royal palace (Building A). This structure, though only partially preserved, shows the monumental scale of early Hittite royal architecture, with stone foundations supporting mud-brick superstructures.

Equally significant was the establishment of religious infrastructure within the new capital. Temple 1, the earliest identified religious structure at Hattuša, dates to this initial phase of settlement. Its basic plan—a rectangular structure with thick walls and a central courtyard—established a template that would be followed in later Hittite religious architecture. The prominent position of this temple within the city plan reflects the centrality of religious practice to Hittite state ideology.

Textual evidence suggests that Ḫattušili I not only rebuilt Hattuša physically but also established it as a ritual center. The "Proclamation of Anitta" (CTH 1) and other early texts indicate that the king transferred cult objects and established regular festivals in the new capital, effectively creating a sacred landscape that legitimized his rule. This integration of political and religious functions would remain characteristic of Hattuša throughout its history.

The decision to establish Hattuša as capital had significant geopolitical implications as well. Located further north than previous centers of power like Kanesh/Neša, Hattuša provided better access to the metal-rich Pontic region and created a buffer against threats from the northern frontier. This positioning reflected Ḫattušili's strategic priorities and anticipated the northern campaigns that would characterize his reign.

Archaeological evidence from contemporary sites in central Anatolia suggests that the establishment of Hattuša as capital was part of a broader process of political centralization. Smaller settlements show signs of abandonment or reduced occupation during this period, indicating population movement toward the new center of power. This demographic shift would have provided the human resources necessary for Ḫattušili's ambitious building projects and military campaigns.

Military Campaigns in Northern Syria

Having secured his capital, Ḫattušili I embarked on a series of military campaigns that would establish the territorial foundations of the Hittite state. His primary focus was northern Syria, a region that offered both economic opportunities and strategic advantages. The textual record of these campaigns, primarily preserved in the "Annals of Ḫattušili I" (CTH 4), provides remarkable insight into early Hittite military operations and imperial ideology.

Ḫattušili's first major Syrian campaign targeted the kingdom of Alalakh in the Amuq Valley. According to his annals, "I, the Great King Tabarna, destroyed Alalakh and Warsuwa. I reached the shore of the Great Sea and washed my weapons in the Great Sea" (KBo 10.1, trans. Beckman 2006: 219). This dramatic image of the king ritually cleansing his weapons in the Mediterranean became a powerful symbol of Hittite imperial reach, one that would be invoked by later kings seeking to emulate Ḫattušili's achievements.

The conquest of Alalakh had significant economic motivations. Control of this region provided access to Mediterranean trade networks and the valuable resources of the Amanus Mountains, particularly timber and metal ores. Archaeological evidence from Alalakh (modern Tell Atchana) confirms a destruction layer dating to approximately 1650 BCE, aligning with the textual account of Ḫattušili's campaign.

Following this initial success, Ḫattušili turned his attention to the middle Euphrates region, targeting the kingdom of Urshu. The siege of Urshu, described in detail in a fragmentary text known as the "Siege of Urshu" (CTH 7), reveals much about early Hittite military tactics and the challenges they faced in projecting power beyond Anatolia:

"The king besieged Urshu for six months. He built siege ramps against it and brought up battering rams. But the inhabitants of Urshu strengthened their wall and raised it higher... The king became angry and said to his troops: 'Why do you delay? Take the city at once!'" (KUB 31.1, trans. Hoffner 2009: 183)

This passage highlights both the sophisticated siege techniques employed by Hittite forces and the frustrations inherent in early imperial expansion. Despite these challenges, Ḫattušili eventually captured Urshu, extending Hittite influence along the crucial Euphrates corridor.

Perhaps the most significant of Ḫattušili's Syrian campaigns was his attack on Aleppo (Hittite Halpa), the dominant power in northern Syria. While he was unable to capture this heavily fortified city, Ḫattušili's assault weakened Yamhad (the kingdom centered on Aleppo) and established the Hittites as major players in Syrian politics. As historian Trevor Bryce notes, "Ḫattušili's campaigns against Yamhad, though not immediately successful in terms of territorial conquest, laid the groundwork for later Hittite domination of the region by demonstrating their military capabilities and establishing precedent for intervention" (Bryce 2005: 97).

These Syrian campaigns were not merely military adventures but reflected a coherent imperial strategy. Control of northern Syria provided economic benefits through access to trade routes and resources, created a buffer zone protecting Anatolia from Mesopotamian powers, and enhanced the king's prestige through association with the ancient urban civilizations of Syria. The campaigns also allowed Ḫattušili to project an image of divinely sanctioned conquest that strengthened his position domestically.

Textual evidence suggests that Ḫattušili developed innovative approaches to governing conquered territories. Rather than attempting direct administration of distant regions, he established treaty relationships with local rulers who acknowledged Hittite supremacy while maintaining substantial autonomy. This system, which would be elaborated by later Hittite kings, balanced the practical limitations of Bronze Age imperial control with the ideological requirements of royal prestige.

Ḫattušili I's military achievements extended beyond Syria. His annals also record campaigns within Anatolia that consolidated Hittite control over central regions and secured the northern frontier against the Kaska peoples. These operations, though less dramatic than the Syrian expeditions, were crucial in establishing the territorial core of the Hittite state.

Administrative Innovations and Legal Codes

The expansion of Hittite territory under Ḫattušili I necessitated administrative innovations to govern an increasingly complex polity. The evidence for these developments comes primarily from the corpus of Hittite laws, the earliest versions of which date to Ḫattušili's reign or shortly thereafter. These texts reveal a sophisticated approach to governance that combined indigenous Anatolian traditions with adaptations from Mesopotamian models.

The Hittite Law Code, preserved in multiple copies and recensions from throughout Hittite history, provides our most comprehensive insight into early Hittite administrative structures. Comprising approximately 200 provisions in its fullest form, the code addresses a wide range of issues, from property rights and family law to criminal penalties and compensation for injuries. Unlike contemporary Mesopotamian codes such as Hammurabi's, the Hittite laws are presented without an ideological prologue, suggesting a more pragmatic approach to legal codification.

Several features of the Hittite laws are especially noteworthy for what they reveal about administrative innovations during this formative period. First, the laws show a remarkable concern for proportionality in punishment, with penalties carefully calibrated to the severity of the offense. For example, Law §1 states:

"If anyone kills a man or woman in a quarrel, he shall bring him for burial and shall give four persons, either men or women respectively, and he shall look to his house for it." (KBo 6.2, trans. Hoffner 1997: 17)

This provision replaces the principle of retaliatory killing with a system of compensation, reflecting a sophisticated understanding of how legal mechanisms could reduce cycles of violence.

The laws also demonstrate administrative flexibility through their provision for alternative penalties based on the status and resources of the offender. Law §9 specifies:

"If anyone blinds a free person or knocks out his tooth, formerly they would pay 40 shekels of silver, but now he shall pay 20 shekels of silver. He shall look to his house for it." (KBo 6.2, trans. Hoffner 1997: 19)

The phrase "formerly... but now" indicates that the law code was periodically revised to reflect changing social and economic conditions, suggesting an adaptive approach to governance.

Perhaps most significant for understanding early Hittite administration is the law code's attention to official misconduct and accountability. Multiple provisions address the responsibilities of various officials and the penalties for failing to fulfill them. Law §50 states:

"If a district governor fails to provide seed grain to a man, and his fields remain unsown, in the place where the fields remain unsown, he shall give him grain corresponding to the neighboring fields." (KBo 6.2, trans. Hoffner 1997: 45)

Such provisions demonstrate the development of a bureaucratic apparatus with defined responsibilities and mechanisms for accountability, essential innovations for governing an expanding state.

Beyond the law codes, administrative innovations are visible in the development of specialized scribal practices during this period. The earliest Hittite texts show clear influence from Old Assyrian and Old Babylonian scribal traditions, but by the end of Ḫattušili's reign, distinctive Hittite documentary practices had emerged. These included standardized formats for administrative records, treaty texts, and royal pronouncements, facilitating consistent governance across the realm.

The "Palace Chronicle" (CTH 8), a text describing events at the royal court during this period, provides glimpses of administrative structures in action. It records the king consulting with a council of dignitaries (the *pankus*) on matters of state importance and delegating specific responsibilities to various officials. While the text has literary dimensions and cannot be read as a straightforward administrative document, it nevertheless indicates the development of formalized decision-making processes.

Archaeological evidence complements the textual record of administrative innovation. The earliest phase of the royal palace at Hattuša includes spaces identifiable as administrative areas, with evidence of record-keeping activities including clay bullae (sealing devices) and storage facilities for tablets. The standardization of ceramic production and distribution visible in the archaeological record similarly suggests increasingly centralized economic management.

Particularly significant is evidence for the development of standardized weights and measures during this period. Excavations at Hattuša and contemporary sites have yielded stone weights conforming to consistent standards, facilitating both internal economic administration and international trade. This standardization represents a crucial administrative innovation that enhanced state capacity to mobilize resources.

The innovations in governance under Ḫattušili I laid foundations for the administrative system that would sustain the Hittite state for centuries. As historian Gary Beckman observes, "The administrative structures established during the formative period of the Hittite state demonstrated a remarkable balance between centralized authority and pragmatic flexibility, characteristics that would contribute significantly to the longevity of Hittite political institutions" (Beckman 2011: 345).

The Succession Crisis and Muršili I

Despite his administrative and military achievements, Ḫattušili I faced a succession crisis that threatened the stability of his nascent state. The "Testament of Ḫattušili I" (CTH 6), a remarkable document in which the aging king addresses this crisis directly, provides unprecedented insight into royal succession dynamics during this formative period.

According to this text, Ḫattušili initially designated his nephew Labarna as his heir, but later disinherited him due to unspecified misconduct. The king then appointed his grandson Mursili as successor, despite his youth and inexperience:

"Behold, I have named Mursili as my son. Seat him upon the throne. He is still young; whatever words I speak to him, keep them in mind... Protect him, and may the gods of heaven and the gods of the netherworld protect him as well!" (KUB 1.16, trans. van den Hout 2003: 194)

This decision to designate a young and presumably malleable successor rather than an experienced adult male relative reveals the tensions inherent in early Hittite succession practices. Ḫattušili appears to have prioritized loyalty and control over traditional patterns of succession, a choice that reflected the personalized nature of authority in this formative period.

The Testament also contains a remarkable passage in which Ḫattušili reflects on the challenges he faced from his own family members:

"My sons, my brothers, my in-laws, my family members, and my troops have become my enemies. You, my servants, be loyal to my son in the future as you have been loyal to me!" (KUB 1.16, trans. Van den Hout 2003: 196)

This statement highlights the factional nature of early Hittite politics and the constant threat of internal opposition, even from within the royal family itself. By appealing directly to his officials and servants, Ḫattušili attempted to create a power base for his chosen successor that extended beyond kinship networks.

Despite these challenges, the succession of Mursili I (r. ca. 1620-1590 BCE) appears to have proceeded as Ḫattušili intended. The young king quickly demonstrated both military capability and political acumen, continuing and expanding upon his grandfather's imperial project. His reign represents both the culmination of Ḫattušili's policies and a significant extension of Hittite power.

Mursili's most dramatic achievement was his campaign against Aleppo, which succeeded where Ḫattušili had failed. The conquest of this powerful Syrian kingdom removed the primary obstacle to Hittite domination of northern Syria and demonstrated the increasing military capabilities of the Hittite state. Archaeological evidence from Aleppo confirms a major destruction event dating to approximately 1600 BCE, aligning with the textual account of Mursili's conquest.

Following this success, Mursili embarked on an even more ambitious expedition against Babylon, approximately 1,200 kilometers from Hattuša. This extraordinary campaign, documented in both Hittite and Babylonian sources, resulted in the sack of Babylon in approximately 1595 BCE, ending the dynasty of Hammurabi. A later Hittite text describes the achievement:

"Formerly Mursili was king, and his sons, brothers, in-laws, family members, and troops were united. And the land was small, but wherever he went on campaign he held the enemy lands in subjection by force. He destroyed the lands one after another, took away their power, and made them borders of the sea. When he came back from Babylon, however, a conspiracy arose against him, and Hantili, his brother-in-law, shed his blood." (KBo 3.1, trans. Beckman 2006: 223)

This passage, while highlighting Mursili's military achievements, also foreshadows the crisis that would follow his reign. The Babylon campaign, while demonstrating the extraordinary reach of Hittite military power, created logistical challenges that may have contributed to political instability at home. Unable to maintain a permanent presence in distant Mesopotamia, Mursili withdrew after looting the city, creating a power vacuum that was quickly filled by the Kassites.

The assassination of Mursili I by his brother-in-law Hantili initiated a period of succession struggles and internal conflict that would last for several generations. This crisis revealed the vulnerability of the personalized authority structure established by Ḫattušili I and demonstrated the need for more formalized succession mechanisms.

The subsequent "Edict of Telipinu" (CTH 19), issued several generations later, would explicitly reference Mursili's murder as the beginning of a dark period in Hittite history:

"When Mursili was king, his sons, brothers, in-laws, family members, and troops were united. He held enemy lands in subjection by force and took away their power, making the sea their border. But when he returned from campaign, Hantili, the cupbearer, was married to Harapshili, the sister of Mursili, and they conspired with Zidanta. They killed Mursili and shed his blood, and then Hantili became king." (KBo 3.1, trans. Hoffner 2009: 182)

Despite this violent end, Mursili's reign represented the high point of the early Hittite state. His campaigns extended Hittite influence from the Mediterranean to Mesopotamia, creating an imperial framework that later kings would struggle to maintain. The administrative innovations begun under Ḫattušili I had provided the organizational capacity for these ambitious military operations, while the establishment of Hattuša as a secure capital created the stable base from which such campaigns could be launched.

The period from Ḫattušili I through Mursili I thus represents the crucial formative phase of Hittite imperial power. Through strategic selection of a capital, ambitious military campaigns, administrative innovation, and careful management of succession, these early kings established patterns that would characterize Hittite statecraft for centuries to come.

Even as the assassination of Mursili initiated a period of instability, the foundations laid during this formative period proved strong enough to sustain the Hittite state through subsequent crises.

As historian Itamar Singer concluded in his analysis of this period, "The achievements of Ḫattušili I and Mursili I established a template for Hittite imperial practice that would be invoked by later kings seeking to legitimate their own rule. Their innovations in governance, military strategy, and territorial control created a framework for Hittite power that, despite periodic crises, would sustain one of antiquity's most resilient states for over four centuries" (Singer 2002: 134).

Chapter 5

THE SACK OF BABYLON AND ITS CONSEQUENCES

The Mesopotamian Campaign: Strategic Ambition and Geopolitical Consequences

Muršili I's expedition against Babylon represents one of the most remarkable military achievements of the Bronze Age. The sheer distance—approximately 1,200 kilometers from Hattuša to Babylon—posed enormous logistical challenges. No previous Anatolian power had projected military force so far into Mesopotamia, and the campaign's success fundamentally altered the geopolitical landscape of the ancient Near East.

The Hittite annals, though fragmentary for this period, emphasize the unprecedented nature of the achievement. One text states: "And in the tenth year [of his reign], King Muršili marched against Babylon and destroyed Babylon. He took the deportees and property of Babylon to Hattuša. After he had destroyed

Babylon, on his return Hantili... [conspired against him]" (KBo 3.57, adapted from Beckman 2000: 219). The terse account belies the complexity of the operation, which required crossing multiple mountain ranges, traversing the Syrian desert, and navigating hostile territories.

Archaeological evidence from several sites along the likely route of the Hittite army reveals destruction layers dating to approximately 1595 BCE. At Tell Bazi on the middle Euphrates, excavations uncovered a burned administrative building containing tablets dated to the final years of Samsu-ditana's reign in Babylon. Similar destruction horizons at Mari and several sites in the Khabur Triangle suggest that the Hittite forces followed the Euphrates corridor southward, securing their supply lines by subduing potential threats along the route.

The motivation behind this ambitious campaign has been debated extensively. Trevor Bryce (2005: 98-99) suggests that "the primary objective was likely the acquisition of prestige and booty rather than territorial control." This interpretation aligns with the Hittite pattern of raid-style warfare, where demonstrating royal power through dramatic victories took precedence over permanent occupation of distant territories. However, Richard Beal (2011: 597) argues that "economic motivations should not be underestimated," noting that control of trade routes connecting Anatolia to Mesopotamia represented a significant strategic advantage.

The campaign's timing coincided with a period of weakness in Babylon. The last king of Hammurabi's dynasty, Samsu-ditana (r. ca. 1625-1595 BCE), faced multiple challenges, including pressure from Kassite groups infiltrating from the Zagros mountains and the expanding power of the Sealand Dynasty in southern Mesopotamia. A fragmentary chronicle from later Babylonian tradition describes the situation: "During the time of Samsu-ditana, the Hittite [king] marched against Akkad" (Chronicle 20, lines 11-12, trans. Glassner 2004: 271).

The End of the Old Babylonian Period: Causes and Consequences

The Hittite sack of Babylon in approximately 1595 BCE marked the end of the Old Babylonian period and terminated the dynasty founded by Hammurabi. This watershed event transformed the political landscape of Mesopotamia and created ripple effects throughout the Near East.

Babylonian sources are largely silent about the details of the city's fall, reflecting the disruption of scribal traditions. However, later Mesopotamian historical consciousness preserved the memory of this catastrophic event. The Babylonian Chronicle series, compiled centuries later, records: "During the time of Samsu-ditana, the Hittites marched against Akkad" (Chronicle 20, lines 11-12, trans. Glassner 2004: 271). The brevity of this entry belies the traumatic impact of the event on Babylonian historical memory.

Archaeological evidence from Babylon itself remains limited due to the high water table that has complicated excavations of the Old Babylonian levels. However, investigations at other major centers in northern Babylonia, including Sippar and Kish, reveal destruction layers dating to this period. At Sippar, the archives of the nadītum priestesses, which had been maintained continuously for generations, abruptly end around 1595 BCE, suggesting significant disruption to institutional continuity.

The Hittite conquest coincided with—and likely exacerbated—other pressures on the Babylonian state. Climate data from lake sediment cores in the region indicate increasing aridity during the 17th and 16th centuries BCE, creating agricultural stress. Economic records show inflation in grain prices in the decades preceding the collapse. Additionally, incursions by Kassite groups from the Zagros foothills had intensified, while the southern marshlands had fallen under control of the independent Sealand Dynasty.

Dominique Charpin (2004: 372-373) characterizes the fall of Babylon as "the culmination of a multi-faceted crisis rather than simply the result of Hittite military action." The Hittite attack, though delivering the final blow to Hammurabi's dynasty, exploited vulnerabilities created by these converging pressures.

In the aftermath of the Hittite withdrawal, a power vacuum emerged in central Mesopotamia. This vacuum was quickly filled by the Kassites, who established a dynasty that would rule Babylon for the next four centuries. The Kassite Chronicle (ABC 21) states: "After the Hittites withdrew, Agum [a Kassite leader] came down and seized Babylon" (trans. Grayson 1975: 156). This transition marked a significant cultural shift, as the Kassites—originally from the Zagros region—introduced new political practices and religious elements while largely adopting Babylonian cultural traditions.

The Hittite sack of Babylon had far-reaching consequences beyond Mesopotamia. Egyptian records from the reign of Thutmose I (ca. 1504-1492 BCE) refer to diplomatic contacts with rulers of Mitanni and Babylon, suggesting that new political configurations had emerged in the power vacuum left by Babylon's fall and Hittite withdrawal. The collapse of centralized authority in Mesopotamia likely contributed to the rise of Mitanni as a major power in northern Syria—ironically creating a formidable opponent that would challenge later Hittite kings.

Hittite Withdrawal and Internal Instability

Despite the spectacular success of the Babylon campaign, the Hittites did not try to incorporate Mesopotamia into their territorial holdings. This decision reflected both practical limitations and strategic priorities. Maintaining control over territories so distant from the Anatolian heartland would have strained the administrative capabilities of the early Hittite state. As Trevor Bryce (2005: 104) notes, "The campaign was conceived as a raid rather than as the first step in establishing a permanent Hittite presence in Mesopotamia."

The Hittite forces withdrew with substantial booty, including the cult statue of Marduk, Babylon's patron deity. A later Babylonian text, the "Marduk Prophecy," appears to reference this event: "For 24 years the dwelling places lay in ruins. The Hittites carried Marduk off to Hana" (trans. Foster 2005: 388-389). The removal of divine images represented both practical plunder—as these statues often contained precious materials—and symbolic domination, demonstrating the victor's power over the defeated city's protective deities.

The logistical challenges of the long return journey to Hattuša likely contributed to the political crisis that followed. The Telipinu Edict, composed approximately a century later, establishes a direct connection between Muršili's return from Babylon and his assassination: "But when he came back from campaign, Hantili, the cupbearer, was married to Harapshili, the sister of Muršili, and they conspired with Zidanta. They killed Muršili and shed his blood" (CTH 19, trans. Hoffner 2009: 182).

This assassination began a period of succession crises and internal conflict that would last for several generations. The violence followed a pattern common to ancient Near Eastern succession disputes, with family members eliminating potential rivals. The Telipinu Edict continues: "So Hantili became king. But when Hantili became old, Zidanta killed Hantili's son Pisheni together with his sons. And then Zidanta became king. But when Zidanta had become king, Ammuna, the son of Zidanta, killed Zidanta, his father" (CTH 19, trans. Hoffner 2009: 182-183).

This cycle of violence reflected the absence of clear succession principles in the early Hittite state. Unlike some contemporary kingdoms that followed primogeniture, the Hittite monarchy employed a more flexible approach to succession. While kingship generally remained within a single extended family, selection among potential heirs could be influenced by multiple factors, including designation by the previous king, approval by a royal council (panku), and simple power politics.

The instability following Muršili's assassination also had significant territorial consequences. Hittite control over Syria rapidly disintegrated, creating opportunities for the emergence of new regional powers. Most notably, the kingdom of Mitanni (also known as Hanigalbat) expanded to fill the vacuum in northern Syria, establishing control over former Hittite client states and key trade routes. Archaeological evidence from Tell Brak, Tell Leilan, and other sites in the Khabur region shows increasing Hurrian cultural influence during this period, reflecting Mitanni's consolidation of power.

The "Dark Age" of Hittite History: Challenges and Adaptations

The period from approximately 1590 to 1430 BCE represents what scholars have traditionally termed the "dark age" of Hittite history. This characterization stems from both the relative scarcity of textual sources and the apparent contraction of Hittite territorial control. However, recent archaeological work and reanalysis of existing texts has begun to nuance this picture, revealing patterns of adaptation and resilience amid undeniable challenges.

The textual record becomes notably sparse after Muršili's assassination. While the names and approximate sequence of kings are known from later king lists and the Telipinu Edict, few contemporary documents survive from the reigns of Hantili I, Zidanta I, Ammuna, and Huzziya I. This documentary gap likely reflects both the political instability of the period and possible disruptions to the scribal institutions that produced and maintained royal archives.

Archaeological evidence from Hattuša indicates that the city remained the royal capital throughout this period, though with some signs of contraction. The excavation of "Building K" on Büyükkale (the royal citadel) revealed multiple rebuilding phases dating to this era, suggesting continued investment in administrative infrastructure despite political turmoil. However, the virtual absence of Hittite material culture at previously controlled sites in northern Syria confirms the textual indications of territorial retreat.

The kings of this period faced multiple external challenges. The Telipinu Edict summarizes the situation during Ammuna's reign (ca. 1550-1530 BCE):

"When Ammuna had become king, his sons, brothers, in-laws, family members, and troops were not united. The enemy lands began to attack him, and the lands one after another were lost. Adaniya became enemy territory, Arzawa became enemy territory, Sallapa became enemy territory, Parduwata became enemy territory, and Ahhiyawa became enemy territory" (CTH 19, trans. Hoffner 2009: 183).

This passage indicates losses on multiple fronts: Adaniya (classical Adana) in Cilicia to the south, Arzawa in western Anatolia, and other territories in various directions. The mention of "Ahhiyawa" is particularly intriguing, as this term likely refers to Mycenaean Greeks or their Anatolian outposts, suggesting early conflict with emerging Aegean powers.

The most significant geopolitical development during this period was the rise of Mitanni as a major power controlling northern Syria and upper Mesopotamia. Texts from Mari and Tell Leilan document the expansion of Hurrian political control under early Mitannian kings, including Parattarna and Shaushtatar. By approximately 1500 BCE, Mitanni had emerged as a formidable empire extending from the Mediterranean to the Zagros mountains, effectively blocking Hittite access to Syria and Mesopotamia.

Despite these challenges, the Hittite state demonstrated remarkable resilience. Internal reforms implemented during this period may have strengthened institutional foundations even as territorial extent contracted. The reign of Telipinu (ca. 1525-1500 BCE) represents a important moment of adaptation. Ascending to the throne after deposing his predecessor Huzziya I, Telipinu confronted both the immediate crisis of political violence and the longer-term challenge of institutional weakness.

The document known as the "Telipinu Edict" (CTH 19) represents both a historical justification for Telipinu's rule and a program of political reform. After recounting the cycle of violence that had plagued the royal family since Muršili's assassination, Telipinu established clear succession principles:

"Let only a prince of first rank, a son, become king. If there is no first-rank prince, then whoever is a son of second rank—let this one become king. If there is no prince, no (male) heir, then whoever is a first-rank daughter—let them take a husband for her, and let him become king" (CTH 19, trans. Hoffner 2009: 185).

This attempt to regulate succession represented a significant step toward institutionalizing royal authority. The edict also reformed the judicial process for handling cases of royal bloodshed, placing such matters before a formal assembly (panku) rather than leaving them to private vengeance.

Archaeologically, Telipinu's reign coincides with renewed building activity at Hattuša and several provincial centers. The expansion of fortifications at sites like Alaca Höyük and Ortaköy suggests efforts to consolidate control over the Anatolian heartland even as more distant territories had been lost. These infrastructure investments show that, despite territorial contraction, the central administration maintained substantial resource mobilization capabilities.

The reforms started by Telipinu created a foundation for the later imperial resurgence under Tudhaliya I/II and Suppiluliuma I. By stabilizing succession mechanisms and strengthening central institutions, Telipinu's initiatives helped the Hittite state weather the geopolitical challenges of the 16th and early 15th centuries BCE. Jared Miller (2013: 4) characterizes this period as "less a dark age than a time of strategic consolidation," noting that many of the institutional features that would characterize the later empire emerged during this challenging interval.

Ideological Adaptations and Cultural Continuity

The political challenges of the post-Muršili era prompted significant ideological adaptations. Royal inscriptions from this period reveal efforts to reframe the relationship between king, elite, and gods in ways that addressed the crisis of legitimacy created by repeated usurpations.

The Telipinu Edict explicitly connects political violence with divine disfavor and ecological disaster:

"See how it was in former times in Hattuša! If the enemy countries ever defeated the troops of Hatti, it was because the gods were angry. And since the gods were angry, there was dying in Hatti. When [kings] performed the festivals, they performed them only partially" (CTH 19, trans. Hoffner 2009: 186).

This passage reflects a sophisticated theological interpretation of political crisis, linking proper ritual observance with state security. By framing the kingdom's troubles as consequences of religious negligence rather than structural weaknesses, Telipinu provided both an explanation for past failures and a program for future success centered on ritual renewal.

The religious texts from this period show increased emphasis on purification rituals and festival performances. The "Instructions for Temple Personnel" (CTH 264), which may date to this era, establishes detailed protocols for maintaining ritual purity:

"The gods' bread shall be pure, and the libation wine shall be pure. The baker shall be pure. He shall have washed his hands and trimmed his nails. He shall be freshly bathed and wearing clean clothes" (trans. Miller 2013: 248-249).

This intensified concern with ritual correctness suggests efforts to address perceived divine displeasure through religious reforms.

Despite political instability, cultural continuity remained strong in several domains. The Hittite legal tradition, first codified under Hattušili I, continued to develop during this period. Comparison of Old Hittite and Middle Hittite versions of the legal code reveals ongoing refinement rather than radical revision, suggesting institutional continuity in the judicial sphere. Similarly, the continued production of texts in both Hittite and Akkadian indicates the maintenance of scribal traditions despite political disruptions.

Material culture shows both continuity and adaptation. Ceramic styles from this period display gradual evolution rather than abrupt changes, suggesting stable production networks despite political turmoil. The archaeological sequence at Hattuša and provincial centers like Maşat Höyük shows no evidence of major destruction or abandonment during this period, indicating that basic economic and administrative functions continued despite succession crises at the highest political level.

International Context and Diplomatic Isolation

The internal challenges facing the Hittite kingdom during this period unfolded against a backdrop of significant international developments. The 16th century BCE witnessed the emergence of new political configurations across the Near East, creating both constraints and opportunities for Hittite rulers.

In Egypt, the expulsion of the Hyksos and the reunification under the early 18th Dynasty (ca. 1550 BCE) initiated a period of Egyptian expansionism into the Levant. Campaigns by Ahmose, Thutmose I, and their successors established Egyptian influence as far north as the Euphrates. The absence of Hittite forces from Syria during this period created a vacuum that Egypt partially filled, particularly in the southern Levant.

More significantly for Hittite interests, the kingdom of Mitanni emerged as the dominant power in northern Syria and upper Mesopotamia. Texts from Tell Brak and other sites document the expansion of Mitannian control under kings Parattarna and Shaushtatar. By approximately 1500 BCE, Mitanni had consolidated an empire stretching from the Mediterranean to the Zagros, effectively blocking Hittite access to Syria and Mesopotamia.

The rise of these powers coincided with the Hittite period of internal instability, creating a challenging international environment. Diplomatic correspondence from this era is sparse, but the absence of Hittite rulers from the international diplomatic networks documented in later periods suggests a degree of isolation. Unlike the vibrant gift exchange and marriage alliances that would characterize the Amarna Age (14th century BCE), the Hittite kingdom during its "dark age" appears to have maintained few formal diplomatic relationships beyond its immediate neighbors.

This diplomatic isolation had significant economic consequences. Control over trade routes connecting Anatolia to Mesopotamia and the Levant had been a key achievement of Hattušili I and Muršili I. The loss of Syrian territories cut the Hittites off from direct access to these networks, forcing a reorientation toward more localized economic patterns. Archaeological evidence from Hittite sites dating to this period shows a decrease in imported luxury goods from Mesopotamia and Egypt, reflecting this commercial constriction.

Toward Imperial Renewal

The foundations for Hittite imperial renewal were laid during the final phases of this challenging period. Under kings Alluwamna (ca. 1500-1490 BCE) and Hantili II (ca. 1490-1480 BCE), the Hittite state began to stabilize internally, creating conditions for the more aggressive external policies that would follow under Tudhaliya I/II (ca. 1430-1410 BCE).

Archaeological evidence from provincial centers like Maşat Höyük (ancient Tapikka) indicates administrative reorganization during this transitional period. The discovery of bullae (clay sealing impressions) bearing royal seals suggests efforts to strengthen central control over regional economies. Similarly, the construction or renovation of provincial palaces and fortifications at sites like Alaca Höyük and Šapinuwa points to renewed investment in territorial administration.

Textually, this period remains poorly documented, creating challenges for precise historical reconstruction. However, fragmentary records suggest initial attempts to reassert Hittite influence in northern Syria under Hantili II and his successor Zidanta II. These efforts achieved limited success but established patterns that more powerful kings would later exploit.

The accession of Tudhaliya I/II around 1430 BCE traditionally marks the end of the Hittite "dark age" and the beginning of the Middle Kingdom period. Drawing on the institutional reforms implemented by his predecessors, Tudhaliya executed campaigns that would begin to restore Hittite influence in Syria and western Anatolia. His reign represents the culmination of a long process of adaptation and recovery that had unfolded over the previous century and a half.

Historiographical Perspectives and Reassessment

Modern scholarly assessments of the Hittite "dark age" have evolved significantly. Earlier generations of Hittitologists, working with limited textual evidence, emphasized political fragmentation and territorial contraction. More recent approaches, integrating archaeological data with close readings of available texts, have highlighted elements of resilience and adaptation during this challenging period.

Itamar Singer's influential 1998 article "From Hattuša to Tarhuntassa" characterized the period as one of "strategic consolidation" rather than simple decline, noting that many institutional features of the later empire emerged during this era. Similarly, Trevor Bryce's reassessment in "Life and Society in the Hittite World" (2002) emphasizes the cultural continuities that persisted despite political disruptions.

Archaeological work at provincial centers has been particularly important in revising older narratives. Excavations at Maşat Höyük, Ortaköy, and Kuşaklı have revealed evidence of continued administrative activity and infrastructure investment during this period, suggesting that the contraction of Hittite power was more geographically selective than previously assumed.

As Andreas Schachner (2017: 79) concludes in his synthesis of recent archaeological work, "The traditional characterization of this period as a 'dark age' primarily reflects gaps in our textual record rather than actual historical conditions. Archaeological evidence shows significant continuities in material culture, settlement patterns, and administrative practices, suggesting that the Hittite state maintained functional capacity despite succession crises at the highest political level."

This reassessment aligns with broader trends in Bronze Age studies, which increasingly emphasize the resilience and adaptability of ancient political systems rather than focusing exclusively on collapse narratives. The Hittite experience during the 16th and early 15th centuries BCE demonstrates how ancient states could weather serious challenges through institutional adaptation and ideological innovation, creating foundations for later resurgence.

The dramatic arc from Muršili's conquest of Babylon through the subsequent period of instability to eventual recovery under Telipinu and his successors illustrates both the vulnerability and resilience of early Bronze Age states. The Hittite kingdom's ability to survive this challenging period—maintaining its core territories and institutional framework despite serious setbacks—helps explain its exceptional longevity in the volatile political landscape of the ancient Near East.

Chapter 6

POLITICAL FRAGMENTATION AND RECOVERY

Crisis and Reform - The Hittite Dark Age

In the aftermath of Muršili I's assassination, the Hittite kingdom entered what scholars have traditionally termed a "dark age" - a period of approximately 150 years characterized by political instability, territorial contraction, and diminished international influence. The historical record for this period is frustratingly fragmentary, with significant gaps in our documentation that have only recently begun to be filled through archaeological discoveries and reinterpretation of existing texts.

What emerges from this patchwork of evidence is a picture of a state in crisis, yet one that possessed remarkable institutional resilience.

Succession Struggles and Weak Kings

The assassination of Muršili I around 1590 BCE marked the beginning of a prolonged period of dynastic instability. His brother-in-law and murderer, Hantili I, seized the throne but was haunted by his deed. The Telepinu Proclamation, our principal source for this period, records Hantili's anxiety: "When I took the throne, the gods sought vengeance for the blood of Muršili." This text, composed nearly a century later, presents the intervening period as one of divine punishment for the crime of regicide.

Hantili's reign (ca. 1590-1560 BCE) was troubled from the outset. The Hurrians, taking advantage of the power vacuum created by Muršili's death, launched raids deep into Hittite territory. According to fragmentary annals, "The Hurrian enemy came and plundered the land of Hatti and carried off the images of the gods to the land of Hurri." Losing divine statues represented both a religious catastrophe and a profound political humiliation.

Archaeological evidence from Hattuša supports textual accounts of Hurrian incursions during this period. Excavations in the Lower City have revealed a destruction layer dating to approximately 1570-1560 BCE, with evidence of burning and hasty abandonment. Pottery fragments and small finds from this stratum show mixed Hittite and Hurrian stylistic elements, suggesting a complex pattern of interaction rather than simple conquest.

Hantili was succeeded by his son Zidanta I, who, continuing the pattern of violence, murdered his father along with his entire family. The Telepinu Proclamation states bluntly: "Zidanta killed Hantili along with his sons, and took the throne." His reign appears to have been brief and is poorly documented in surviving sources.

The next ruler, Ammuna (ca. 1550-1530 BCE), inherited a diminished kingdom. The Telepinu Proclamation characterizes his reign as one of continued territorial losses: "In the days of Ammuna, all the lands became hostile. The armies of Adaniya, Arzawa, Šallapa, Parduwata, and Aḫḫiyawa came and plundered the lands of Hatti." These territories encompassed much of western and southern Anatolia, indicating a significant contraction of Hittite control to its central Anatolian heartland.

Ammuna's death precipitated another succession crisis. His son Tittiya briefly claimed the throne but was murdered by Ḫuzziya I, who then eliminated several other royal family members. This pattern of violence culminated in the reign of Telepinu (ca. 1525-1500 BCE), who deposed Ḫuzziya but, breaking with tradition, spared his life and sent him into exile.

Trevor Bryce has characterized this period as one in which "the Hittite royal house was devouring itself from within." The succession of murders, coups, and counter-coups severely undermined the stability of the state. Each violent transition created opportunities for both internal and external enemies, while consuming the attention and resources of the central administration.

Contemporary Hittite documents frame these events in religious terms, seeing the political chaos as divine punishment for bloodshed within the royal family.

The Telepinu Proclamation states: "Behold, this is what the shedding of blood does. The gods took revenge for the blood of Muršili on the person of Hantili, on his person, on his sons, on his household, on his servants, and on his land."

Recent scholarship, however, has emphasized structural factors behind the succession crises. Petra Goedegebuure's analysis of Old Hittite political terminology suggests that the kingdom lacked clear succession principles during this period.

The title of tuhkanti (crown prince) appears inconsistently in texts, indicating an ad hoc approach to designating heirs. Without established rules governing succession, ambitious members of the royal family had both opportunity and incentive to pursue power through violence.

Archaeological evidence from provincial centers offers a more nuanced picture of this period than textual sources alone might suggest. While political chaos engulfed the royal court, administrative continuity is evident at sites like Maşat Höyük (ancient Tapikka), where archives dating to this period show ongoing bureaucratic functions. Seal impressions and administrative texts demonstrate that, despite succession struggles at the center, provincial governance maintained significant continuity.

Loss of Syrian Territories

The territorial losses suffered during this period were most pronounced in northern Syria, where Hattušili I and Muršili I had established Hittite dominance through their military campaigns. The vacuum created by Muršili's assassination and the subsequent Hittite withdrawal provided opportunities for local powers to reassert independence.

Aleppo (Ḫalab), which had been conquered by Muršili I, quickly broke free from Hittite control. Archaeological evidence from Tell Atchana (ancient Alalakh) indicates that by approximately 1570 BCE, local dynasties had reestablished themselves throughout northwestern Syria. Level VII at Alalakh, dating to this period, shows no evidence of Hittite political control, though Hittite cultural influences persist in architectural styles and ceramic traditions.

The economic consequences of losing control over northern Syria were significant. As Itamar Singer has emphasized, "Access to Syrian trade routes represented one of the primary motivations for Hittite expansion under the early kings." Northern Syria served as the critical interface between Anatolia and the wealthy civilizations of Mesopotamia and the eastern Mediterranean. Control of this region had given the Hittites access to luxury goods, raw materials (particularly metals), and international diplomatic networks.

Textual evidence from Mari and other Mesopotamian sites indicates that by the mid-16th century BCE, Hittite merchants and diplomats had largely disappeared from Syrian commercial centers. The vacuum created by Hittite withdrawal was quickly filled by emerging regional powers, particularly the Hurrian kingdom of Mitanni.

The loss of Syrian territories also had significant ideological implications. Under Hattušili I and Muršili I, control over northern Syria had been framed as evidence of divine favor and royal legitimacy. The inability of their successors to maintain these conquests thus represented not merely a strategic setback but a challenge to the ideological foundations of royal authority.

The Hurrian Challenge and Mitanni Expansion

The most significant external threat to the Hittite kingdom during this period came from the Hurrian populations of northern Mesopotamia and eastern Anatolia. The Hurrians had been present in the region since the third millennium BCE, but it was only in the 16th century BCE that they coalesced into a major political power under the leadership of an Indo-Aryan military elite.

The kingdom of Mitanni (also known as Hanigalbat in Assyrian sources and Naharina in Egyptian texts) emerged as the dominant Hurrian state around 1550 BCE. From its heartland in the Khabur River valley of northern Mesopotamia, Mitanni expanded rapidly, taking advantage of the power vacuum created by the Hittite withdrawal from Syria and the temporary weakness of Egypt during its Second Intermediate Period.

By approximately 1530 BCE, Mitanni had established control over most of northern Syria and was pressing against the southeastern frontiers of the Hittite kingdom. The Telepinu Proclamation refers obliquely to these threats: "The enemy came from across the frontier and overwhelmed the land." Archaeological evidence from sites along the upper Euphrates, including Carchemish and Emar, confirms Mitannian political control during this period.

The Mitannian threat was not limited to military pressure. Hurrian cultural and religious influences penetrated deeply into Hittite society during this period.

Eva von Dassow's analysis of religious texts from the 15th and 14th centuries BCE reveals extensive adoption of Hurrian deities and ritual practices into Hittite cult. The goddess Šauška, the storm god Tešub, and other Hurrian deities were incorporated into official Hittite worship, reflecting both cultural exchange and political accommodation.

Linguistic evidence also points to significant Hurrian influence during this period. Annelies Kammenhuber's study of the Hittite lexicon identified numerous Hurrian loanwords entering the language during the 16th and 15th centuries BCE, particularly in the domains of ritual practice, music, and material culture. This linguistic borrowing suggests intensive cultural contact, likely facilitated by the movement of Hurrian populations into Hittite territory.

Archaeological evidence from central Anatolian sites corroborates this picture of Hurrian cultural penetration. Excavations at Alaca Höyük, Maşat Höyük, and other provincial centers have yielded ceramics and small finds showing Hurrian stylistic influences dating to this period. At Hattuša itself, the so-called "Building A" on Büyükkale (the royal acropolis) contains architectural elements and artifacts showing clear Hurrian inspiration, dating to approximately 1530-1500 BCE.

The Mitannian challenge was not solely external. Evidence suggests that Hurrian populations within Hittite territory may have served as a "fifth column" during this period. The Telepinu Proclamation refers to "men of Hurri" participating in court intrigues and succession disputes. While these references are ambiguous, they suggest that Hurrian elements within the Hittite realm may have aligned themselves with Mitannian interests.

By the early 15th century BCE, Mitanni had emerged as one of the great powers of the Near East, controlling a territory stretching from the Mediterranean coast to the Zagros Mountains. Egyptian records from the reign of Thutmose III (ca. 1479-1425 BCE) describe diplomatic exchanges and military confrontations with Mitanni, confirming its status as a major international actor. The Amarna letters, dating to the 14th century BCE, provide further evidence of Mitannian diplomatic influence throughout the region.

For the weakened Hittite kingdom, Mitannian expansion represented an existential threat. As Horst Klengel has observed, "The rise of Mitanni effectively reversed the geopolitical situation established by Hattušili I and Muršili I, transforming the Hittites from expansionist power to defensive state." This reversal contributed significantly to the crisis of legitimacy facing Hittite rulers during this period.

Telepinu's Reforms and Constitutional Changes

Against this backdrop of internal instability and external threat, Telepinu (ca. 1525-1500 BCE) emerged as a reformer whose policies would shape Hittite political institutions for centuries to come. His most significant contribution was the document known as the Telepinu Proclamation, which established clear principles for royal succession and governance.

The Proclamation begins with a historical review, contrasting the glory of early kings like Hattušili I and Muršili I with the chaos that followed: "Formerly Labarna was Great King. And then his sons, his brothers, his in-laws, his family members, and his troops were united. And the land was small, but wherever he went on campaign, he held the enemy lands in submission by force of arms."

This idealized past is contrasted with the period following Muršili's assassination: "But when they began to oppose the word of the king, then the lands began to diminish. And when they came from campaign, each nobleman would attack a city and destroy it." This passage identifies factional conflict within the elite as a primary cause of Hittite decline.

The core of Telepinu's reform was the establishment of clear succession principles. The Proclamation states: "Let only a prince of the first rank, a son, become king. If there is no first-rank prince, let a son of the second rank take kingship. If there is no prince, no (male) heir, then whoever is a first-rank son-in-law, let them take him as husband for a daughter and let him become king."

This succession formula aimed to eliminate the ambiguity that had fueled previous conflicts. By establishing a clear order of precedence - first sons, then sons-in-law - Telepinu sought to remove the incentive for violence among royal family members. As Gary Beckman has noted, "The Telepinu Proclamation represents the first documented attempt in world history to establish constitutional principles governing royal succession."

Beyond succession rules, the Proclamation addressed broader issues of governance. It established the panku (assembly of nobles) as a judicial body with authority to try cases of royal bloodshed: "If any king does evil against a brother or sister, you who are the assembly shall judge him." This provision created an institutional check on royal power, albeit a limited one focused specifically on preventing violence within the royal family.

The Proclamation also addressed administrative reforms, emphasizing the importance of maintaining provincial control: "Let the governor of each province regularly perform the service obligations of his province. Let him not oppress the people of his province, but protect them." This passage suggests efforts to strengthen provincial administration after the territorial losses of the previous decades.

Archaeological evidence supports the textual account of administrative reforms under Telepinu. Excavations at provincial centers like Maşat Höyük show evidence of architectural renovation and administrative reorganization dating to approximately 1520-1500 BCE. The distribution of standardized administrative seals at multiple sites suggests efforts to reassert central control over provincial governance.

Scholars have debated the effectiveness of Telepinu's reforms. The traditional view, articulated by Oliver Gurney and others, held that the Proclamation successfully stabilized Hittite succession practices, creating the foundation for the imperial resurgence of the 15th and 14th centuries BCE. More recent assessments, including those by Jared Miller and Mary Bachvarova, have emphasized the limits of these reforms.

Miller points out that violent succession disputes continued to occur periodically throughout Hittite history, suggesting that the Proclamation's principles were honored inconsistently. Bachvarova emphasizes the ideological dimension of the text, arguing that it should be understood as "a work of political rhetoric rather than constitutional law in the modern sense."

Despite these qualifications, the Telepinu Proclamation represents a significant innovation in ancient Near Eastern political thought. Unlike earlier Mesopotamian and Egyptian royal texts, which typically framed kingship in purely religious terms, the Proclamation acknowledges the practical, institutional dimensions of governance. It recognizes that political stability requires not just divine favor but effective institutions and clear rules.

Telepinu's reforms extended beyond succession principles to include religious innovations. Several ritual texts attributed to his reign describe efforts to reorganize cult practices and standardize festival calendars. The so-called "Telepinu Myth," while not directly connected to the historical king, gained prominence during this period and reflects similar concerns with establishing order amid chaos.

The archaeological record from Hattuša shows evidence of building activity during Telepinu's reign, including renovations to the royal acropolis (Büyükkale) and the construction of new temple facilities. These projects suggest efforts to reassert royal authority through monumental architecture after the instability of previous decades.

In foreign affairs, Telepinu adopted a pragmatic approach, focusing on securing Hittite borders rather than pursuing the expansionist policies of Hattušili I and Muršili I. A treaty between Telepinu and Išputahšu of Kizzuwatna (Cilicia) established a defensive alliance against Hurrian expansion, representing an early example of the treaty diplomacy that would become a hallmark of later Hittite statecraft.

Reassessing the "Dark Age"

Traditional historiography has characterized the period between Muršili I and Tudhaliya I/II (ca. 1590-1430 BCE) as a "dark age" of Hittite history. This framing, influenced by the negative portrayal in the Telepinu Proclamation itself, emphasizes political instability, territorial losses, and cultural decline.

Recent scholarship has challenged this narrative, offering a more nuanced assessment. Trevor Bryce suggests that "the concept of a Hittite dark age reflects the limitations of our sources more than historical reality." While political instability at the center is well-documented, archaeological evidence indicates significant continuity in material culture and administrative practices throughout this period.

Itamar Singer's influential reassessment emphasizes the creative adaptations that occurred during this challenging period: "Far from being simply an era of decline, the so-called dark age witnessed crucial institutional innovations that would provide the foundation for later imperial resurgence." Telepinu's reforms represent the most visible of these innovations, but archaeological evidence suggests broader patterns of adaptation throughout Hittite society.

Provincial sites like Maşat Höyük, Ortaköy (ancient Šapinuwa), and Kuşaklı (ancient Šarišša) show evidence of continuous occupation and administrative activity throughout this period. The persistence of Hittite administrative practices in these provincial centers suggests that, despite succession crises at the capital, the basic infrastructure of the state remained intact.

Linguistic and textual evidence also points to important cultural developments during this period. The increased use of the Hittite language (rather than Akkadian) for administrative and religious texts dates to the late 16th and early 15th centuries BCE. Similarly, the codification of Hittite laws appears to have begun during this period, with the earliest versions of the Hittite legal code dating to approximately 1500 BCE.

Petra Goedegebuure's analysis of political terminology suggests that this period witnessed the evolution of more sophisticated concepts of kingship and governance. Terms like Tabarna (title of the king) and Tawananna (title of the queen) acquired more precise institutional meanings during this era, reflecting efforts to formalize royal authority in response to succession crises.

Archaeological evidence from cult centers indicates significant religious developments during this period. Excavations at Yazılıkaya, the rock sanctuary near Hattuša, have revealed evidence of ritual activity dating to the 16th century BCE, predating the monumental relief sculptures of the 13th century. This suggests that the site's importance as a religious center developed during the so-called "dark age."

Integrating Hurrian religious elements into Hittite cult practice, while partly reflecting political pressure from Mitanni, also represented a creative cultural synthesis. Maciej Popko's analysis of religious texts from this period identifies a pattern of "selective adaptation," in which Hurrian deities and rituals were incorporated into Hittite practice while being reinterpreted within a Hittite theological framework.

Even the territorial contractions of this period allow for reassessment as strategic adaptations rather than simple decline. The withdrawal from Syria allowed the Hittite state to concentrate resources on securing its Anatolian heartland. As Andreas Schachner notes, "The focus on central Anatolia during this period laid the groundwork for the more sustainable imperial system that would emerge under Tudhaliya I/II and his successors."

Transition to Imperial Resurgence

The reforms initiated by Telepinu created conditions for the Hittite imperial resurgence that began under Tudhaliya I/II (ca. 1430-1410 BCE). While there remains a gap of approximately 70 years between Telepinu and Tudhaliya in our documentation, archaeological evidence suggests gradual recovery during this intervening period.

The accession of Tudhaliya I/II traditionally marks the beginning of the Middle Kingdom period in Hittite history. Drawing on the institutional foundations established by Telepinu, Tudhaliya initiated campaigns that began to restore Hittite influence in Syria and western Anatolia. A fragmentary text known as the

"Annals of Tudhaliya" describes military campaigns against Arzawa in western Anatolia and diplomatic initiatives in northern Syria.

Archaeological evidence from Hattuša shows significant building activity during Tudhaliya's reign, including the construction of a new palace complex on Büyükkale and the expansion of the city's fortifications. These projects reflect both increased resources and renewed confidence after the challenges of the previous century.

The religious policies of Tudhaliya I/II built upon developments from the "dark age" period. Texts from his reign describe efforts to systematize cult practices, integrating Hurrian elements into a coherent Hittite framework. The so-called "Festival of the Month" (CTH 591), attributed to his reign, represents an attempt to standardize religious observances throughout the kingdom.

In foreign affairs, Tudhaliya confronted the continuing challenge posed by Mitanni. Rather than directly challenging Mitannian power, he adopted a strategy of diplomatic encirclement, establishing alliances with Kizzuwatna (Cilicia) and Aleppo. These diplomatic initiatives laid the groundwork for the more aggressive anti-Mitannian policies that would be pursued by his successors Arnuwanda I and Tudhaliya III.

Conclusion

The period between Muršili I's assassination and Telepinu's reforms represents one of the most challenging phases in Hittite history. Succession struggles, territorial losses, and external threats combined to create a profound crisis for the Hittite state. Yet this period also witnessed crucial adaptations and innovations that would shape Hittite institutions for centuries to come.

Telepinu's reforms, particularly his establishment of clear succession principles, represented a significant innovation in ancient political thought. By acknowledging the institutional dimensions of governance and establishing formal procedures for managing succession, Telepinu created foundations for greater political stability.

The traditional characterization of this period as a "dark age" reflects both the limitations of our sources and the negative portrayal in the Telepinu Proclamation itself. Archaeological evidence reveals significant continuities in material culture and administrative practices, suggesting that the Hittite state maintained functional capacity despite political challenges at the center.

The Hittite experience during this period illustrates both the vulnerability and resilience of early Bronze Age states. The assassination of Muršili I triggered a cascade of succession crises that severely weakened the kingdom, yet the basic institutional framework established by earlier kings proved durable enough to survive these challenges.

This resilience helps explain one of the most remarkable features of Hittite history: the kingdom's ability to recover from near-collapse and reemerge as a major imperial power by the mid-15th century BCE. The reforms and adaptations that occurred during the so-called "dark age" created institutional foundations for this imperial resurgence, demonstrating how periods of crisis can generate innovations that enable long-term survival.

As we transition to examining the Middle Kingdom period under Tudhaliya I/II and his successors, it is important to recognize the continuities that link this era of renewed expansion to the challenging period that preceded it. The Hittite imperial system that would dominate Anatolia until 1180 BCE built directly upon institutional innovations that emerged during the kingdom's darkest hour.

Chapter 7

TUDḫALIYA I/II AND IMPERIAL RESTORATION

The Middle Kingdom (c. 1500-1400 BCE)

Imperial Resurgence

The transition from the Old Kingdom to what scholars term the Middle Kingdom period (ca. 1500-1400 BCE) represents one of the most remarkable recoveries in ancient Near Eastern history. Following decades of political instability and territorial contraction, the Hittite state under Tudhaliya I/II put into action a process of systematic reconquest and institutional renewal that would establish foundations for the subsequent imperial period.

The historical record for the early phases of this recovery remains fragmentary. The so-called "Deeds of Tudhaliya" (CTH 142), preserved only in later copies, provides our primary textual evidence for the military campaigns that reestablished Hittite control over central Anatolia. According to this document, Tudhaliya confronted a coalition of enemies described as the "Assuwan Confederacy" in western Anatolia:

"When the men of Assuwa rose up against me, the Storm God, my lord, delivered them into my hand. I defeated them and pursued them to the sea. I brought back to Hattuša 10,000 infantry and 600 teams of horses."

While the numbers are likely exaggerated, archaeological evidence confirms increased Hittite influence in western Anatolia during this period. Excavations at sites like Beycesultan (Level IVa) show destruction layers dating to approximately 1430 BCE, followed by architectural features suggesting Hittite administrative presence.

The reconquest extended beyond western Anatolia to include the restoration of Hittite authority in the Upper Land (northeastern Anatolia) and the Kaska frontier region to the north. The fragmentary "Annals of Arnuwanda I" (CTH 143) describe campaigns against Kaska groups who had occupied Hittite territories during the preceding period of weakness:

"The enemy from Kaska had taken the cities of the Upper Land. But I, Arnuwanda, the Great King, went against them with chariotry and infantry. I recaptured the cities that the Kaska people had taken, and I resettled them with people of Hatti."

Archaeological surveys in north-central Anatolia confirm the reestablishment of Hittite administrative centers during this period. At sites like Maşat Höyük (ancient Tapikka) and Ortaköy (ancient Sapinuwa), excavations have revealed administrative complexes dating to the Middle Kingdom period, demonstrating the systematic nature of this territorial reconsolidation.

The Hittite reconquest faced significant challenges from the kingdom of Mitanni, which had emerged as the dominant power in northern Syria during the Hittite "dark age." Tudhaliya I/II and his successor Arnuwanda I pursued a strategy of diplomatic encirclement, establishing alliances with polities on Mitanni's periphery. The treaty between Tudhaliya and Sunaššura of Kizzuwatna (CTH 41) exemplifies this approach:

"Thus speaks Tudhaliya, Great King, King of Hatti: I have taken Sunaššura, King of Kizzuwatna, as my brother and ally. He shall be my friend and the enemy of my enemy."

This diplomatic offensive created conditions for more direct confrontation with Mitanni under subsequent rulers. Trevor Bryce observes that "the restoration of Hittite power in Anatolia under Tudhaliya I/II and Arnuwanda I was a necessary precondition for the more ambitious Syrian campaigns of their successors" (Bryce 2005: 129).

Military Innovation

The military resurgence of the Hittite kingdom during the Middle Kingdom period coincided with significant technological and organizational innovations. The most consequential development was the transformation of chariot warfare, which evolved from the relatively lightweight vehicles of the Old Kingdom to more robust platforms capable of supporting multiple warriors.

Archaeological evidence for this transformation comes from both pictorial representations and surviving equipment. The rock relief at İmamkulu, dating to approximately 1400 BCE, depicts a chariot carrying two warriors—a driver and a combatant—representing what military historian Robert Drews terms "the mature form of Bronze Age chariotry" (Drews 1993: 104). Excavations at Hattuša have yielded fragments of chariot fittings showing increased structural reinforcement compared to earlier examples.

Textual evidence confirms the importance of these developments. The "Instructions for the Royal Bodyguard" (CTH 262) contains detailed provisions for the maintenance and deployment of chariot forces:

"The chariot warriors shall keep their weapons, their chariots, and their teams in good order. The overseer of a thousand shall inspect them monthly. Any man whose equipment is found deficient shall make good the deficiency from his own resources."

The size of Hittite chariot forces increased substantially during this period. While Old Kingdom texts mention units of several hundred chariots, Middle Kingdom military records describe forces of up to 1,000 chariots. This expansion required significant logistical infrastructure, including specialized workshops for vehicle production and facilities for breeding and training horses.

Infantry organization also evolved during this period. The "Instructions for the Commander of the Border Guards" (CTH 261) describes a hierarchical structure with units organized in decimal formations (groups of 10, 100, and 1,000). Archaeological evidence from frontier fortresses like Kuşaklı (ancient Sarissa) reveals barracks facilities designed to accommodate these standardized units.

Weapons technology saw significant innovation during the Middle Kingdom. Metallurgical analysis of bronze artifacts from this period shows increased tin content compared to earlier examples, resulting in harder, more durable alloys. The "Palace Inventory Texts" (CTH 241-250) document large stockpiles of standardized weapons, including:

"5,000 spears with bronze heads, 2,000 bows with horn reinforcement, 10,000 arrows with bronze points, 500 bronze helmets of the new type..."

The reference to "the new type" of helmets is notable, suggesting conscious technological innovation. Archaeological discoveries at sites like Boğazköy and Kuşaklı have yielded examples of conical helmets with cheek pieces, representing a substantial improvement over earlier designs.

Defensive architecture underwent parallel developments. The fortifications at Hattuša were substantially expanded during the Middle Kingdom, with the addition of what archaeologists term the "Upper City." These new defenses incorporated postern tunnels, caponiers, and other sophisticated features that military historian Yigael Yadin described as "two millennia ahead of their time" (Yadin 1963: 71).

Perhaps the most significant military innovation of this period was organizational rather than technological. The Hittites developed a sophisticated system for mobilizing and sustaining forces in the field. The "Instructions for the BĒL MADGALTI" (Provincial Governor, CTH 261) detail procedures for mustering troops from provincial populations:

"When the word of the king comes for a campaign, you shall immediately muster the troops of your province. Every man liable for service shall provide his own weapons and rations for three months. You shall record their names on wooden tablets and send one copy to the palace."

This system of provincial mobilization allowed the Hittite state to field larger forces than would have been possible using only professional soldiers. Richard Beal notes that "the Hittite military system represented a sophisticated balance between a permanent professional core and a broader provincial levy" (Beal 1992: 427).

The cumulative effect of these military innovations was to create forces capable of both reconquering lost territories and projecting power beyond Anatolia's borders. As Mary Bachvarova observes, "The military developments of the Middle Kingdom created the capacity for the more ambitious imperial projects of Suppiluliuma I and his successors" (Bachvarova 2016: 152).

Administrative Reorganization

The territorial expansion of the Middle Kingdom period necessitated significant administrative innovations. The Hittite state developed more sophisticated mechanisms for controlling territory, extracting resources, and maintaining political allegiance across its growing domains.

At the center of this administrative system stood the king, whose role evolved significantly during this period. Royal titles expanded to emphasize universal claims, with Tudhaliya I/II and his successors adopting the full titulary: "Great

King, Hero, Beloved of the Storm God, King of Hatti Land." Practical innovations accompanied this ideological assertion of supreme authority in governance.

The palace administration grew more complex, with specialized officials responsible for distinct aspects of state activity. The "Palace Chronicle" (CTH 8) describes the organization of the royal court under Tudhaliya I/II:

"These are the officials who stand before the king: the Chief of the Wine Stewards, the Chief of the Table-Men, the Chief of the Heralds, the Chief of the Palace Attendants, the Chief of the Scribes on Wooden Tablets, the Chief of the Scribes on Clay Tablets..."

Archaeological evidence from Hattuša confirms this administrative elaboration. The excavation of Building A on Büyükkale (the citadel) revealed a complex that German archaeologist Peter Neve identified as the central chancellery of the Hittite state. This facility included specialized storage areas for different types of documents, workspaces for scribes, and reception areas for official business.

The most significant administrative innovation of the Middle Kingdom period was the development of a more formalized provincial system. The text known as the "Instructions for the BĒL MADGALTI" (CTH 261) provides detailed guidelines for provincial governors, addressing matters ranging from judicial procedures to border security:

"You shall judge cases according to the law. You shall not take bribes. You shall not show favoritism to anyone, whether he is a relative or a friend... You shall maintain the border posts and watchtowers. You shall send scouts across the border every day to observe enemy movements..."

This document reveals a sophisticated conception of delegated authority, with provincial governors exercising substantial power while remaining accountable to the central administration. The archaeological identification of provincial centers like Maşat Höyük (ancient Tapikka) has provided physical evidence for this system, with discoveries including administrative archives that document communication between local officials and the central government.

The Middle Kingdom period also saw innovations in resource management. The "Land Donation Texts" (CTH 222) document royal grants of agricultural land to officials and military officers, creating a class of service-holders dependent on royal favor:

"Thus speaks My Sun Arnuwanda, Great King: Because Huzziyas the chariot-fighter has served me well, I have given to him the village of Hariyasas with all its fields, vineyards, and dependents. He shall hold it free of all obligations, and his sons shall inherit it after him, as long as they continue to serve the king of Hatti."

This system of land grants served multiple purposes: rewarding service, ensuring the loyalty of elites, and establishing royal representatives in provincial areas. Jared Miller argues that "the land donation system represented a sophisticated solution to the challenge of maintaining elite loyalty while extending state control into peripheral regions" (Miller 2013: 77).

The administration of conquered territories evolved during this period, with the development of what scholars term the "Hittite imperial system." Rather than imposing direct rule, the Hittites typically established treaty relationships with subordinate rulers. The treaty between Arnuwanda I and the rulers of Hayasa (CTH 42) exemplifies this approach:

"You shall be my ally. The enemy of the King of Hatti shall be your enemy, and the friend of the King of Hatti shall be your friend. You shall send troops when the King of Hatti summons them, and you shall pay the tribute established in this tablet."

This flexible approach to imperial control allowed the Hittites to extend their influence without overextending their administrative capacity. As Gary Beckman notes, "The Hittite imperial system prioritized political loyalty and resource extraction over cultural homogenization or direct administration" (Beckman 1999: 54).

The administrative innovations of the Middle Kingdom created institutional foundations for the subsequent imperial period. By developing more sophisticated mechanisms for controlling territory, mobilizing resources, and maintaining political allegiance, Tudhaliya I/II and his successors established a system capable of supporting more ambitious imperial projects.

The Rise of the "Great Kings"

The Middle Kingdom period witnessed the emergence of what scholars term the "Great Kings" system—a network of diplomatic relationships among the major powers of the ancient Near East. This system, which would reach its full elaboration during the subsequent imperial period, fundamentally altered the political landscape of the region.

The Hittite rulers of this period consciously positioned themselves as peers of other major kings, particularly the pharaohs of Egypt and the kings of Mitanni and Babylon. The adoption of the title "Great King" (LUGAL.GAL) by Tudhaliya I/II represented both an ideological claim and a practical assertion of status in interstate relations.

Archaeological evidence for this development comes from the discovery of cuneiform tablets at sites like Tell el-Amarna in Egypt and Maşat Höyük in Anatolia. These archives document diplomatic correspondence between royal courts, conducted according to elaborate protocols that emphasized the equality of "Great Kings" while maintaining their superiority over lesser rulers.

The letter from Tudhaliya I/II to an unnamed Egyptian pharaoh (possibly Amenhotep II) exemplifies this diplomatic language:

"Thus speaks Tudhaliya, Great King, King of Hatti: Say to the King of Egypt, Great King, my brother: For me all goes well. For you, your household, your wives, your sons, your country, your magnates, your horses, your chariots, may all go well!"

This formulation, with its greeting between "brothers" and parallel wishes for well-being, established a framework of formal equality between the major powers. Trevor Bryce observes that "the diplomatic protocols of the Great Kings system represented a sophisticated mechanism for managing interstate relations in the absence of overarching authority" (Bryce 2003: 89).

The Great Kings system involved more than formal correspondence. Archaeological discoveries have documented substantial gift exchange between royal courts. The "Palace Inventory Texts" (CTH 241-250) record luxury items received from foreign rulers:

"One gold cup inlaid with lapis lazuli, gift of the King of Egypt. One chariot overlaid with silver, with two horses equipped with trappings of red leather, gift of the King of Mitanni. Twenty garments of fine linen with purple borders, gift of the King of Babylon."

These exchanges served multiple purposes: demonstrating wealth and status, establishing personal connections between rulers, and creating material expressions of diplomatic relationships. As Amanda Podany notes, "Gift exchange created tangible bonds between courts, transforming abstract political relationships into personal obligations" (Podany 2010: 312).

The emergence of the Great Kings system coincided with increased competition for influence in strategically important regions, particularly Syria. The fragmentary "Deeds of Arnuwanda I" (CTH 143) describes diplomatic initiatives aimed at countering Mitannian influence:

"When the people of Nuhašše inclined toward the King of Mitanni, I sent messengers with many gifts to their king. I reminded him of the friendship that had existed between his father and my father Tudhaliya. He returned to the allegiance of Hatti, and I confirmed him in his kingship."

This episode illustrates the complex interplay between diplomacy and power politics that characterized the Great Kings system. While maintaining formal equality with other major powers, the Hittite rulers sought advantage through relationships with smaller states in contested regions.

The diplomatic activities of the Middle Kingdom period laid foundations for the more ambitious international initiatives of Suppiluliuma I and his successors. By establishing Hatti's position within the Great Kings system, Tudhaliya I/II and Arnuwanda I created conditions for the subsequent expansion of Hittite influence throughout the eastern Mediterranean world.

As Itamar Singer observed, "The diplomatic innovations of the Middle Kingdom period were as significant as the military and administrative developments in enabling Hittite imperial resurgence" (Singer 2011: 98). The Great Kings system provided a framework within which the Hittites could legitimately assert their interests and extend their influence beyond Anatolia.

Institutional Continuity and Innovation

The transformation of the Hittite state during the Middle Kingdom period represented a complex blend of continuity and innovation. While introducing significant new administrative and military capabilities, Tudhaliya I/II and his successors maintained fundamental aspects of Hittite political culture established during the Old Kingdom.

Religious institutions exemplify this pattern of innovative conservation. The Middle Kingdom period saw substantial elaboration of cult practices, with increased Hurrian influence evident in both pantheon and ritual. The "Festival Texts" (CTH 591-724) document new ceremonies introduced during this period, including the purulli spring festival and the AN.TAH.ŠUM festival cycle.

Yet these innovations were framed as restorations of ancient tradition. The colophon to a ritual text from Arnuwanda I's reign is characteristic:

"This is a copy of an old tablet. Because the original had become damaged, Arnuwanda, Great King, ordered that it be rewritten according to the words of Allitaḫ, the elderly priest from Zithara."

This rhetorical emphasis on continuity with the past served important political functions. As Mary Bachvarova notes, "The Hittite state legitimized innovation by presenting it as restoration, maintaining the fiction of an unchanging tradition while adapting to new circumstances" (Bachvarova 2016: 205).

Similar patterns appear in legal institutions. The Middle Kingdom version of the Hittite Laws (CTH 291-292) incorporated significant innovations, particularly regarding property rights and obligations associated with land grants. Yet these changes were presented as clarifications of existing principles rather than innovations. The prologue maintains the traditional attribution to earlier kings:

"These are the words of the Tabarna, the Great King: If anyone commits an offense, shall he not make restitution according to the word of the king?"

Political institutions demonstrated the same blend of continuity and innovation. The panku assembly established by Telepinu continued to function, but its role evolved from potential check on royal power to instrument of royal authority. The "Protocol for the Royal Bodyguard" (CTH 262) describes the assembly's participation in state ceremonies:

"When the king enters the chamber of the panku, the bodyguards shall stand at the doorway with their weapons at the ready. No one shall approach the king without permission."

This evolution reflects what political scientist Jack Goldstone terms "adaptive traditionalism"—the capacity to introduce substantial innovations while maintaining the appearance of continuity with established traditions. As Goldstone observes, "The most successful premodern states were those that could innovate while claiming to preserve tradition" (Goldstone 1991: 37).

The architectural development of Hattuša during this period provides physical expression of this dynamic. The expansion of the city to include the "Upper City" represented a substantial innovation, nearly doubling the urban area and introducing new monumental structures. Yet this development incorporated traditional elements, with temples in the Upper City maintaining conventional layouts while increasing in scale and elaboration.

The German archaeologist Jürgen Seeher describes this pattern as "innovative conservatism," noting that "the architects of Middle Kingdom Hattuša introduced significant innovations in urban planning while maintaining continuity in the design of individual structures" (Seeher 2006: 142).

Perhaps the most significant continuity between the Old Kingdom and Middle Kingdom periods was the central role of the royal family in state governance. Despite the administrative elaboration described above, the Hittite state remained fundamentally dynastic in character. The "Palace Chronicle" (CTH 8) describes how royal family members occupied key positions:

"The king appointed his brother Zidanza as Chief of the Wine Stewards, his son Arnuwanda as Chief of the Charioteers, and his brother-in-law Himuili as Chief of the Bodyguard."

This continued reliance on kinship networks as the foundation of state administration created both strengths and vulnerabilities. While ensuring loyalty among top officials, it also perpetuated the succession conflicts that had plagued the Old Kingdom. The assassination of Tudhaliya the Younger (son of Arnuwanda I) around 1400 BCE demonstrated the persistent challenge of managing succession within this dynastic system.

The institutional developments of the Middle Kingdom created foundations for the subsequent imperial period under Suppiluliuma I and his successors. By blending innovation with claims to tradition, Tudhaliya I/II and Arnuwanda I established more robust administrative, military, and diplomatic capabilities while maintaining the legitimizing frameworks of Hittite political culture.

Conclusion: Foundations of Empire

The Middle Kingdom period represents a crucial transitional phase in Hittite history. Following the political fragmentation and territorial contraction of the "dark age," Tudhaliya I/II and his successors systematically reconstructed Hittite power through military reconquest, administrative reorganization, and diplomatic innovation.

The reconquest of central Anatolia established a secure territorial base for subsequent imperial expansion. The development of more sophisticated military technologies and organizational systems created forces capable of projecting power beyond Anatolia's borders. Administrative innovations provided mechanisms for controlling territory and extracting resources across an expanding domain. The emergence of the Great Kings system positioned Hatti as a legitimate peer of other major powers in the ancient Near East.

These developments created conditions for the dramatic imperial expansion that would occur under Suppiluliuma I (ca. 1350-1322 BCE). As Itamar Singer observes, "The achievements of Suppiluliuma I, often portrayed as revolutionary, in fact represented the culmination of processes set in motion during the Middle Kingdom period" (Singer 2011: 142).

Archaeological evidence confirms this interpretation. Excavations at Hattuša reveal substantial building activity during the Middle Kingdom, establishing the urban framework that would support the imperial capital. Provincial centers like Maşat Höyük and Kuşaklı demonstrate the extension of administrative infrastructure throughout the kingdom. International connections are documented by imported goods found in Middle Kingdom contexts, including Egyptian scarabs, Mycenaean pottery, and Mesopotamian cylinder seals.

The Middle Kingdom thus represents not merely a period of recovery from earlier setbacks, but a creative phase of state formation that established foundations for subsequent imperial development. By systematically addressing the military, administrative, and diplomatic challenges facing the kingdom, Tudhaliya I/II and his successors transformed the Hittite state into a more robust and capable political entity.

This transformation occurred within a broader regional context of increasing interstate competition and connection. The second half of the second millennium BCE witnessed the emergence of what scholars term the "international age"—a period characterized by intensive diplomatic, commercial, and cultural exchanges among the major powers of the eastern Mediterranean and Near East. The innovations of the Hittite Middle Kingdom positioned Hatti to take part fully in this emerging international system.

As we transition to examining the imperial period under Suppiluliuma I and his successors, it is important to recognize the continuities that link these eras. The Hittite Empire that would dominate Anatolia and northern Syria until its collapse around 1180 BCE built directly upon the institutional foundations established during the Middle Kingdom. Understanding these foundations is essential for comprehending both the achievements and limitations of Hittite imperial power.

Chapter 8

ŠUPPILULIUMA I: THE GREAT CONQUEROR

Šuppiluliuma I and the Creation of Empire

The transformation of the Hittite kingdom into a true empire occurred under the reign of Šuppiluliuma I (ca. 1350-1322 BCE), whose achievements fundamentally altered the geopolitical landscape of the Late Bronze Age Near East. While his predecessors had established the foundations for imperial expansion, it was Šuppiluliuma who executed the ambitious program of conquest and diplomatic maneuvering that positioned Hatti as a genuine rival to Egypt for regional hegemony.

The Destruction of Mitanni and Conquest of Syria

The kingdom of Mitanni had dominated northern Mesopotamia and Syria for nearly two centuries, effectively blocking Hittite expansion southward since the Old Kingdom period. Archaeological evidence from sites like Tell Brak and Tell

Fekheriye confirms Mitanni's control of this strategic region, with distinctive palace complexes and administrative centers demonstrating their political dominance (Akkermans and Schwartz 2003: 327-329).

The "Deeds of Šuppiluliuma," compiled by his son Muršili II, describes the strategic approach that ultimately dismantled this longstanding rival:

"My father sent troops and chariots against the lands of Išuwa, and they attacked Išuwa. And again he sent Lupakki and Tarhunta-zalma to the land of Amka, and they attacked Amka and brought back captives and possessions to my father. But when the king of Egypt heard of the attack on Amka, he was afraid, and he asked my father for his son to take in marriage." (KBo 5.6)

This passage reveals Šuppiluliuma's methodical approach to dismantling Mitanni's sphere of influence. Rather than launching a direct assault on Mitanni's heartland, he first targeted peripheral territories and Egyptian-controlled regions in Syria, testing the responses of both major powers while securing strategic positions for subsequent campaigns.

The decisive campaign against Mitanni came after careful preparation. Šuppiluliuma negotiated an alliance with Artatama II, a rival claimant to the Mitannian throne, effectively exploiting internal divisions within the kingdom. He also secured his northern and western frontiers through treaties with the Kaska peoples and Arzawan states, allowing him to concentrate his forces eastward. The Hittite king then executed what historian Trevor Bryce (2005: 159) calls "one of the most audacious military maneuvers of the ancient world"—crossing the Euphrates River and attacking the Mitannian capital of Waššukanni from an unexpected direction.

The "Deeds" describes this campaign in vivid terms:

"When my father became king, the kings who were his equals in rank were these: Hurri-land, Egypt-land, Babylon-land, Assyria-land, and Ahhiyawa-land. And when my father attacked the king of Hurri-land, he defeated the king of Hurri-land... he crossed the Euphrates and went to Waššukanni. And the king of Hurri-land, Tušratta, fled; he did not come to oppose my father." (KBo 5.6)

Archaeological evidence supports this textual account. Excavations at Tell Brak (ancient Nagar) reveal a destruction layer dating to approximately 1340 BCE, followed by the appearance of Hittite-style administrative practices and material culture (Oates et al. 1997: 142-143). Similar patterns appear at other sites throughout northern Syria, confirming the dramatic shift in political control described in the texts.

The conquest of Mitanni created a power vacuum in northern Syria that Šuppiluliuma moved quickly to fill. He captured key Syrian cities, including Aleppo, Alalakh, and eventually Carchemish, which he made the seat of a secondary Hittite royal line under his son Piyaššili/Šarri-Kušuh. The strategic importance of these conquests cannot be overstated—they secured valuable trade routes connecting Anatolia to Mesopotamia and the Mediterranean coast, provided access to resources like timber and minerals, and created a buffer zone protecting Hittite core territories.

As historian Itamar Singer (2011: 167) observes, "Šuppiluliuma's Syrian conquests represented not merely territorial acquisition but a fundamental restructuring of regional power relations. By eliminating Mitanni as an independent actor, he created a bipolar system dominated by Hatti and Egypt."

The Amarna Letters and International Diplomacy

The Amarna archive, discovered in 1887 at Tell el-Amarna in Egypt, provides extraordinary insight into the diplomatic interactions of the Late Bronze Age "Great Powers." This collection of over 350 cuneiform tablets primarily represents diplomatic correspondence between the Egyptian court and various Near Eastern kingdoms during the reigns of Amenhotep III and Akhenaten (ca. 1390-1336 BCE). Among these tablets are several letters exchanged between the Hittite and Egyptian courts that illuminate the complex relationship between these competing powers.

EA 41, a letter from Šuppiluliuma to Pharaoh Akhenaten, exemplifies the formal diplomatic language that characterized Great King correspondence:

"Say to Naphurureya [Akhenaten], Great King, King of Egypt, my brother: Thus says Šuppiluliuma, Great King, King of Hatti, your brother. With me all goes well. With you may all go well. With your household, with your wives, with your sons, with your magnates, with your troops, with your chariots, with your land, may all go very well." (EA 41)

This elaborate greeting formula reflects what scholar Raymond Cohen (1996: 18) terms "the brotherhood of kings"—a diplomatic fiction that positioned the rulers of major powers as equals regardless of their actual relative strength. The exchange of greeting gifts mentioned in these letters—gold, lapis lazuli, fine textiles, and specialty crafts—served to materialize these relationships, with each gift requiring reciprocation of equal or greater value.

The Amarna letters reveal the multipolar international system within which Šuppiluliuma operated. In addition to Egypt and Hatti, this system included Babylonia, Assyria, and initially Mitanni, with each power maintaining diplomatic relations with the others through regular correspondence and embassy exchanges. Mario Liverani (2001: 176) characterizes this as "a system of balanced multipolarity," noting that "no single power could achieve hegemony without triggering coalition formation among its rivals."

Šuppiluliuma's diplomatic skill is evident in his ability to manipulate this system to Hittite advantage. His correspondence with Babylonia (preserved in Hittite archives) shows how he isolated Mitanni diplomatically before attacking it militarily. Similarly, his letters to Egypt maintained peaceful relations on the southern front while he concentrated on eastern campaigns. The Hittite king also exploited Egyptian domestic turmoil during Akhenaten's religious reforms, timing his Syrian campaigns to coincide with periods of Egyptian distraction.

The international diplomatic system documented in the Amarna archive operated according to established conventions that helped regulate interstate conflict. As political scientist Raymond Cohen observes, "These conventions included rules for royal succession recognition, protocols for embassy reception, and norms regarding territorial control" (Cohen 1996: 24). Šuppiluliuma's innovation lay not in creating new diplomatic forms but in manipulating existing ones with unprecedented skill.

The Egyptian Queen's Marriage Proposal

Perhaps the most dramatic diplomatic episode of Šuppiluliuma's reign—and one of the most remarkable events in ancient Near Eastern history—was the request by an Egyptian queen for a Hittite prince to become her husband and pharaoh. This extraordinary incident is recorded in the "Deeds of Šuppiluliuma" and the "Plague Prayers" of Muršili II:

"When the people of Egypt learned of the destruction of Amka, they were afraid. And since, in addition, their lord Nibhururiya had died, the queen of Egypt, who was Dahamunzu, sent a messenger to my father and wrote to him thus: 'My husband has died. I have no son. But they say that you have many sons. If you would give me one of your sons, he would become my husband. I will never take a servant of mine and make him my husband.'" (KBo 5.6)

This request came while Šuppiluliuma was besieging Carchemish. His initial reaction was disbelief—such a proposal was unprecedented in interstate relations, where royal women were sent to foreign courts, but royal men were not. The Hittite king sent his chamberlain Hattuša-ziti to Egypt to verify the request:

"Go and bring me the true word back. Perhaps they deceive me. Perhaps they have a son of their lord." (KBo 5.6)

When the Egyptian messenger Hani arrived with confirmation, Šuppiluliuma eventually agreed to send his son Zannanza to Egypt. The outcome was disastrous—the Hittite prince was killed en route, likely on the orders of Ay or Horemheb, Egyptian officials who themselves had designs on the throne.

The identity of "Dahamunzu" (clearly a Hittite rendering of the Egyptian title *ta hemet nesu*, "the king's wife") has been debated extensively. Most scholars now believe she was Ankhesenamun, widow of Tutankhamun, whose sudden death around 1327 BCE created a succession crisis in Egypt. This identification is supported by the chronological alignment between Tutankhamun's death and Šuppiluliuma's siege of Carchemish, as well as archaeological evidence from Tutankhamun's tomb, suggesting a hasty burial consistent with political turmoil.

The episode illustrates both the opportunities and limitations of Šuppiluliuma's imperial ambitions. The marriage would have represented an extraordinary diplomatic coup, effectively making Egypt a Hittite client state without military conquest. Its failure, however, demonstrated the limits of Hittite power projection beyond Syria and the strength of Egyptian institutional resistance to foreign influence.

The aftermath of Zannanza's murder shaped Hittite-Egyptian relations for decades. Šuppiluliuma launched punitive raids into Egyptian-controlled territories in Syria, capturing numerous prisoners. When these captives brought plague back to Hatti, resulting in the deaths of both Šuppiluliuma and his successor Arnuwanda II, Muršili II interpreted this as divine punishment for breaking previous treaties with Egypt—a view expressed in his famous "Plague Prayers":

"My father sent infantry and chariotry, and they attacked the border region of Egypt, the land of Amka. And again, he sent, and again they attacked. When the Egyptians became frightened, they asked outright for a son of my father for kingship. But when my father gave them his son, they killed him as they led him there. My father became angry, he went to war against Egypt, he attacked Egypt, and he smote the infantry and chariotry of the land of Egypt." (KUB 14.14)

This episode highlights how deeply religious conceptions shaped Hittite diplomatic practice. Despite his anger at Egyptian treachery, Muršili felt compelled to make offerings to Egyptian deities to resolve the plague, demonstrating the interconnection between international relations and religious obligation in Hittite thought.

Establishment of Hittite Vassal Kingdoms

The territorial acquisitions resulting from Šuppiluliuma's campaigns created significant administrative challenges. Unlike the Assyrians of later centuries, the Hittites did not develop a system of provinces governed directly by officials dispatched from the capital. Instead, Šuppiluliuma established what scholars term an "imperial commonwealth" (Beckman 1999: 3)—a hierarchical network of vassal states bound to the Hittite crown through formal treaties.

The most comprehensive study of these arrangements remains Gary Beckman's *Hittite Diplomatic Texts* (1999), which identifies three distinct categories of vassal relationships: directly administered territories, states ruled by members of the Hittite royal family, and client kingdoms governed by local dynasties under Hittite suzerainty.

The first category included regions like Lower Land and Kizzuwatna, which were incorporated into the Hittite administrative system and governed by officials called *BĒL MADGALTI* ("lord of the watchtower"). The second category is exemplified by Carchemish, where Šuppiluliuma installed his son Piyaššili/Šarri-Kušuh as viceroy:

"My father installed Šarri-Kušuh, son of the Great King Šuppiluliuma, in lordship in the land of Carchemish." (KBo 3.4)

Archaeological excavations at Carchemish confirm the establishment of a secondary Hittite royal center there, with monumental architecture and administrative documents reflecting both Hittite imperial styles and local Syrian traditions (Woolley and Barnett 1952: 234-238). This arrangement created a buffer zone between Hittite core territories and potential threats from Egypt or Assyria, while maintaining more direct control than possible through local client rulers.

The third category—client kingdoms governed by local dynasties—was the most common arrangement, particularly in more distant territories. The relationship between Hatti and these vassals was formalized through written treaties, many of which have survived in the Hittite archives. These documents followed a standard structure, including historical prologue, stipulations, divine witness list, and curses against treaty violation.

The treaty between Šuppiluliuma and Niqmaddu II of Ugarit exemplifies this arrangement:

"Thus says My Sun Šuppiluliuma, Great King, King of Hatti: I have taken Niqmaddu, King of Ugarit, as my vassal... He shall pay 500 shekels of gold as his annual tribute... If an enemy attacks the King of Hatti, and the King of Hatti writes to the King of Ugarit, the King of Ugarit shall come to his aid with his infantry and chariotry..." (RS 17.340)

Archaeological evidence from Ugarit confirms the implementation of these treaty terms. The city maintained its distinctive local culture and administrative systems while integrating into the Hittite economic and military sphere. Ugaritic texts document the delivery of tribute to Hatti and the participation of Ugaritic forces in Hittite military campaigns (Yon 2006: 21-24).

The vassal system offered several advantages over direct administration. It reduced the need for Hittite administrative personnel, leveraged local knowledge and legitimacy, and created buffer zones protecting core territories. However, it also created potential instability, as vassals might rebel or be subverted by rival powers. To mitigate these risks, Šuppiluliuma implemented several control mechanisms:

The effectiveness of these control mechanisms varied considerably across time and space. Trevor Bryce (2003: 48) observes that "the Hittite imperial system was characterized by cycles of rebellion and reconquest, particularly in frontier regions," noting that territories like Išuwa and Azzi-Hayaša in northeastern Anatolia required repeated military interventions to maintain Hittite control.

Despite these challenges, the vassal system established by Šuppiluliuma proved remarkably durable. Many of the political arrangements he created—particularly in Syria—survived not only his reign but the entire imperial period, collapsing only with the broader systemic crisis around 1180 BCE that ended the Late Bronze Age political order.

Imperial Ideology and Royal Self-Representation

The expansion of Hittite power under Šuppiluliuma was accompanied by significant developments in royal ideology and self-representation. The title "My Sun," previously used occasionally in Hittite royal discourse, became standardized in this period as the primary form of address for the king in diplomatic correspondence and vassal treaties. This solar imagery positioned the Hittite king as a universal sovereign whose authority, like the sun's light, extended across all lands.

Šuppiluliuma's monumental building programs at Hattuša reinforced this imperial ideology. The construction of the Great Temple complex and expansion of the royal acropolis created architectural expressions of imperial power visible to both residents and foreign visitors. Excavations directed by Peter Neve (1992: 15-32) revealed how these building projects transformed the urban landscape of the capital, creating processional routes and ceremonial spaces that showcased royal authority.

The king's conquest narratives, preserved in the "Deeds" compiled by Muršili II, present Šuppiluliuma as an instrument of divine will. His victories are attributed not merely to military skill but to the support of the Storm God:

"The Storm God, my lord, showed his divine power, and my father defeated the entire army of the Hurrian enemy." (KBo 5.6)

This religious framing of imperial expansion served important legitimizing functions, positioning conquest not as aggression but as the fulfillment of divine mandate. It also integrated newly conquered territories into the Hittite religious system by asserting the Storm God's superiority over local pantheons.

Archaeological evidence from provincial centers like Alaca Höyük and Šapinuwa demonstrates how imperial ideology was projected beyond the capital. Monumental gateways decorated with relief sculptures, standardized administrative buildings, and religious installations created visible markers of Hittite presence throughout the empire (Mielke 2011: 182-185).

Long-term Consequences of Šuppiluliuma's Conquests

The empire created by Šuppiluliuma I fundamentally altered the trajectory of Hittite history and transformed the geopolitical landscape of the ancient Near East. His conquests more than doubled the territory under Hittite control, created access to valuable resources and trade routes, and positioned Hatti as Egypt's primary rival for regional hegemony.

Incorporating Syrian territories had profound economic impacts. Texts from Ugarit document the intensification of Mediterranean trade networks following Hittite conquest, with Hittite officials facilitating commercial exchanges with Cyprus, the Aegean, and Egypt (Singer 1999: 634-639). The tribute from Syrian vassals—gold, silver, copper, and luxury goods—enriched the Hittite court and supported further imperial projects.

Culturally, Šuppiluliuma's conquests sped up processes of syncretism and hybridization that had been underway since the Old Kingdom. Syrian religious concepts and artistic conventions entered the Hittite cultural sphere, while Hurrian traditions previously adopted from Mitanni were reinforced through the incorporation of Hurrian populations. This cultural synthesis is visible in the religious texts of the imperial period, which frequently present deities in both their Hittite and Hurrian aspects.

The administrative and diplomatic systems developed to manage Šuppiluliuma's conquests created institutional frameworks that would govern Hittite foreign relations for the remainder of the imperial period. The three-tiered vassal system, the treaty formulary, and the mechanisms of imperial control established during his reign became standard features of Hittite governance under his successors.

However, Šuppiluliuma's achievements also created significant challenges. The expanded imperial frontiers required constant military attention, stretching Hittite resources and creating vulnerability to simultaneous threats on multiple fronts. The complex vassal system demanded sophisticated diplomatic management and regular shows of force to maintain stability. Relations with Egypt remained hostile following the Zannanza affair, creating a persistent security threat on the southern frontier.

As historian Theo van den Hout (2013: 35) observes, "The empire created by Šuppiluliuma represented both the fulfillment of long-standing Hittite ambitions and the creation of new vulnerabilities. The imperial structure he established would require continuous maintenance by his successors."

Conclusion: The Foundations of Imperial Power

Šuppiluliuma I's reign marked the transformation of Hatti from a regional kingdom into a genuine empire with interests and influence extending throughout the eastern Mediterranean world. Through military conquest, diplomatic maneuvering, and administrative innovation, he created a political structure that would dominate Anatolia and northern Syria for more than a century.

The destruction of Mitanni eliminated a longstanding rival and opened Syria to Hittite domination. The establishment of a sophisticated vassal system created mechanisms for controlling this expanded territory while accommodating local political traditions. The development of new forms of imperial ideology provided conceptual frameworks justifying and sustaining Hittite hegemony.

These achievements rested on foundations laid during the Middle Kingdom period—military reforms, administrative developments, and diplomatic innovations begun by Tudhaliya I/II and his successors. What distinguished Šuppiluliuma was not the creation of entirely new imperial forms, but the systematic and ambitious application of existing capabilities to transform Hatti's regional position.

The empire he created would face significant challenges under his successors. Muršili II would confront rebellions throughout the imperial periphery. Muwatalli II would fight Egypt to a costly draw at Kadesh. Hattušili III would struggle to legitimize his usurpation of the throne. Yet the fundamental imperial structure established by Šuppiluliuma would endure until the broader systemic collapse that ended the Late Bronze Age around 1180 BCE.

As we transition to examining the mature imperial period under Šuppiluliuma's successors, it is essential to recognize his foundational role in creating the political, military, and ideological frameworks that defined Hittite imperial power. The achievements and limitations of subsequent rulers can only be understood against the backdrop of the imperial system he established.

Chapter 9

INTERNATIONAL RELATIONS AND THE GREAT POWER SYSTEM

The Club of "Great Kings": An Exclusive International Order

The imperial achievement of Šuppiluliuma I secured Hatti's position within what scholars have termed the "Great Powers Club" of the Late Bronze Age—an exclusive group of states whose rulers addressed each other as equals and collectively dominated the geopolitical landscape of the ancient Near East. This elite circle, which Egyptologist Trevor Bryce (2003: 78) describes as "the world's first documented international system," consisted primarily of four major powers: Hatti, Egypt, Babylonia, and Assyria, with Mitanni initially included before its dismemberment by the Hittites.

The concept of the "Great King" (Hittite: LUGAL.GAL, Akkadian: šarru rabû) emerged as a specific diplomatic status designation rather than merely a grandiose royal title. Texts from the Amarna archives and the Hittite capital reveal that this status carried concrete diplomatic implications, including the right to address other Great Kings as "brother" and to expect reciprocal treatment in correspondence and gift exchange.

"The very concept of international relations in the Late Bronze Age was predicated on the fiction of fraternal equality among a select group of rulers," notes diplomatic historian Raymond Cohen (2000: 15). "Outside this charmed circle, political entities existed in various states of subordination to one or another of the Great Powers."

This system of diplomatic parity among Great Kings is explicitly articulated in a letter from Hattušili III to the Assyrian king Adad-nirari I, who had apparently claimed Great King status that the Hittite ruler was unwilling to recognize:

"As for the greeting tablet which you sent me, you did not write to me as one Great King writes to another Great King. But are we not equals, you and I? [...] Or did you not know that in Hatti, kingship is the concern of the gods?" (KBo I 14, translation adapted from Beckman 1999: 146)

The archaeological and textual evidence demonstrates that this Great Powers system was remarkably stable for over two centuries (ca. 1400-1180 BCE), despite significant conflicts between its members. Even during periods of open warfare, the conceptual framework of Great King parity remained intact. After the Battle of Kadesh, Ramesses II and Hattušili III returned to addressing each other as "brothers" despite their previous violent confrontation.

Several structural features supported this stability. First, the geographic separation between power centers (Hattuša, Thebes/Pi-Ramesse, Babylon, and Assur) made complete conquest of one Great Power by another logistically challenging. Second, the shared interest in maintaining predictable diplomatic protocols facilitated conflict resolution. Third, the system provided mechanisms for status recognition that helped accommodate rising powers like Assyria, which gradually transitioned from peripheral status to full Great King recognition during the 13th century BCE.

The material expression of Great King status took multiple forms. Royal residences featured standardized architectural elements that signaled membership in this elite club. International gift exchange involved specific prestige goods—gold, lapis lazuli, fine textiles—that circulated almost exclusively among Great Kings. Most visibly, royal iconography across these diverse cultures adopted shared motifs signaling membership in this exclusive group, including specific postures, regalia, and symbolic scenes depicting royal power.

Diplomatic Protocols and Royal Correspondence

The interaction between Great Kings was governed by elaborate protocols that structured everything from the format of written communication to the procedures for receiving foreign envoys. These protocols, far from being mere ceremony, constituted the operational framework of international relations in the Late Bronze Age.

The extensive diplomatic correspondence preserved in the Amarna and Hattuša archives reveals a highly formalized system of communication. Letters between Great Kings followed a standard format beginning with elaborate salutations that established the relationship between sender and recipient:

"Say to Naphuriya [Akhenaten], Great King, King of Egypt, my brother, my son-in-law, whom I love and who loves me: Thus says Šuppiluliuma, Great King, King of Hatti, your brother, your father-in-law, who loves you and whom you love. For me all goes well. For you, for your household, for your wives, for your sons, for your magnates, for your troops, for your chariots, and in your country, may all go very well." (EA 41, translation adapted from Moran 1992: 114)

Such formulaic openings served crucial diplomatic functions. They publicly reaffirmed the status relationship between rulers, acknowledged family connections created through marriage alliances, and established the peaceful intent of the communication. Deviations from these formulas—such as the omission of "brother" or the alteration of greeting order—could signal diplomatic displeasure or even constitute a casus belli.

The physical format of diplomatic correspondence also followed strict conventions. Letters between Great Kings were typically written on large, high-quality tablets in Akkadian, the diplomatic lingua franca of the period. They were often enclosed in clay envelopes bearing seal impressions that authenticated the sender's identity. The Amarna letters reveal Egyptian scribes maintained archives recording previous correspondence, allowing them to check whether incoming letters adhered to established precedents.

Diplomatic missions themselves operated according to elaborate protocols. The Tale of Wenamun from Egypt and various Hittite texts describe the reception of foreign envoys, including formal greeting ceremonies, provision of appropriate accommodations, and the staging of audiences with the king. The frequency of complaints in the diplomatic corpus about envoys being detained or inadequately honored indicates how seriously these protocols were taken.

Historian Mario Liverani (2001: 128) observes that "the diplomatic system of the Late Bronze Age operated as a self-contained semiotic universe with its own rules, expectations, and symbolic vocabulary." This system allowed rulers separated by vast distances and cultural differences to engage in meaningful communication through shared diplomatic conventions.

An interesting feature of this diplomatic system was the "messenger immunity" that protected envoys even during periods of hostility. In a letter to the Babylonian king Kadašman-Enlil, the Hittite king Hattušili III invokes this principle:

"It is not the custom that messengers should be killed. Messengers between Great Kings pass to and fro without hindrance, and no one harms them. If a Great King is angry with another Great King, he returns his messenger to him with an angry message, but he does not kill the messenger." (KUB III 71, translation adapted from Beckman 1999: 132)

The complexity of diplomatic protocol is further illustrated by the elaborate gift exchange system that accompanied official correspondence. Gifts were carefully recorded, with expectations of reciprocity precisely calibrated to the status of the participants. When these expectations were violated—as when Assyrian king Aššur-uballiṭ I complained that the gifts he received from Egypt were inadequate—diplomatic incidents could ensue.

Marriage Diplomacy and Alliance Systems

Among the most powerful instruments of Late Bronze Age diplomacy was the practice of inter-dynastic marriage, through which Great Kings cemented alliances by exchanging royal women. These marriages created kinship bonds between ruling houses, transformed political relationships into family obligations, and established channels for ongoing influence.

The marriage between Šuppiluliuma's daughter and the Egyptian pharaoh Akhenaten represents perhaps the most significant example of this practice. This union, documented in both the Amarna letters and Hittite texts, transformed the relationship between the two greatest powers of the age. By becoming Akhenaten's father-in-law, Šuppiluliuma established a hierarchical element within the otherwise equal Great King relationship, as he could now address the pharaoh as both "brother" and "son-in-law."

Marriage diplomacy followed strict status rules. Great Kings would send their daughters to marry other Great Kings or important vassals but would not allow their sons to marry foreign princesses, which would imply subordination. This asymmetry is explicitly addressed in a famous exchange between the Babylonian king Kadašman-Enlil and the Egyptian pharaoh:

"As to the daughter of the King of Babylon whom you requested in marriage, my messenger does not know which one is my sister whom my father gave to you... Send a dignitary who knows my sister whom my father gave to you and let him identify her. You wrote to me: 'From time immemorial, no daughter of the King of Egypt has been given in marriage to anyone.' Why not? You are a king, and you do as you please. If you were to give a daughter, who would say anything about it?" (EA 4, translation adapted from Moran 1992: 8-9)

The pharaoh's refusal to send an Egyptian princess abroad—justified with the claim that "from time immemorial" no Egyptian princess had been given in marriage—demonstrates the political significance attached to these unions. When Šuppiluliuma received the request from an Egyptian queen (likely Ankhesenamun) for a Hittite prince to become her husband following Tutankhamun's death, his initial disbelief was so great that he sent an envoy to verify the unprecedented request.

These marriage alliances created complex kinship networks that spanned political boundaries. Royal women who married foreign kings often maintained their cultural identities and religious practices, becoming channels for cultural exchange. The Hittite queen Puduhepa, for instance, maintained correspondence with her son-in-law Ramesses II, sometimes intervening in diplomatic matters based on her family connection.

Archaeological evidence complements the textual record of these diplomatic marriages. The grave goods of foreign princesses sometimes include distinctive items from their homelands, while palace areas associated with royal women occasionally show architectural or artistic elements reflecting their origins. At Tell el-Amarna, areas of the palace complex may have been designated for the Mitannian and Babylonian wives of Akhenaten, complete with facilities for their entourages.

The alliance systems constructed through marriage diplomacy created multilayered relationships between states. A typical pattern involved a Great King sending daughters to marry both peer rulers and important vassals, creating a network of kinship ties that reinforced political hierarchies. Šuppiluliuma I employed this strategy systematically, marrying daughters not only to the Egyptian pharaoh but also to rulers of strategically important vassal states like Carchemish and Amurru.

"Marriage alliances served as the sinews of the international system," argues historian Amanda Podany (2010: 251), "transforming abstract diplomatic relationships into concrete family obligations with emotional as well as political dimensions."

Trade Networks and Economic Integration

The diplomatic system of the Late Bronze Age both facilitated and was sustained by extensive networks of trade that connected the Great Powers economically as well as politically. These trade networks operated at multiple levels, from state-directed exchange of prestige goods to private commercial ventures that crossed political boundaries.

At the highest level was the exchange of gifts between Great Kings—a practice that blurred the line between diplomacy and trade. The inventories of such gifts, meticulously recorded in texts from Amarna and Hattuša, reveal the circulation of extraordinary wealth:

"I herewith send as your greeting-gift: 1 gold cup, 500 shekels of pure gold in 5 containers, 30 garments of fine linen with multicolored trim, 10 teams of horses, 10 chariots with all their equipment, and 30 male and female servants." (EA 14, translation adapted from Moran 1992: 27-28)

While framed as gifts, these exchanges followed implicit rules of reciprocity and value equivalence. When these expectations were violated—as when the Assyrian king complained about receiving only "5 teams of horses" from Egypt—diplomatic friction resulted. Great Kings maintained specialists who assessed the value of incoming gifts and advised on appropriate reciprocation.

Below this elite gift exchange operated state-sanctioned trade in strategic commodities. The Hittite archives document the importation of tin (essential for bronze production), iron (still rare and treated as a precious metal), and copper from Assyria and Cyprus. Egypt provided gold, papyrus, and finished luxury goods, while Babylonia specialized in textiles and lapis lazuli imported from Afghanistan. Merchants operating under royal authority often conducted this trade, with special privileges and protections.

The archaeological record provides abundant evidence for this long-distance trade. Shipwrecks like Uluburun off the Turkish coast (ca. 1320 BCE) have yielded cargoes that match exactly the inventories described in texts: copper and tin ingots, glass beads, ebony, ivory, Baltic amber, and Mycenaean pottery. The diverse origins of these goods—spanning three continents—demonstrates the geographical scope of Late Bronze Age trade networks.

A remarkable feature of this period was the degree of economic integration across political boundaries. Standardized weights and measures facilitated commerce between different regions, while widely accepted forms of currency (primarily silver, measured by weight) enabled complex transactions. In vassal states like Ugarit, archives document international commercial operations involving merchants from multiple political entities operating under various legal jurisdictions.

The treaties negotiated by Šuppiluliuma I and his successors frequently included provisions regulating trade, establishing customs duties, and protecting merchants. A treaty between Hattušili III and Ramesses II included specific provisions for commercial exchange:

"The merchant of the land of Egypt shall be protected in the land of Hatti, and the merchant of the land of Hatti shall be protected in the land of Egypt." (KUB III 121, translation adapted from Beckman 1999: 97)

This economic integration created interdependencies that sometimes constrained political action. When Hittite king Hattušili III faced grain shortages during a famine, he wrote to Ramesses II requesting emergency shipments of grain—despite their history of conflict. The Egyptian pharaoh complied, recognizing the mutual benefits of economic cooperation even between former enemies.

Archaeologist Kristian Kristiansen (2018: 142) observes that "the Late Bronze Age world system represented the first truly integrated international economy in human history, with specialized production centers, long-distance trade networks, and financial mechanisms that transcended political boundaries."

The Diplomatic Revolution of the 13th Century BCE

The system established during Šuppiluliuma's reign reached its fullest development in the 13th century BCE, when his grandson Hattušili III negotiated the world's first recorded peace treaty with Ramesses II of Egypt in 1259 BCE. This remarkable document, preserved in both Egyptian hieroglyphic and Akkadian cuneiform versions, transformed the relationship between the two greatest powers of the age from endemic hostility to structured peace.

The treaty's preamble establishes the equality of the two Great Kings and frames their agreement as divinely sanctioned:

"The treaty which Ramesses, Beloved of Amun, Great King, King of Egypt, Hero, concluded on a silver tablet with Hattušili, Great King, King of Hatti, his brother, for establishing good peace and good brotherhood between them forever." (KUB III 119, translation adapted from Beckman 1999: 90)

The substantive provisions included mutual defense obligations, extradition arrangements for fugitives, and guarantees for legitimate succession in both kingdoms. Most significantly, the treaty established a permanent peace between empires that had been intermittently at war for nearly a century.

A series of dynastic marriages reinforced this diplomatic revolution. Ramesses II married two Hittite princesses, with the first union celebrated in his 34th regnal year (ca. 1246 BCE) and commemorated in stelae erected throughout Egypt. These marriages created family bonds between the ruling houses and established regular communication between the royal courts.

The transformation of Egyptian-Hittite relations exemplifies the sophistication of Late Bronze Age diplomacy at its height. Former enemies became allies, with their relationship structured through multiple, overlapping mechanisms: formal treaty obligations, kinship bonds through marriage, regularized diplomatic contact, and economic exchange. When Hattušili III faced a succession crisis late in his reign, Ramesses II offered support to his preferred heir, demonstrating how thoroughly intertwined the interests of the Great Powers had become.

This integration extended to cultural and religious spheres as well. Following her marriage to Ramesses II, the Hittite princess (given the Egyptian name Maathorneferure) brought Hittite deities and religious specialists to Egypt. These foreign cults were accommodated within Egyptian religious frameworks, creating new syncretic forms. Similarly, Egyptian medical knowledge, literary motifs, and artistic conventions traveled to Hatti through diplomatic channels, influencing Hittite cultural development.

Historian Marc Van De Mieroop (2016: 137) argues that "the Egyptian-Hittite peace represents the culmination of Late Bronze Age diplomatic practice—a moment when the abstract principles of the Great Powers system were fully articulated and institutionalized in ways that transcended the personalities of individual rulers."

The Limits of Ancient Internationalism

Despite its sophistication, the international system of the Late Bronze Age operated within significant constraints. The diplomatic frameworks established during Šuppiluliuma's reign and elaborated by his successors ultimately could not prevent the systemic collapse that ended the Bronze Age around 1180 BCE.

Several structural limitations undermined the stability of the Great Powers system. First, while diplomatic protocols created mechanisms for conflict management, they provided no means for resolving fundamental power competitions. The Egyptian-Hittite peace came only after decades of warfare had demonstrated that neither side could achieve decisive victory, not through the intervention of international institutions.

Second, the personalized nature of ancient diplomacy—focused on relationships between individual rulers rather than between states as abstract entities—created vulnerability during succession periods. When a Great King died, established relationships had to be reconstructed with his successor, creating recurring moments of systemic instability.

Third, the economic integration that underpinned diplomatic relationships also created channels for systemic contagion. When one region experienced political collapse, trade disruptions could trigger cascading failures throughout the network. Archaeological evidence suggests this may have contributed to the Bronze Age collapse, as the fall of Mycenaean centers disrupted Mediterranean trade networks that sustained other regions.

Perhaps most fundamentally, the Great Powers system remained basically hierarchical despite its emphasis on equality among the elite club members. Most political entities existed as vassals or subjects of the Great Kings, with limited agency in international affairs. This structural inequality created persistent instability, as subordinate polities sought opportunities to assert independence or switch allegiance between competing Great Powers.

"The internationalism of the Late Bronze Age was real but limited," notes historian Mario Liverani (2014: 291). "It created mechanisms for elite cooperation without fundamentally transforming the competitive logic of imperial politics."

Conclusion: The Diplomatic Legacy of Šuppiluliuma I

The international system that emerged during Šuppiluliuma's reign represented a remarkable achievement in the history of diplomacy. Through military conquest and diplomatic innovation, the Hittite king transformed Hatti from a regional power into a central player in the world's first documented international system. The diplomatic frameworks established during his reign—the Great Kings club, formalized correspondence protocols, marriage alliances, and regulated trade networks—created structures that would govern international relations throughout the eastern Mediterranean for more than a century.

These achievements had lasting historical significance beyond the Bronze Age. When the Neo-Assyrian and Neo-Babylonian empires emerged after the Dark

Age that followed the Bronze Age collapse, they consciously revived many elements of Late Bronze Age diplomatic practice. The Achaemenid Persian Empire later adapted these traditions for governing its vast multicultural domain. Even the Hellenistic kingdoms established after Alexander's conquests drew on diplomatic precedents with roots in the system Šuppiluliuma helped create.

"The diplomatic revolution of the Late Bronze Age established conceptual frameworks and practical mechanisms that would influence international relations for millennia," argues historian Raymond Cohen (2000: 157). "The notion of a community of states governed by shared protocols, the practice of formalized treaty-making, and the concept of diplomatic immunity all have roots in the system that reached maturity under Šuppiluliuma and his successors."

As we turn to examining the challenges faced by Šuppiluliuma's immediate successors, it is essential to recognize that his legacy lay not only in the territories he conquered but in the diplomatic frameworks he helped establish. The Hittite Empire would endure for another century and a half, navigating the complex international environment through the diplomatic instruments he had helped forge.

Chapter 10

Muršili II and the Consolidation of Empire

The death of Šuppiluliuma I in 1322 BCE, followed by the brief reign of his son Arnuwanda II who succumbed to the same plague epidemic, created a moment of profound vulnerability for the newly expanded Hittite Empire. When Muršili II ascended the throne, likely in 1321 BCE, he faced challenges that would have overwhelmed a lesser ruler. As the young king himself recorded in the introduction to his Comprehensive Annals:

"When my father, Šuppiluliuma, went to his fate and my brother Arnuwanda, who was king after my father, also went to his fate, at that time the enemy lands all around heard: 'The king of Hatti is dead, and a child has become king in Hatti.' Then all the enemy lands began to attack me." (KBo 3.4 i 1-8)

This remarkable document, composed in the first person and covering the first ten years of Muršili's reign, provides an unusually detailed window into the challenges of imperial consolidation. The young king, likely in his early twenties when he took the throne, inherited an empire substantially expanded by his father but now threatened by rebellions across multiple frontiers.

The Challenges of Succession

The circumstances of Muršili's accession highlight the vulnerability inherent in imperial succession. Šuppiluliuma I had designated his son Arnuwanda as crown prince, who duly succeeded to the throne but reigned for only about a year before succumbing to the plague that had claimed his father. With the death of Arnuwanda II, the succession passed to his younger brother Muršili, who had not been groomed for kingship.

Muršili's youth and inexperience made him an obvious target for challengers both within and beyond the empire's borders. His Comprehensive Annals repeatedly emphasize his initial vulnerability, creating a narrative arc that highlights his growth into effective leadership. This rhetorical strategy served both to document historical events and to legitimize his rule through demonstrated achievement.

The plague that had killed both his father and brother continued to ravage the Hittite homeland during the early years of Muršili's reign. In his famous "Plague Prayers," composed later in his reign, the king reflects on this devastating epidemic:

"The plague has now continued for twenty years in Hatti. Since Šuppiluliuma, my father, died, and since my brother Arnuwanda died, the plague has not been eliminated from Hatti." (KUB 14.8 obv. 21-24)

This text reveals both the duration of the epidemic and its profound impact on Hittite society. The plague not only killed the previous two kings but also decimated the population, reducing military manpower and agricultural productivity at precisely the moment when the empire faced multiple external challenges.

The administrative continuity that helped Muršili navigate these initial challenges owed much to experienced officials who had served his father. Foremost among these was Zida, described in the texts as "the Chief of the Wine Stewards," who appears to have functioned as a regent or chief minister during the king's early years. Other senior officials mentioned in texts from this period include Nuwanza, the army commander, and Mittannamuwa, the Chief Scribe, whose expertise in diplomatic correspondence proved crucial for managing foreign relations.

Archaeological evidence from Hattuša provides material context for this transitional period. Building activity in the capital slowed markedly during the early years of Muršili's reign, likely reflecting both the impact of the plague and the diversion of resources to military campaigns. Excavations at the royal citadel (Büyükkale) show that several construction projects begun under Šuppiluliuma I were completed only several years into Muršili's reign, suggesting initial delays followed by renewed administrative capacity.

Suppressing Rebellions on Multiple Fronts

The most immediate challenge facing the young king was the wave of rebellions that erupted across the empire. Vassal states that had submitted to Šuppiluliuma I saw in his death and the succession of an untested ruler an opportunity to reassert their independence. The Comprehensive Annals document rebellions in Arzawa in western Anatolia, among the Kaška peoples of the northern frontier, in the Upper Land to the northeast, and in Syria.

The western front proved exceptionally dangerous. The kingdom of Arzawa, centered in southwestern Anatolia, had been subdued by Šuppiluliuma I but never fully integrated into the imperial system. Under its king Uhha-ziti, Arzawa not only declared independence but formed a coalition with neighboring states including Ahhiyawa (possibly a Mycenaean Greek power) and Millawanda (classical Miletus). This coalition represented a serious threat to Hittite control of western Anatolia.

Muršili's response demonstrates sophisticated strategic thinking. Rather than attempting to address all fronts simultaneously, he prioritized threats based on their severity and proximity to the Hittite heartland. His Comprehensive Annals describe his reasoning:

"Since the king of Arzawa had been hostile to my father, and now he has become hostile to me as well, I will go against him first. The land of the Kaška people, which has become hostile, can wait." (KBo 3.4 i 20-24)

This prioritization allowed Muršili to concentrate his limited forces for maximum effect, addressing the most serious threats sequentially rather than dispersing his resources.

The campaign against Arzawa in Muršili's third year (ca. 1319 BCE) marked his first major military success. After crossing the difficult terrain of Mount Lawasa, he engaged and defeated Uhha-ziti's forces near the Astarpa River. The Hittite army then advanced on Apasa (classical Ephesus), the Arzawan capital, forcing Uhha-ziti to flee to islands offshore. A timely earthquake, which Muršili interpreted as divine intervention by the Storm God, further demoralized the Arzawan population:

"When I reached Apasa, his royal residence, Uhhaziti did not come against me in battle. The Storm God, my lord, showed his divine power: a thunderbolt fell, and my army saw it, and the land of Arzawa saw it. The thunderbolt went and struck the land of Arzawa, and it struck Apasa, Uhhaziti's city. It struck Uhhaziti on the knee, and he became ill." (KBo 3.4 ii 14-22)

This dramatic event, whether an actual earthquake or a literary embellishment, became central to Muršili's narrative of divinely sanctioned victory. The king presented himself not merely as a military commander but as the agent of the Storm God's will, a theme that would recur throughout his reign.

Following the defeat of Arzawa, Muršili implemented a comprehensive reorganization of western Anatolia. Rather than attempting direct rule over this distant region, he established a system of vassal states under rulers loyal to Hatti. The land of Mira-Kuwaliya was granted to Mashuiluwa, a prince who had earlier sought refuge at the Hittite court. The Seha River Land was placed under Manapa-Tarhunta, who had abandoned the Arzawan coalition at a critical moment. The region of Hapalla received a similar arrangement.

This pragmatic approach to imperial governance—maintaining local rulers while binding them through formal treaties to the Hittite crown—became a hallmark of Muršili's reign. It allowed him to extend Hittite influence with minimal administrative overhead, a crucial consideration given the empire's limited manpower.

With the western frontier secured, Muršili turned his attention to the northern threat posed by the Kaška peoples. Unlike the organized kingdoms of western Anatolia and Syria, the Kaška represented a different kind of challenge. Semi-nomadic tribal groups occupying the Pontic mountain region, they had long raided Hittite territories and periodically seized border settlements.

Muršili's campaigns against the Kaška, documented in both the Comprehensive Annals and the "Deeds of Šuppiluliuma" (which he commissioned), show a systematic approach to frontier security. Rather than attempting to conquer and directly administer Kaška territory—a task that had defeated even his father—Muršili focused on punitive expeditions, the recovery of Hittite settlements, and the establishment of defensive infrastructure.

The king's seventh year saw intensive campaigns in the north, with operations against multiple Kaška groups:

"I, My Majesty, went to the land of Tipiya, and the Kaška of Tipiya came against me in battle. The Storm God, my lord, and the Sun Goddess of Arinna, my lady, and all the gods ran before me, and I defeated the Kaška of Tipiya." (KBo 3.4 iii 44-48)

These campaigns followed a consistent pattern: Muršili would lead the army into Kaška territory, defeat any forces that opposed him, burn settlements, seize livestock and captives, and then withdraw after extracting oaths of submission from local leaders. While these operations did not permanently eliminate the Kaška threat, they secured the northern frontier sufficiently to allow Muršili to address challenges elsewhere.

Archaeological evidence from northern Hittite sites like Maşat Höyük (ancient Tapikka) confirms the pattern of destruction and rebuilding described in the texts. Excavations have revealed multiple burn layers dating to this period, followed by reconstruction phases showing Hittite architectural features. This material evidence demonstrates both the intensity of the conflict and the Hittite determination to maintain control of these frontier regions despite repeated Kaška incursions.

The eastern frontier, particularly the region known as the Upper Land, presented yet another challenge. This area had been under Hittite control during Šuppiluliuma's reign but had experienced significant disruption during the plague years. Local rulers had asserted independence, and Azzi-Hayasa, a kingdom to the northeast, had seized Hittite territories.

Muršili's campaigns in this region, conducted primarily in his fifth and sixth regnal years, focused on restoring Hittite control over key fortresses and trade routes. The Comprehensive Annals describe operations against the fortress of Ura, which had been seized by a local ruler named Hutupianza:

"I, My Majesty, went to Mount Nanni and besieged Ura. When the people of Ura saw that I had besieged the city, they became afraid, and they came forth to me and fell at my feet." (KBo 4.4 i 27-30)

These eastern campaigns secured the Upper Land and reestablished Hittite control over the crucial routes connecting central Anatolia to northern Mesopotamia. The restoration of these trade corridors had significant economic implications, ensuring Hittite access to essential resources including metals and luxury goods.

Perhaps the most serious challenge to Muršili's authority came from Syria, where his father had established a network of vassal states and installed his son Piyassili (also known as Šarri-Kušuh) as viceroy of Carchemish. Following Šuppiluliuma's death, several Syrian vassals attempted to break away from Hittite control, sometimes with Egyptian encouragement.

The situation became particularly critical when Piyassili died, creating a leadership vacuum in the Syrian territories. Muršili responded decisively, appointing his nephew Šahurunuwa as the new viceroy of Carchemish and personally leading campaigns to suppress rebellions in northern Syria.

The most significant of these campaigns targeted Nuhassi, a kingdom that had shifted its allegiance to Egypt. The Annals describe Muršili's response:

"The people of Nuhassi had sworn an oath to My Majesty, but they broke their oath to me and went over to the king of Egypt. I, My Majesty, went to Nuhassi, defeated them, and brought back captives and possessions to Hattusa." (KBo 4.4 iv 31-36)

This campaign demonstrated both Muršili's military capability and his determination to maintain the Syrian territories that had been his father's most significant conquest. By reestablishing Hittite control over northern Syria, Muršili secured valuable trade routes and created a buffer zone protecting Anatolia from potential Egyptian or Assyrian aggression.

Archaeological evidence from Syrian sites like Tell Atchana (ancient Alalakh) and Ugarit confirms the continuation of Hittite influence during this period. Administrative texts from Ugarit document ongoing tribute payments to Hatti and the presence of Hittite officials overseeing local governance. Material culture shows a blend of local Syrian traditions with Hittite influences, reflecting the empire's policy of allowing cultural autonomy while maintaining political control.

Administrative Innovations and Imperial Governance

Beyond military campaigns, Muršili II made significant contributions to Hittite administrative practices and imperial governance. Building on foundations established by his father, he developed more sophisticated systems for managing the empire's diverse territories and populations.

The vassal treaty system, already a feature of Hittite diplomacy under Šuppiluliuma I, was refined and expanded under Muršili. These treaties followed a consistent format: a historical prologue establishing the relationship between Hatti and the vassal state, detailed stipulations regarding obligations on both sides, divine witnesses, and curses for violation. The treaty with Tuppi-Tešub of Amurru exemplifies this approach:

"When your father Aziru came to my father Šuppiluliuma in Hatti, he abandoned the king of Egypt and placed himself under the authority of my father. My father received him kindly and imposed on him a fixed yearly tribute... Now that my father has gone to his fate, I, Muršili, Great King, have not altered the word of my father. I have confirmed it." (CTH 62)

This emphasis on continuity with arrangements made by Šuppiluliuma served both practical and ideological purposes. It reassured vassals that agreements would be honored across generations while reinforcing Muršili's legitimacy as his father's heir.

The administration of conquered territories followed a tiered system that balanced central control with local autonomy. Directly administered provinces in Anatolia were governed by officials called BĒL MADGALTI ("lord of the watchtower"), who reported directly to the king. More distant territories were typically governed through vassal arrangements, with local rulers maintaining their positions while acknowledging Hittite overlordship.

Regions of particular strategic importance received special treatment. In northern Syria, the viceroyalty of Carchemish functioned as a secondary administrative center, managing Hittite interests throughout the region. Similarly, the "Lower Land" in southern Anatolia was placed under governors with expanded authority, reflecting its importance as a buffer zone against potential threats from the south.

Muršili's administrative innovations extended to the legal sphere as well. During his reign, the Hittite law code underwent significant revision, with many penalties reduced from earlier versions. For example, Law §25 states:

"If anyone blinds a free person or knocks out his tooth, formerly they would pay 40 shekels of silver, but now he shall pay 20 shekels of silver."

This reduction in penalties reflects a more pragmatic approach to justice, emphasizing compensation over punishment. It also suggests a shift toward a more centralized legal system, with royal courts playing a greater role in dispute resolution.

Religious administration received particular attention during Muršili's reign. The plague that had killed his father and brother was interpreted as divine punishment for neglected religious obligations. In response, Muršili conducted a comprehensive inventory of cult practices throughout the empire, restoring neglected festivals and clarifying ritual responsibilities.

His "Plague Prayers" reveal this concern with proper religious observance:

"O gods, whatever sin has brought about the plague in Hatti, I have now confessed it before you. Perhaps we have done something against the gods? It is true, we have done something. But does a man ever overstep his god's command? Does he not overstep it?" (KUB 14.8 rev. 21-25)

This theological reflection led to practical administrative actions, including the reorganization of temple personnel, the restoration of interrupted cult practices, and the establishment of new festivals. Archaeological evidence from Hattuša shows increased investment in temple construction and renovation during the latter part of Muršili's reign, supporting the textual evidence for religious revival.

The economic administration of the empire also saw innovations under Muršili. Land donation texts from his reign reveal a systematic approach to rewarding loyal officials with grants of agricultural land, creating a class of service-holders dependent on royal favor. These grants typically included tax exemptions and specified that the land would revert to the crown if service obligations were not fulfilled.

Palace administration became more elaborate during Muršili's reign, with specialized departments overseeing different aspects of state activity. The archives from Hattuša reveal a complex bureaucracy with departments dedicated to diplomatic correspondence, religious affairs, military logistics, and economic administration. The increased volume of administrative texts dating from this period suggests both greater bureaucratic activity and more systematic record-keeping.

Cultural Achievements and Historical Consciousness

Beyond his military and administrative accomplishments, Muršili II made significant contributions to Hittite cultural and intellectual life. His reign saw remarkable developments in historical writing, religious thought, and artistic expression that would influence subsequent generations.

Perhaps Muršili's most distinctive cultural contribution was his development of Hittite historiography. The Comprehensive Annals represent a sophisticated approach to historical narrative, combining chronological precision with ideological framing. Unlike the more propagandistic royal inscriptions of contemporary civilizations, Muršili's Annals acknowledge setbacks and difficulties while placing events within a coherent narrative of divine support and royal achievement.

The king also commissioned the "Deeds of Šuppiluliuma," a detailed account of his father's reign compiled from earlier sources. This text, while celebrating Šuppiluliuma's achievements, also served to establish continuity between father and son, legitimizing Muršili's rule by connecting it to his father's more established authority.

This historical consciousness extended beyond royal inscriptions to include what might be called "constitutional" documents. The "Indictment of Madduwatta" (CTH 147), likely compiled during Muršili's reign, recounts the treacherous actions of a western Anatolian ruler who repeatedly violated agreements with Hatti. While ostensibly focused on a specific individual, the text establishes principles regarding vassal obligations and the consequences of betrayal.

Muršili's religious writings reveal sophisticated theological reflection. His "Plague Prayers" wrestle with questions of divine justice, human responsibility, and the relationship between sin and punishment. Unlike the more formulaic prayers of many ancient Near Eastern traditions, these texts express genuine anguish and uncertainty:

"What is this that you have done, O gods? A plague you have let into the land of Hatti, and the land of Hatti has been badly oppressed by the plague... The matter of the plague weighs heavily upon me." (KUB 14.8 obv. 14-18)

This personal voice, unusual in ancient royal inscriptions, reveals Muršili's distinctive approach to religious expression. His prayers combine traditional invocations with heartfelt appeals, creating texts that function both as ritual performances and as expressions of genuine religious sentiment.

The artistic achievements of Muršili's reign are more difficult to assess due to the limited archaeological evidence specifically datable to this period. However, several significant monuments can be attributed to his patronage, including renovations to the Great Temple at Hattuša and possibly early work at the rock sanctuary of Yazılıkaya.

The most distinctive artistic development of this period was the increased use of Luwian hieroglyphic writing alongside cuneiform for monumental inscriptions. While cuneiform remained the primary script for administrative and religious texts, hieroglyphic inscriptions became more common for public monuments, particularly in regions with significant Luwian-speaking populations.

This linguistic development reflects broader cultural patterns during Muršili's reign. The Hittite Empire had always been multilingual, with Hittite, Luwian, Hattic, Hurrian, and other languages used in different contexts. Under Muršili, this linguistic diversity became more systematically integrated into imperial administration, with specific languages used for particular purposes and contexts.

The cultural achievements of Muršili's reign extended to legal thought as well. The revisions to the Hittite law code mentioned earlier reflect not merely practical adjustments but evolving conceptions of justice and social order. The emphasis on compensation over punishment and the reduced penalties for various offenses suggest a more pragmatic approach to maintaining social harmony.

Legacy and Historical Significance

By the time of Muršili II's death around 1295 BCE, after approximately 25 years on the throne, he had transformed the Hittite Empire from a fragile inheritance threatened by rebellions on multiple fronts to a consolidated imperial system with secure borders and effective governance structures. His achievements established foundations that would sustain Hittite power for nearly another century.

The territorial integrity of the empire had been restored, with rebellions suppressed in Anatolia and Syria. The reorganization of western Anatolia into vassal states created a more stable frontier, while the reestablishment of Hittite control in Syria secured valuable trade routes and created a buffer against Egyptian expansion. Even the perennially troublesome northern frontier had been secured sufficiently to prevent major Kaška incursions.

Administratively, Muršili refined the imperial governance system developed by his father, creating more sophisticated mechanisms for controlling diverse territories. The tiered administrative structure—with directly governed provinces in the heartland, secondary administrative centers like Carchemish for distant regions, and vassal arrangements for peripheral territories—proved remarkably effective at balancing central control with local autonomy.

The diplomatic and legal precedents established during Muršili's reign would influence Hittite international relations for generations. His refinement of the vassal treaty system created a framework for managing imperial relationships that subsequent kings would follow with only minor modifications. His approach to international disputes, combining military force with diplomatic engagement, established patterns that would characterize Hittite foreign policy throughout the empire period.

Religiously, Muršili's efforts to restore proper cult observance and his theological reflections on divine justice influenced subsequent Hittite religious practice. His plague prayers established a tradition of royal confessional prayer that later kings would emulate when facing similar crises. His reorganization of cult personnel and festival schedules created religious structures that would endure throughout the empire period.

Culturally, Muršili's contributions to Hittite historical writing established traditions that subsequent generations would build upon. His Comprehensive Annals became a model for royal historical narratives, while his commission of the "Deeds of Šuppiluliuma" established the practice of compiling historical records of previous reigns. This historical consciousness contributed to the remarkable continuity of Hittite political culture despite periodic crises.

Muršili's legacy is perhaps best measured by the stability he created. Despite inheriting a precarious situation—with an empire overextended by his father's conquests, ravaged by plague, and threatened by rebellions on multiple fronts—he not only preserved the Hittite state but strengthened it. The half-century following his reign would represent the height of Hittite imperial power, a period made possible by his patient work of consolidation and institutionalization.

As historian Trevor Bryce observes, "Muršili II's achievement lay not in dramatic new conquests but in the methodical consolidation of what his father had won. His patient rebuilding of imperial structures created the foundations for Hittite power throughout the 13th century BCE" (Bryce 2005: 197).

Archaeological evidence confirms this assessment. Sites throughout the Hittite realm show increased prosperity and stability during the latter part of Muršili's reign and into the subsequent period. Urban centers expanded, trade networks flourished, and material culture shows greater standardization, all indicating effective imperial integration.

Muršili II's reign thus represents a crucial phase in Hittite imperial development—the transition from conquest to consolidation, from the charismatic authority of Šuppiluliuma I to the institutionalized power of the mature empire. Through military skill, administrative innovation, and cultural achievement, Muršili transformed his father's conquests into a sustainable imperial system that would dominate Anatolia and northern Syria for generations to come.

Conclusion

The reign of Muršili II (ca. 1321-1295 BCE) marks a pivotal chapter in Hittite history, bridging the dramatic conquests of his father Šuppiluliuma I and the imperial zenith that would follow under his successors. Ascending to the throne as a young man during a time of crisis—with the empire ravaged by plague and threatened by rebellions across multiple frontiers—Muršili demonstrated remarkable resilience and strategic vision.

His systematic suppression of rebellions in western Anatolia, among the Kaška peoples of the north, in the Upper Land to the east, and in Syria restored the territorial integrity of the empire. Rather than pursuing new conquests, he focused on securing what his father had won, creating more sustainable governance structures adapted to the realities of Bronze Age imperial administration.

Muršili's administrative innovations refined the imperial system developed by his father. His vassal treaties, provincial governance structures, and legal reforms created frameworks that balanced central control with necessary local autonomy. His religious reforms addressed the spiritual crisis triggered by the plague while reinforcing the king's role as intermediary between human and divine realms.

Perhaps most distinctively, Muršili's historical writings—including his Comprehensive Annals and the "Deeds of Šuppiluliuma" that he commissioned—reveal a sophisticated historical consciousness unusual for his era. These texts not only documented events but reflected on their meaning, establishing traditions of royal historiography that would influence subsequent generations.

By the time of his death around 1295 BCE, Muršili had transformed a precarious inheritance into a consolidated empire with secure borders, effective administration, and renewed religious foundations. His patient work of rebuilding and institutionalization created the stability that would allow the Hittite Empire to reach its zenith in the 13th century BCE.

As we turn to examining the achievements and challenges of Muršili's successors, we will see how the foundations he established supported further imperial development while creating new tensions that would eventually contribute to the empire's transformation and ultimate collapse. The consolidated empire he created would face new challenges—from Egyptian rivalry to Assyrian expansion to internal succession disputes—that would test the resilience of Hittite imperial structures in the century to come.

Chapter 11

Muwatalli II and the Egyptian Confrontation

The Transfer of the Capital to Tarḫuntašša

Among the most dramatic and consequential decisions of Muwatalli II's reign was the relocation of the Hittite capital from Ḫattuša to a new southern site called Tarḫuntašša. This unprecedented move—no previous Hittite king had abandoned the traditional capital—reveals much about both the practical challenges and ideological dimensions of imperial governance during this period.

The primary textual evidence for this transfer comes from the "Apology of Ḫattušili III," where Muwatalli's brother and eventual successor describes the event:

"When my brother Muwatalli, at the command of his god, moved down from Ḫattuša to the Lower Land and took up residence in Tarḫuntašša, he left me in the land of Ḫakpiš and made me its king. He took the gods of Ḫatti and the dead [ancestors] from Ḫattuša and settled them in Tarḫuntašša. But he left the goddess Inara in Ḫattuša and installed me as her priest." (KBo VI 29 ii 1-8)

This brief passage reveals several crucial aspects of the transfer. First, Muwatalli justified the move as divinely ordained ("at the command of his god"), suggesting religious motivations. Second, the relocation involved not just administrative functions but also the physical transfer of divine images and possibly royal funerary installations ("the gods of Ḫatti and the dead"). Third, the move was not total—some cults remained at Ḫattuša under Ḫattušili's supervision.

The exact location of Tarḫuntašša remains uncertain, though most scholars place it somewhere in the Konya Plain of south-central Anatolia. Archaeological candidates include Kızıldağ, where rock reliefs depict a king named Hartapu who later claimed the title "Great King of Tarḫuntašša," or possibly the substantial Bronze Age settlement at Kınık Höyük. As archaeologist Dirk Paul Mielke (2011: 184) notes, "The identification of Tarḫuntašša remains one of the most tantalizing unsolved problems in Hittite geography."

The transfer of the capital had significant consequences for imperial administration. Muwatalli established a tripartite division of the empire: the south (including Tarḫuntašša) under his direct rule; the north-central region around Ḫakpiš governed by his brother Ḫattušili; and the Syrian territories administered through the Carchemish viceroyalty established by Šuppiluliuma I. This arrangement created a more distributed governance structure that acknowledged the empire's expanded scale.

Archaeological evidence from Ḫattuša indicates the city was not abandoned entirely. Limited construction continued, and administrative archives remained active, suggesting that some bureaucratic functions continued there. As archaeologist Andreas Schachner (2019: 121) notes, "The continued architectural activity at Ḫattuša during this period, though reduced, indicates that Muwatalli's relocation was not as complete as textual sources might suggest."

The capital transfer also had significant long-term consequences. After Muwatalli's death, his son Urḫi-Tešub (Mursili III) briefly ruled from Tarḫuntašša before being overthrown by Ḫattušili III, who restored Ḫattuša as the capital. However, Tarḫuntašša remained an important center, eventually becoming a semi-autonomous kingdom ruled by Muwatalli's son Kurunta. The famous "Bronze Tablet" treaty between Tudḫaliya IV and Kurunta (c. 1235 BCE) granted Tarḫuntašša extensive privileges, creating a potential rival power center within the empire.

"The creation of Tarḫuntašša," observes historian Trevor Bryce (2005: 230), "introduced a fundamental division within the Hittite realm that would have profound consequences for the final century of imperial history. What began as an administrative solution to imperial overextension ultimately created competing centers of power that weakened central authority."

The Road to Kadesh: Causes of the Egyptian Conflict

The confrontation between Hittite and Egyptian forces at Kadesh in 1274 BCE represented the culmination of nearly a century of geopolitical competition. Understanding this pivotal battle requires examining the long-term structural causes as well as the immediate triggers that led Ramesses II and Muwatalli II to commit their forces to this decisive encounter.

The fundamental cause of Hittite-Egyptian conflict lay in competing imperial ambitions in Syria-Palestine, a region that offered both powers critical strategic and economic advantages.

This competition had intensified during the reign of Šuppiluliuma I (c. 1350-1322 BCE), who had dramatically expanded Hittite influence in Syria at the expense of Egypt's traditional sphere of influence. As Egyptologist Anthony Spalinger (2005: 211) notes, "Šuppiluliuma's Syrian campaigns fundamentally altered the regional balance of power, creating conditions for the later confrontation at Kadesh."

The immediate background to the battle involved a series of Egyptian attempts to reassert control over territories lost during the late 18th Dynasty. After the death of Tutankhamun and the brief reign of Ay, the general Horemheb had ascended to the Egyptian throne (c. 1319 BCE) and begun rebuilding Egyptian military capacity. His successors Ramesses I and Seti I continued this process, with Seti conducting campaigns in Syria that reclaimed some territories, including briefly Kadesh itself.

A key factor in the escalating tensions was the unstable status of vassal states in the border regions. Cities like Amurru and Kadesh had shifted allegiance between the great powers multiple times. An inscription of Seti I from Karnak describes his campaign against Kadesh:

"The wretched chief of Kadesh had entered into the town of Kadesh, and he gathered to himself the chiefs of every foreign land to the limits of the sea... His Majesty defeated them through the fame of his father Amun, who gave to him valor and victory." (KRI I, 12-17)

Despite this temporary success, Kadesh appears to have returned to the Hittite orbit by the time of Muwatalli II's reign. The ruler of Amurru, Benteshina, also appears to have switched allegiance from Egypt to Hatti, providing Ramesses II with a pretext for military intervention.

Diplomatic exchanges before the battle remain poorly documented, but the Egyptian "Poem of Pentaur" suggests that Ramesses believed Hittite spies had deliberately misled him:

"Two Shasu came from the tribes of Shasu to speak to His Majesty: "Our brothers who are chiefs of the tribes with the Fallen One of Hatti have sent us to His Majesty saying: 'We will be servants of Pharaoh and will flee from the Fallen One of Hatti.'" But they spoke these words to His Majesty falsely, for the Fallen One of Hatti had sent them to spy where His Majesty was." (KRI II, 16-17)

While this account may exaggerate Hittite duplicity for propaganda purposes, it suggests that intelligence operations and misinformation played important roles in the lead-up to the confrontation.

By the spring of 1274 BCE, both rulers had assembled substantial forces. Ramesses II led an army of approximately 20,000 men organized into four divisions named after Egyptian deities (Amun, Re, Ptah, and Seth), supported by Sherden mercenaries and numerous chariots. Muwatalli commanded a coalition that included Hittite forces and contingents from several vassal states, with perhaps 15,000-18,000 troops and a particularly strong chariot arm.

As historian Mark Healy (1993: 22) observes, "Both rulers had compelling reasons to risk a decisive engagement. Ramesses sought to cement his legitimacy through military glory and restore Egyptian prestige in Syria. Muwatalli needed to demonstrate that Hatti could defend its imperial possessions against Egyptian aggression."

The Battle of Kadesh: Military Analysis and Consequences

The Battle of Kadesh in 1274 BCE represents one of the best-documented military engagements from the ancient world. Egyptian sources include temple inscriptions at Abydos, Karnak, Luxor, Abu Simbel, and the Ramesseum, as well as the literary "Poem of Pentaur" preserved on papyrus. While Hittite records of the battle are more fragmentary, they provide crucial counterpoints to the Egyptian narrative.

The battle unfolded around the city of Kadesh on the Orontes River (modern Tell Nebi Mend in Syria). Ramesses II approached from the south with his army divided into four divisions marching separately. The Egyptian advance guard captured two Hittite scouts who, under torture, claimed that the Hittite army was still far to the north near Aleppo. This information was false—Muwatalli had positioned his forces on the east side of Kadesh, concealed by the city and a nearby forest.

As the lead Egyptian division (Amun) established camp northwest of Kadesh, two more Hittite scouts were captured who revealed the truth: the Hittite army was nearby and ready for battle. Before Ramesses could fully react, Muwatalli launched 2,500 chariots across the Orontes, striking the Re division as it marched north and driving the survivors back into the camp of Amun.

The Egyptian "Bulletin" inscription describes the resulting crisis:

"Now His Majesty had halted on the north of the city of Kadesh, on the western side of the Orontes. Then came one to tell His Majesty: 'Behold, the fallen one of Hatti has come together with the many countries who are with him... They stand equipped and ready for battle behind Kadesh the Old.' When His Majesty heard this, he became like his father Montu, Lord of Thebes... His Majesty mounted his chariot 'Victory-in-Thebes,' and he dashed forth alone by himself." (KRI II, 125-131)

While the Egyptian accounts emphasize Ramesses' personal courage in rallying his forces, the tactical situation was indeed dire. The Hittite chariot attack had nearly succeeded in overwhelming the Egyptian position. What saved the Egyptians appears to have been the arrival of reinforcements—the "ne'arin" troops mentioned in Egyptian texts, possibly a coastal contingent that arrived from the direction of Amurru.

Military historian Richard A. Gabriel (2002: 129) provides this tactical analysis: "The Hittite plan—to ambush and destroy the Egyptian army in detail as it marched in separated divisions—was tactically sound but ultimately unsuccessful. The failure to completely overwhelm the Amun division before reinforcements arrived proved decisive."

The battle continued through the afternoon, with the Egyptians gradually stabilizing their position. A counterattack by Egyptian chariots, possibly supported by the newly arrived reinforcements, pushed the Hittite forces back across the Orontes. By evening, the fighting had ended with the Egyptian army intact but unable to capture Kadesh itself.

The Hittite chariot tactics at Kadesh demonstrate the effectiveness of Muwatalli's military reforms. The lighter, more maneuverable Hittite chariots, each carrying two men proved superior to the heavier Egyptian vehicles in the initial phase of battle. However, the Hittites could not maintain this advantage once the element of surprise was lost.

Archaeological evidence from contemporary Hittite sites has yielded examples of the military equipment employed at Kadesh. Excavations at Kuşaklı (ancient Sarissa) have uncovered arrowheads, spear points, and scale armor consistent with the forces described in textual sources. Chariot fittings and horse trappings from various sites demonstrate the sophisticated metallurgical technology supporting Hittite military power.

Both sides claimed victory in their official accounts. The Egyptian inscriptions portray Ramesses as triumphant through personal valor:

"His Majesty slew the entire force of the Fallen One of Hatti, together with his great chiefs and all his brothers, as well as all the chiefs of all the countries that had come with him... His Majesty slaughtered them in their places; they sprawled before his horses; and his Majesty was alone, none other with him." (KRI II, 137-139)

The fragmentary Hittite accounts suggest a different outcome, indicating that Muwatalli considered himself victorious by preventing the Egyptian reconquest of Kadesh and maintaining Hittite control over northern Syria.

Modern scholarly consensus views the battle as a tactical draw but a strategic Hittite victory. As historian Trevor Bryce (2006: 257) concludes: "Despite the extravagant claims of the Egyptian records, Ramesses failed to achieve his objective of capturing Kadesh and reestablishing Egyptian control over Amurru. Muwatalli successfully defended Hittite territory and maintained the imperial boundaries established by his predecessors."

The military consequences of Kadesh were significant for both powers.

As archaeologist Christine Lilyquist (2003: 157) observes, "The material remains associated with the battle—from chariot fittings to weaponry—reveal the substantial investment both empires made in military technology, suggesting that the confrontation at Kadesh represented the culmination of long-term strategic planning rather than an impulsive clash."

Diplomatic Aftermath and Territorial Arrangements

The Battle of Kadesh did not immediately resolve the Hittite-Egyptian conflict. For approximately 16 years following the battle, relations remained hostile, with both powers conducting military operations in the contested border regions. Ramesses II undertook at least four more campaigns in Syria-Palestine, reaching as far north as Dapur on the Euphrates in his eighth regnal year.

During this period, internal developments within both empires gradually shifted priorities away from direct confrontation. In Egypt, Ramesses focused increasingly on monumental building projects and securing the western frontier against Libyan incursions. Within the Hittite Empire, Muwatalli's death around 1272 BCE triggered a succession crisis between his son Urḫi-Tešub (who ruled as Mursili III) and his brother Ḫattušili III, who eventually seized the throne around 1267 BCE.

The usurpation created legitimacy problems for Ḫattušili III, who sought international recognition to consolidate his position. As historian Itamar Singer (2002: 78) notes, "Ḫattušili's diplomatic initiatives toward Egypt were partly motivated by his need for external validation of his controversial accession to power."

Simultaneously, geopolitical realignments created new incentives for Egyptian-Hittite cooperation. The rising power of Assyria under Adad-nirari I and Shalmaneser I threatened both empires' interests in Syria. Economic considerations also favored peace, as the prolonged conflict disrupted valuable trade networks.

These factors culminated in the famous Egyptian-Hittite peace treaty of 1259 BCE. This remarkable document—preserved in both Egyptian hieroglyphic inscriptions at Karnak and in Akkadian cuneiform on clay tablets from Ḫattuša—represents one of the earliest fully preserved international peace treaties in world history.

The treaty established "good peace and good brotherhood" between the two powers and included several key provisions.

The Akkadian version states:

"Ramesses, the Great King, King of Egypt, shall never attack the land of Hatti to take possession of a part (of this country). And Ḫattušili, the Great King, King of Hatti, shall never attack the land of Egypt to take possession of a part (of that country)." (CTH 91)

Significantly, the treaty did not specify precise territorial boundaries, suggesting that both sides accepted the post-Kadesh status quo. This arrangement left northern Syria under Hittite control, with Egyptian influence predominating in Palestine and southern Syria. The kingdom of Amurru, which had defected to the Hittites before Kadesh, remained within the Hittite sphere.

The treaty was reinforced through dynastic marriage. In his 34th regnal year (c. 1245 BCE), Ramesses II married a Hittite princess, daughter of Ḫattušili III and Queen Puduhepa. The diplomatic correspondence surrounding this marriage has been preserved in the Hittite archives, documenting the elaborate negotiations over dowry, status, and ceremonial arrangements.

Queen Puduhepa's letter to Ramesses illustrates the personal dimension of this diplomatic alliance:

"You, my brother, have written to me saying: "My sister, send your daughter to be my wife, to be the Queen of Egypt." Heaven forbid that I should refuse to send her! I shall send her. But my brother has not written to me about the status of the wife he already has, and I do not know how things stand with the daughter of the King of Babylon or the daughter of the King of Zulabi whom my brother has taken as wives." (KUB XXI 38)

Archaeological evidence confirms the significance of this diplomatic revolution. At Pi-Ramesses in Egypt, Hittite-style pottery and metalwork appear in contexts dating to the later reign of Ramesses II. Similarly, Egyptian imports increase at Hittite sites after the treaty, suggesting expanded trade relations.

The territorial arrangements established after Kadesh proved remarkably stable. For the remaining decades of the 13th century BCE, the Hittite-Egyptian frontier saw little conflict, with both powers respecting each other's spheres of influence. This stability allowed both empires to address other challenges—Egypt focusing on its western frontier and monumental construction, while the Hittites confronted internal succession disputes and the growing Assyrian threat from the east.

As historian Marc Van De Mieroop (2016: 137) observes, "The post-Kadesh settlement demonstrates how warfare and diplomacy functioned as complementary tools of statecraft in the Late Bronze Age. The battle established the parameters within which a mutually beneficial peace could be negotiated."

The long-term consequences of these arrangements extended beyond the immediate participants. The treaty established a model for international relations that influenced subsequent diplomatic practice in the ancient Near East. Its emphasis on dynastic legitimacy, mutual defense, and regulated conflict resolution reflected sophisticated concepts of international law that would reappear in later periods.

For the Hittite Empire specifically, the resolution of the Egyptian conflict allowed Ḫattušili III and his successors to focus on consolidating control over Anatolia and addressing the Assyrian threat. The resources previously committed to the southern frontier could be redirected to other imperial priorities, temporarily strengthening the empire's position.

"The diplomatic achievement following Kadesh," notes historian Amanda Podany (2010: 301), "represents perhaps the most significant legacy of Muwatalli's reign. His military leadership preserved Hittite territorial integrity against Egyptian expansion, creating conditions for the peaceful accommodation that would define international relations for the remainder of the 13th century BCE."

Conclusion: Muwatalli's Legacy

Muwatalli II's reign marked a pivotal moment in Hittite imperial history. His administrative innovations—particularly the capital transfer to Tarḫuntašša and the tripartite division of imperial governance—demonstrated creative responses to the challenges of managing an expanded empire. His military leadership at Kadesh preserved Hittite control over northern Syria against Egyptian expansionism, while establishing the conditions for the eventual diplomatic resolution under his successor.

The territorial and administrative arrangements established during his reign would have lasting consequences, both positive and negative. The creation of Tarḫuntašša as an alternative power center eventually contributed to internal divisions within the empire, particularly during the reign of Tudḫaliya IV. However, the successful defense of imperial boundaries and the stabilization of the southern frontier provided the Hittite state with valuable breathing room during a period of increasing international pressures.

Archaeological evidence from the final decades of the 13th century BCE suggests that these achievements helped sustain Hittite imperial power for nearly another century before the final collapse around 1180 BCE. Sites throughout the empire show continued prosperity and administrative continuity, with substantial building programs at Ḫattuša and other centers reflecting imperial confidence.

As historian Theo van den Hout (2013: 35) concludes, "Muwatalli II's reign represents both the culmination of Hittite imperial expansion and the beginning of creative adaptation to the challenges of late Bronze Age international politics. His innovations in governance, military organization, and religious practice demonstrate the remarkable flexibility that characterized Hittite imperial administration at its height."

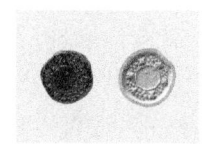

Chapter 12

ḪATTUŠILI III AND THE EGYPTIAN PEACE

The Coup Against Urḫi-Tešup and Civil War

The death of Muwatalli II around 1272 BCE precipitated one of the most dramatic succession crises in Hittite history. According to Hittite dynastic principles, the throne passed to his son Urḫi-Tešup, who took the throne name Mursili III. The new king inherited an empire at its territorial peak but faced immediate challenges to his authority, particularly from his uncle Ḫattušili, who had served as a senior military commander and administrator under Muwatalli II.

The historical sources for this period derive primarily from Ḫattušili's own account, the so-called "Apology" (CTH 81), which presents a decidedly partisan view of events. According to this text, Urḫi-Tešup's reign began with a deliberate campaign to undermine his uncle's position:

"When my brother Muwatalli went to his fate, I did not in any way do evil to Urḫi-Tešup, the son of my brother... But when he became hostile to me, he took away from me the towns of the Upper Land which Muwatalli had given me, and he gave me other towns" (Apology of Ḫattušili III, §10a-10b, trans. Van den Hout 2003: 203).

Archaeological evidence from this period suggests significant administrative disruption. Tablet archives at Ḫattuša show a marked decrease in administrative documentation, while provincial centers demonstrate changes in official personnel. Excavations at sites in the "Upper Land" (north-central Anatolia) reveal evidence of changing administrative practices, with seal impressions indicating the replacement of officials loyal to Ḫattušili with new appointees (Glatz and Matthews 2005: 55-58).

Urḫi-Tešup's decision to return the capital to Ḫattuša from Tarḫuntašša represented a significant reversal of his father's policies. This move had practical administrative advantages but also carried powerful symbolic significance, potentially signaling a broader rejection of Muwatalli's innovations.

Excavations at Ḫattuša confirm renewed building activity during this period, including modifications to the royal citadel and temple complexes (Seeher 2006: 131-135).

The conflict between Urḫi-Tešup and Ḫattušili escalated over approximately seven years (ca. 1272-1265 BCE). Ḫattušili maintained his power base in the north, particularly around the city of Hakpiš, while Urḫi-Tešup controlled the capital and central administration. The "Apology" describes the final confrontation:

"For seven years I submitted to him, but when he sought to destroy me, we went to battle. The Storm-god, my lord, and Ištar, my lady, delivered him into my hand. I banished him from the land of Ḫatti and sent him across the sea" (Apology of Ḫattušili III, §11, trans. Van den Hout 2003: 204).

The "battle" referenced may have been less a military engagement than a palace coup. The lack of archaeological evidence for widespread destruction during this period suggests a relatively contained conflict, focused on elite power centers rather than a general civil war. Urḫi-Tešup was exiled rather than executed, initially to the Syrian territories and later, according to Egyptian sources, to Egypt itself (Singer 2002: 97-98).

Ḫattušili's seizure of power created significant legitimacy problems. As the brother of the previous king, his claim to the throne violated the succession principles established by Telepinu centuries earlier. The extensive justifications offered in his "Apology" reflect this legitimacy deficit. Ḫattušili attempted to resolve these issues through multiple strategies: divine endorsement (particularly from the goddess Ištar/Šauška), marriage to Puduḫepa (a priestess of Ištar), and the rapid appointment of his son Tudḫaliya as crown prince.

The international implications of this coup were significant. Urḫi-Tešup's flight to Egypt created potential for Egyptian intervention in Hittite affairs. As historian Trevor Bryce (2005: 266) notes, "Ramesses II now held a valuable political asset—a legitimate claimant to the Hittite throne whom he could use as a bargaining counter in his dealings with the usurper or even restore to the Hittite throne as his own puppet ruler."

This political vulnerability became a key factor motivating Ḫattušili's subsequent diplomatic initiatives toward Egypt. His need to neutralize the threat posed by the exiled legitimate king contributed significantly to the peace negotiations that would follow.

The Egyptian-Hittite Peace Treaty: Terms and Significance

The Egyptian-Hittite peace treaty of 1259 BCE stands as one of the most remarkable diplomatic achievements of the Late Bronze Age. Copies were produced in both Hittite and Egyptian versions, with the Hittite version inscribed in Akkadian (the diplomatic lingua franca) on clay tablets, while the Egyptian version was carved in hieroglyphics on temple walls at Karnak and later at the Ramesseum. This dual preservation offers historians a rare opportunity to compare different linguistic versions of the same diplomatic instrument.

The treaty negotiations likely began around 1262 BCE and concluded approximately three years later. The initiative appears to have come from the Hittite side, motivated by Ḫattušili's need to secure international recognition for his rule and neutralize the threat posed by the exiled Urḫi-Tešup. From the Egyptian perspective, the continued military stalemate in Syria made peace an attractive option, particularly as Ramesses II faced emerging threats from Libya in the west.

The treaty's preamble establishes its historical context, referencing previous relationships between the two powers:

"Behold, Ḫattušili, Great King, King of the land of Ḫatti, has established himself in a treaty with Ramesses II, Great King, King of the land of Egypt, effective from this day, to establish good peace and good brotherhood between us forever" (Treaty between Ḫattušili III and Ramesses II, §1, trans. Beckman 1999: 97).

The treaty was sealed with religious sanctions, invoking the gods of both kingdoms as witnesses and guarantors:

"As for these words which are on this silver tablet for the land of Ḫatti and the land of Egypt—whoever does not observe them, the thousand gods of the land of Ḫatti and the thousand gods of the land of Egypt shall destroy his house, his land, and his servants" (Treaty between Ḫattušili III and Ramesses II, §31, trans. Beckman 1999: 103).

The significance of this treaty extends beyond its immediate political context. As historian Mario Liverani (2001: 19) observes, "The Egyptian-Hittite treaty represents the culmination of Late Bronze Age diplomatic practice, combining elements of alliance, non-aggression, and mutual recognition in a comprehensive international instrument."

Several features make this treaty particularly noteworthy: First, it established a durable peace between former enemies. Despite occasional tensions, the peace established in 1259 BCE held for the remainder of both kingdoms' existence. The treaty succeeded in transforming the relationship from one of endemic conflict to stable cooperation. Second, it exemplifies the sophisticated diplomatic system of the Late Bronze Age. The use of Akkadian as a diplomatic language, the exchange of messengers, the involvement of royal women, and the elaborate protocol all reflect the developed international system of the period. Third, the treaty's provisions for mutual defense created a genuine alliance structure that would influence subsequent events. When Assyria began threatening Hittite interests in the Upper Euphrates region during the reign of Tudḫaliya IV, Egyptian diplomatic support (though not direct military intervention) appears to have been forthcoming.

Finally, the treaty's emphasis on dynastic legitimacy helped secure Ḫattušili's position both domestically and internationally. By gaining Ramesses II's recognition, Ḫattušili neutralized the threat posed by the exiled Urḫi-Tešup and strengthened his own somewhat tenuous claim to the throne.

Archaeologically, the treaty's impact is visible in the material culture of both kingdoms. Egyptian objects appear more frequently in Hittite contexts after this period, while evidence of increased trade flows can be detected in port cities along the eastern Mediterranean coast. The stable political environment facilitated economic exchange that benefited both powers and their vassals.

Royal Marriages and Cultural Exchange

Dynastic marriage reinforced the peace treaty between Ḫattušili III and Ramesses II. In the 13th year of Ramesses' reign (ca. 1246 BCE), a Hittite princess—daughter of Ḫattušili and Puduḫepa—was sent to Egypt as a bride for the pharaoh. This marriage represented the culmination of complex negotiations documented in the correspondence between Puduḫepa and Ramesses II preserved in the Hittite archives.

The Hittite queen played a central role in these negotiations, as evidenced by her letter to Ramesses:

"As for what my brother wrote to me saying: 'My brother has not sent the gift(s) of greeting'—you are a Great King. Why do you speak in this manner? If there were a daughter available, would you not give her to my brother because of a mere greeting gift? I will give her to him, and we will establish a relationship between our countries" (KUB 21.38, trans. Hoffner 2009: 281-282).

The marriage alliance had profound significance for both kingdoms. For the Hittites, it represented Egyptian recognition of their equal status in the international system. For Egypt, it created a valuable diplomatic connection with a former enemy. The Hittite princess, renamed Maathorneferure in Egyptian, received the title "Great Royal Wife," indicating her high status at the Egyptian court.

This marriage initiated a period of increased cultural exchange between the two powers. Egyptian influence appears in Hittite art and iconography from this period, while Hittite religious concepts may have influenced certain aspects of Egyptian practice. The exchange of physicians, mentioned in the correspondence between the two courts, suggests intellectual and scientific exchange as well.

A letter from Ḫattušili III to Ramesses II illustrates the medical exchanges that occurred:

"Concerning the physician and the exorcist about whom my brother wrote to me—behold, I am sending them to my brother. And concerning the physician for the eyes about whom I wrote to my brother, saying: 'Send him to me'—let my brother not hold him back. Let my brother send him to me quickly, so that he may prepare the medicine" (KUB 21.38, trans. Hoffner 2009: 283).

Archaeological evidence for this cultural exchange comes from both Egyptian and Hittite contexts. At Pi-Ramesses, Ramesses II's capital in the eastern Nile Delta, Hittite-style pottery and artifacts have been discovered. Similarly, Egyptian luxury goods appear in increased quantities at Hittite sites during this period, particularly at Ḫattuša itself.

Additional dynastic marriages followed the marriage alliance between the Hittites and Egypt. A second Hittite princess was sent to Egypt around 1239 BCE. These marriages created kinship bonds between the ruling houses that reinforced the diplomatic relationship established by the treaty.

As historian Billie Jean Collins (2007: 104) notes, "The royal marriages between Hatti and Egypt transformed former enemies into family members, adding a personal dimension to international relations that helped sustain peace between the powers for the remainder of the Late Bronze Age."

The Apology of Ḫattušili III: Political Autobiography

The so-called "Apology" of Ḫattušili III represents one of the most remarkable political texts to survive from the ancient Near East. Composed around 1250 BCE, this first-person narrative recounts Ḫattušili's career from his youth through his seizure of power from Urḫi-Tešup. The text serves multiple purposes: justifying Ḫattušili's usurpation, establishing divine sanction for his rule, and securing the succession for his son Tudḫaliya IV.

The "Apology" begins with Ḫattušili's early life and his relationship with the goddess Ištar/Šauška of Šamuḫa:

"When my father Mursili made me a priest of the Storm-god, I was still a child. Since the goddess Ištar sent my father the message through a dream: 'Take him under my service, let him be my priest,' my father took me under the service of the goddess while I was still a child, and I served her as a priest" (Apology of Ḫattušili III, §1, trans. van den Hout 2003: 199).

This divine connection becomes a central theme throughout the text. Ḫattušili repeatedly attributes his successes to divine favor, particularly from Ištar, while presenting setbacks faced by his opponents as evidence of divine displeasure. This theological framework serves to legitimize his unconventional path to power.

The text recounts Ḫattušili's military service under his brother Muwatalli II, emphasizing his loyalty and accomplishments:

"When my brother Muwatalli went to the land of Arzawa, he left me in the Upper Land, and he made me military governor of the Upper Land and placed border troops under my command. Then the Kaška enemy, the enemy from

Piššuru, the enemy from Išḫupitta—these three enemies invaded my territory" (Apology of Ḫattušili III, §3, trans. Van den Hout 2003: 200).

Ḫattušili describes his successful defense of these territories and his brother's gratitude, establishing his credentials as a capable military leader and loyal servant of the state. This section serves to contrast with the later portrayal of Urḫi-Tešup as ungrateful and incompetent.

The central portion of the text focuses on Ḫattušili's conflict with Urḫi-Tešup, presenting the latter's actions as both unjust and impious:

"But when he sought to destroy me and the goddess, my lady, he took from me the fortress of Šamuḫa, the city of the goddess... But the goddess, my lady, did not permit it, and she handed him over to me" (Apology of Ḫattušili III, §10c-11, trans. Van den Hout 2003: 204).

By framing the conflict in religious terms, Ḫattušili transforms his usurpation into a divinely sanctioned act of justice rather than a violation of legitimate succession principles.

The "Apology" concludes with Ḫattušili's establishment of his son Tudḫaliya as heir, again emphasizing divine approval:

"The goddess, my lady, took me by the hand and helped me, and I installed Tudḫaliya, my son, in kingship. I presented him to the Storm-God, my lord. May the Storm-god, my lord, and Šauška of Šamuḫa, my lady, and all the gods protect Tudḫaliya, my son, and may they extend his years and days" (Apology of Ḫattušili III, §13, trans. Van den Hout 2003: 205).

The "Apology" represents a sophisticated example of political propaganda. As historian Gary Beckman (2005: 223) observes, "Ḫattušili's 'Apology' represents the most developed example of political autobiography from the ancient Near East, skillfully combining historical narrative, religious legitimation, and dynastic propaganda."

Several aspects of this text deserve particular attention: First, it demonstrates the central role of religious legitimation in Hittite political ideology. Ḫattušili's relationship with Ištar/Šauška provides the theological framework justifying his unconventional path to power. Second, the text reveals the importance of historical precedent in Hittite political thought. Ḫattušili carefully positions his actions within established patterns, comparing himself to earlier kings who faced similar challenges. Third, the "Apology" illustrates the sophisticated literary culture of the Hittite court. The text employs complex narrative strategies, careful characterization, and persuasive rhetoric to present Ḫattušili's case to multiple audiences.

Finally, the preservation and distribution of this text suggest its importance for Hittite political culture. Multiple copies have been found at Ḫattuša, indicating that it was intended for circulation among the elite and perhaps public reading in ceremonial contexts.

The "Apology" must be read critically as a historical source, given its obvious bias. However, it provides invaluable insights into Hittite political thought and the challenges faced by a usurper king seeking to establish legitimacy. The text's emphasis on divine favor, military accomplishment, and dynastic continuity reflects core values of Hittite royal ideology.

Ḫattušili's Reign: Achievements and Legacy

Ḫattušili III's reign (ca. 1267-1237 BCE) represented a period of diplomatic innovation and internal consolidation for the Hittite Empire. Having secured power through controversial means, Ḫattušili focused on stabilizing his rule through multiple strategies: religious patronage, diplomatic initiatives, and administrative reforms.

The religious dimension of Ḫattušili's rule centered on the cult of Ištar/Šauška, the goddess who had allegedly supported his rise to power. Excavations at Šamuḫa (possibly modern Kayalıpınar) have revealed evidence of substantial temple construction during this period (Müller-Karpe 2017: 79-82). The king's wife, Puduḫepa, played a crucial role in religious affairs, serving as high priestess and overseeing a comprehensive inventory and reorganization of state cults documented in the "festival lists" preserved in the Ḫattuša archives.

Puduḫepa's influence extended beyond religious matters into diplomacy and administration. As historian Maciej Popko (1995: 142) notes, "Queen Puduḫepa represents perhaps the most powerful female figure in Hittite history, actively participating in diplomatic correspondence, judicial proceedings, and cultic reforms." Her seal appears alongside her husband's on state documents, including the Egyptian-Hittite peace treaty, indicating her formal role in governance.

Administratively, Ḫattušili's reign saw efforts to strengthen central control while accommodating regional interests. The reorganization of provincial administration included the appointment of loyal officials to key positions and the formalization of relationships with semi-autonomous regions like Tarḫuntašša, now governed by Ḫattušili's nephew Kurunta under a detailed treaty arrangement.

The archaeological record from this period shows evidence of prosperity and stability across the empire. Urban centers in central Anatolia and northern Syria demonstrate continuous occupation with minimal destruction layers, suggesting effective security and governance. Trade networks appear to have flourished, with imported goods from Egypt, Cyprus, and Mesopotamia appearing in increased quantities at Hittite sites.

Ḫattušili's diplomatic achievements extended beyond the Egyptian peace treaty. Relations with Babylonia were strengthened through correspondence and gift exchange, while potential threats from Assyria were monitored through intelligence networks. The Hittite diplomatic corps developed sophisticated practices for managing these relationships, as evidenced by the extensive diplomatic correspondence preserved in the Ḫattuša archives.

When Ḫattušili died around 1237 BCE, he left his son Tudḫaliya IV a stable empire with secure borders and valuable international alliances. The successful transition of power to Tudḫaliya, despite the irregular circumstances of Ḫattušili's own accession, suggests that his efforts to legitimize his dynasty had largely succeeded.

As historian Itamar Singer (2011: 408) concludes, "Ḫattušili III's reign represents a masterful example of political rehabilitation. Having seized power through questionable means, he succeeded in transforming himself from usurper to respected international statesman through a combination of diplomatic skill, religious patronage, and effective governance."

Conclusion: The Hittite Empire at Its Height

The period from Šuppiluliuma I through Ḫattušili III (ca. 1350-1237 BCE) represents the zenith of Hittite imperial power. Through military conquest, diplomatic innovation, and administrative adaptation, the Hittite kings transformed their kingdom into a genuine empire capable of competing with Egypt for regional dominance.

The Hittites demonstrated remarkable flexibility in governance, developing varied administrative approaches for different regions and populations. This pragmatism allowed them to maintain control over a diverse empire without excessive military commitment.

Hittite diplomatic practice evolved sophisticated mechanisms for managing international relationships, from formal treaties to dynastic marriages. These diplomatic tools helped stabilize imperial frontiers and resolve conflicts that might otherwise have required military intervention.

The Hittite religious system integrated diverse traditions while maintaining core theological principles. This religious synthesis supported imperial ideology while accommodating local practices, facilitating cultural integration across the empire.

In terms of the military, the Hittites adapted to changing strategic challenges through innovations in chariotry, infantry organization, and siege warfare. These adaptations allowed the Hittites to project power across substantial distances despite limited manpower compared to rivals like Egypt.

As the 13th century BCE progressed, however, new challenges would emerge. The rise of Assyria, climate changes affecting agricultural productivity, and disruptions to Mediterranean trade networks would test the resilience of the imperial system developed during this period. The successors of Ḫattušili III would face these challenges with varying degrees of success, ultimately failing to prevent the empire's collapse around 1180 BCE.

CHAPTER 13

TUDḫALIYA IV AND THE BEGINNING OF DECLINE

Assyrian Resurgence and Loss of Eastern Territories

The relative stability achieved through the Egyptian-Hittite peace treaty of 1259 BCE masked growing challenges on the empire's eastern frontiers. When Tudḫaliya IV (ca. 1237-1209 BCE) ascended to the throne following his father Ḫattušili III's death, he inherited an empire that appeared formidable from the outside but faced mounting structural pressures. Chief among these was the dramatic resurgence of Assyrian power under Tukulti-Ninurta I (1243-1207 BCE), which fundamentally altered the geopolitical landscape of the Near East.

The Assyrian threat had been building gradually since the reign of Adad-nirari I (1307-1275 BCE), who had begun the process of rebuilding Assyrian military capabilities. However, it was under Shalmaneser I (1274-1245 BCE) that Assyria emerged as a significant regional power, systematically dismantling the remnants of Mitanni and establishing direct control over northern Mesopotamia. By the time Tukulti-Ninurta I came to power, Assyria possessed both the military capability and territorial base to challenge Hittite interests directly.

The first major confrontation occurred around 1235 BCE when Tudḫaliya attempted to intervene in support of Babylonia against Assyrian aggression. The Hittite forces suffered a devastating defeat, as recorded in Tukulti-Ninurta's victory inscription:

"I defeated Tudḫaliya, king of Ḫatti. I captured 28,800 Hittite troops on the other side of the Euphrates and carried them off to Assyria. I conquered the lands of Subartu to their full extent." (KBo 12.39)

While this account likely exaggerates the scale of victory, archaeological evidence from sites along the upper Euphrates, including destruction layers and the subsequent appearance of Assyrian administrative materials, confirms a significant shift in political control. The defeat forced Tudḫaliya to recognize new geopolitical realities, as reflected in a letter found at Ugarit (RS 34.165), where he acknowledges Tukulti-Ninurta as "Great King, my brother," a title previously denied to Assyrian rulers.

The loss of influence in northern Mesopotamia had cascading effects on Hittite power. Control over eastern trade routes diminished, reducing access to tin, essential for bronze production, and luxury goods that supported elite gift exchange networks. The kingdom of Išuwa, long a buffer state between Hittite and Assyrian spheres of influence, shifted its allegiance to Assyria, creating a direct threat to the Hittite heartland.

Particularly concerning was the Assyrian encroachment on Carchemish, the seat of a Hittite viceroyalty established by Šuppiluliuma I. Tudḫaliya's desperate attempts to shore up this vital region are evident in a treaty with his cousin Šaušgamuwa of Amurru (CTH 105), which includes specific provisions against allowing Assyrian merchants passage through his territory:

"The King of Assyria is the enemy of My Sun [the Hittite king]; so he must be your enemy. No merchant of yours shall go to Assyria, and you shall allow no merchant of Assyria to enter your land or pass through your land. If an Assyrian merchant comes to your land, seize him and send him to My Sun. Let this be an obligation upon you."

Archaeological evidence from Carchemish (modern Karkamış) supports textual indications of increased fortification during this period. The citadel walls were strengthened, and storage facilities expanded, suggesting preparation for potential siege. Despite these efforts, Hittite control over Syria became increasingly tenuous, requiring constant diplomatic and military intervention to maintain.

Macqueen (2003:152) argues that the eastern losses represented more than just territorial reduction: "The Assyrian advance effectively dismantled the buffer zone that had protected the Hittite heartland for generations. Without this strategic depth, the empire became increasingly vulnerable to both military threats and economic disruption."

The Kaška Problem and Northern Frontiers

While Assyrian expansion threatened the eastern territories, the northern frontier presented an equally persistent challenge in the form of the Kaška peoples. These semi-nomadic groups had troubled Hittite kings since the Old Kingdom period, but during Tudḫaliya IV's reign, their incursions intensified, stretching imperial resources and threatening the core agricultural regions of the Upper Land.

The Kaška occupied the mountainous Pontic region north of the Hittite heartland, an area characterized by dense forests and difficult terrain. Unlike the urban-based states of Syria and Mesopotamia, the Kaška operated as a decentralized confederation of tribes without permanent settlements or centralized authority. This political structure made them simultaneously less threatening as a unified force but more difficult to defeat decisively or incorporate into the imperial system through standard treaty relationships.

A fragmentary text from Tudḫaliya's reign (KUB 23.11) describes the situation:

"The Kaška people have no regard for oaths. They continually come to plunder the land of Ḫatti. They take our subjects captive and make them their own. They have no loyalty. They do not recognize lordship."

Archaeological evidence from northern settlements like Maşat Höyük (ancient Tapikka) reveals a pattern of destruction and rebuilding throughout the 13th century BCE. Excavations have uncovered multiple burn layers interspersed with periods of Hittite administrative presence, suggesting a cycle of Kaška raids, Hittite reconquest, and subsequent abandonment. The archive of clay tablets discovered at the site includes urgent requests for military reinforcements and reports of Kaška movements, painting a picture of constant vigilance and periodic crisis.

Tudḫaliya IV attempted various strategies to address the Kaška threat. Military campaigns were launched regularly, as documented in the annalistic fragments (KBo 16.36+), but these typically resulted in temporary withdrawals rather than permanent subjugation. The terrain favored the defenders, allowing Kaška forces to retreat into forested mountains when confronted with superior Hittite forces.

A more innovative approach involved the construction of a line of fortified settlements along the frontier zone, creating what Glatz and Matthews (2005:55) have termed a "defensive depth strategy." Archaeological surveys have identified a network of medium-sized administrative centers with substantial fortifications, spaced approximately one day's march apart. These sites, including Šapinuwa (modern Ortaköy) and Kuşaklı (ancient Šarišša), functioned as forward bases for military operations and as administrative centers for managing the complex frontier zone.

The northern problem was further complicated by its economic implications. The Pontic region contained valuable resources, particularly metals and timber, essential for maintaining Hittite military capabilities. Texts from the period (KUB 40.80) refer to expeditions sent to secure copper sources in Kaška territory, highlighting the strategic importance of maintaining at least partial access to these regions.

Singer (1985:109) notes that the Kaška represented more than just a military threat: "They embodied the antithesis of the Hittite imperial model—tribal rather than urban, decentralized rather than hierarchical, mobile rather than settled. This fundamental incompatibility made traditional imperial integration strategies largely ineffective."

By the final decades of the 13th century BCE, the situation had deteriorated significantly. A letter found at Ugarit (RS 88.2009) from the last Hittite king, Šuppiluliuma II, requests urgent grain shipments "because there is famine in the midst of my lands," suggesting that Kaška disruption of agricultural production in the northern territories had created food shortages throughout the empire.

Economic Difficulties and Administrative Strain

The territorial pressures on both eastern and northern frontiers contributed to broader economic difficulties that undermined the imperial system during Tudḫaliya IV's reign. However, these external challenges were exacerbated by internal structural problems that had been building throughout the Empire Period.

Climate data derived from dendrochronology, pollen analysis, and stable isotope studies from lake sediments across Anatolia indicate a period of increasing aridity beginning around 1250 BCE. This climatic shift reduced agricultural productivity in key grain-producing regions, particularly the central Anatolian plateau. Paleobotanical remains from Kaman-Kalehöyük show evidence of crop failures and shifts to more drought-resistant but less productive barley varieties during this period.

The Hittite administrative response to these agricultural challenges is documented in a series of inventory texts (CTH 240-250) that record increasingly detailed management of grain reserves. These texts show a progressive centralization of storage facilities and stricter rationing systems. An edict of Tudḫaliya IV (KBo 6.26) establishes standardized measurements for grain distributions and imposes severe penalties for officials who misappropriate food supplies:

"If any governor or official takes grain from the storehouses beyond what is allocated by the seal of the king, he shall replace it threefold, and the king shall determine his punishment."

Disruptions compounded the economic strain to international trade networks that had flourished during the stable period following the Egyptian-Hittite peace treaty. Maritime trade in the eastern Mediterranean became increasingly hazardous, as evidenced by the dramatic increase in shipwrecks dating to the late 13th century BCE. The famous Uluburun shipwreck, discovered off the coast of southern Turkey and dating to approximately 1320 BCE, provides a snapshot of the complex exchange networks that connected the Hittite Empire to Cyprus, Egypt, the Levant, and the Aegean. By Tudhaliya's reign, such connections were becoming more tenuous.

A letter from the king of Ugarit to Tudhaliya IV (RS 94.2523) reports: "Ships from the west no longer reach our shores as before. The merchants say the sea routes are threatened by ships of unknown origin that attack without warning." This reference likely relates to early manifestations of the "Sea Peoples" phenomenon that would later contribute to the regional collapse around 1180 BCE.

The combined effects of agricultural stress and trade disruption created severe fiscal challenges for the imperial administration. The Hittite state had traditionally relied on a combination of direct agricultural production from royal estates, tribute from vassal kingdoms, and taxes collected in kind from provincial territories. As these revenue streams diminished, the empire struggled to maintain its military capabilities and administrative infrastructure.

Evidence for this fiscal strain appears in several forms. Temple inventory texts from Tudhaliya's reign (CTH 530) show a pattern of "borrowing" precious metals from religious institutions, presumably to meet immediate state needs. A significant debasement of silver content in items from late 13th-century contexts has been detected through XRF analysis, suggesting metal shortages. Perhaps most telling is the reduction in scale and quality of royal construction projects compared to earlier periods, with greater use of reused materials and less elaborate architectural ornamentation.

The administrative response to these challenges involved increased bureaucratization and record-keeping. The number of administrative texts increases dramatically during Tudḫaliya's reign, with more detailed tracking of resources, personnel, and obligations. Van den Hout (2020:175) argues that this represents "crisis management through documentation—an attempt to maintain control through ever more precise accounting as actual resources diminished."

This administrative intensification created its own problems, however. The expanded bureaucracy required to manage the complex recording systems consumed resources that might otherwise have been directed to military or economic needs. The proliferation of specialized administrative roles created opportunities for corruption and internal competition, as evidenced by several legal texts addressing conflicts between officials (KBo 16.58).

Beckman (2013:97) summarizes the situation: "The late Hittite Empire presents a paradox—increasingly sophisticated administrative capabilities deployed in service of a progressively weakening economic foundation. The system became more complex even as the resources needed to sustain that complexity diminished."

Late Hittite Monumental Architecture and Propaganda

Facing these multiple challenges, Tudḫaliya IV launched an ambitious program of monumental construction and religious reform that scholars have interpreted as both practical responses to imperial difficulties and ideological statements meant to reinforce royal authority in uncertain times.

The most significant architectural project of Tudḫaliya's reign was the rock sanctuary of Yazılıkaya, located just northeast of the capital Ḫattuša. While the site had religious significance in earlier periods, Tudḫaliya transformed it into a monumental statement of royal ideology integrated with religious authority. The sanctuary comprises two natural chambers in the limestone outcrop, elaborated with relief carvings showing processions of deities culminating in images of the storm god Tešub embracing Tudḫaliya himself, visually equating the king with the divine.

Harmanşah (2015:109) interprets Yazılıkaya as "a deliberate fusion of landscape, religious narrative, and royal presence—creating a permanent statement of the king's divine mandate in the living rock itself." The iconography emphasizes continuity with tradition while introducing subtle innovations that elevate royal status. Particularly notable is the relief showing Tudḫaliya with the protective embrace of his personal deity Šarruma, a visual metaphor for divine legitimation at a time when practical authority may have been questioned.

Within Ḫattuša itself, Tudḫaliya undertook extensive rebuilding projects, particularly in the Upper City. Archaeological excavations reveal a systematic program of temple construction, with at least 31 new or rebuilt temples arranged in a planned layout. The standardized design of these structures, sometimes called "templum duplex" with twin cellae, represented a departure from earlier more varied architectural traditions. Seeher (2006:78) suggests this standardization served both practical purposes—allowing faster construction through repeatable designs—and ideological ones, creating a unified sacred landscape under royal control.

The most impressive defensive construction was the expansion of Ḫattuša's fortification system. The massive walls, reaching heights of 8-10 meters and extending over 6 kilometers, incorporated innovative features including postern tunnels, elaborate gateways with sculptural programs, and defensive planning that utilized the natural topography. The Sphinx Gate, Lion Gate, and King's Gate combined defensive functionality with propagandistic sculpture, presenting images of divine guardians and royal power to visitors and residents alike.

Complementing these architectural statements was an expansion of written propaganda. Tudḫaliya commissioned numerous inscriptions emphasizing his divine favor and military successes, even when the actual political situation suggested otherwise. The "Autobiography of Tudḫaliya" (CTH 81), though fragmentary, presents the king as restorer of proper religious observance and defender of Hittite traditions:

"When I, Tudḫaliya, Great King, sat upon the throne of my father, I found that the festivals of the gods had been neglected. The offerings were reduced, the temples were in disrepair. I restored all that had been forgotten. I increased the offerings beyond what they had been before."

Religious reform featured prominently in Tudḫaliya's ideological program. The king undertook a systematic inventory and reorganization of cult practices throughout the empire, documented in the detailed cult inventories (CTH 525-530). These texts record standardized offerings, festival procedures, and divine images for hundreds of local cults, representing an unprecedented centralization of religious authority under royal control.

The culmination of this religious program was the "Song of Ullikummi" (CTH 345), a mythological text revised during Tudḫaliya's reign that subtly reframes older Hurrian myths to emphasize themes of legitimate succession and divine order restored through proper action. The narrative, which describes the storm god's victory over chaotic forces threatening cosmic order, serves as a mythological parallel to the king's self-presentation as restorer of proper order in troubled times.

McMahon (2011:128) argues that these propagandistic efforts reveal the underlying anxieties of the period: "The very scale and intensity of Tudḫaliya's ideological program suggests deep concern about the stability of royal authority. The insistence on divine sanction reads as an attempt to establish through religious means what could no longer be secured through military or economic power alone."

Archaeological evidence suggests these efforts had limited success beyond the capital region. Provincial centers show declining investment in monumental architecture during this period, with repairs rather than new construction being the norm. At sites like Kuşaklı-Šarišša, temples were maintained but not expanded, while administrative buildings show evidence of repurposing for more practical storage functions.

The contrast between the elaborate ideological program centered on Ḫattuša and the pragmatic adaptations in provincial territories highlights the growing disconnect between imperial self-presentation and administrative reality. As Bryce (2019:231) notes, "Tudḫaliya's monuments speak to us of an empire still confident in its divine mission, while the archaeological record beyond the capital tells a different story of adaptation to diminishing resources and reduced horizons."

The Final Decades: Arnuwanda III and Šuppiluliuma II

Following Tudḫaliya IV's death around 1209 BCE, his son Arnuwanda III ruled briefly before being succeeded by his brother Šuppiluliuma II (ca. 1207-1180 BCE), the last documented Hittite king. The final decades of the empire saw an acceleration of the challenges that had emerged under Tudḫaliya, coupled with new threats that ultimately proved insurmountable.

The most significant new development was the appearance of maritime raiders—the "Sea Peoples" of Egyptian texts—who disrupted coastal settlements and trade networks throughout the eastern Mediterranean. While their exact identity remains debated, archaeological evidence from coastal sites in Cilicia and northern Syria shows destruction layers dating to this period, often followed by new material culture assemblages suggesting population replacement or significant cultural disruption.

A fragmentary letter from Ugarit, likely addressed to Šuppiluliuma II shortly before the city's destruction around 1185 BCE, captures the atmosphere of crisis:

"My father, behold, the enemy ships came here; my cities were burned, and they did evil things in my country. Does not my father know that all my troops and chariots are in the Land of Hatti, and all my ships are in the Land of Lukka? They have not arrived back yet, so the country is abandoned to itself. May my father know it: seven ships of the enemy have come here and have done very grave damage to us." (RS 20.238)

The final years of Šuppiluliuma II's reign are poorly documented due to the abrupt end of the archival tradition at Ḫattuša. The last dated texts describe desperate measures to secure grain supplies and defensive preparations against unspecified enemies approaching from multiple directions. Archaeological evidence from Ḫattuša itself reveals hasty fortification repairs and the organized evacuation of administrative archives and religious objects, suggesting a planned abandonment rather than sudden destruction.

The final abandonment of Ḫattuša around 1180 BCE marked the effective end of the Hittite Empire as a centralized political entity. The causes were multiple and interconnected: climate change reducing agricultural productivity, disruption of trade networks, pressure from Assyria in the east and Kaška in the north, the breakdown of the vassal system in Syria, and ultimately the appearance of new population groups amid a broader regional collapse.

Ironically, some of the very strengths that had allowed the empire to flourish—its complex administrative systems, specialized economic integration, and elaborate religious institutions—may have reduced its adaptability in the face of multiple simultaneous challenges. As Cline (2014:173) argues, "The very interconnectedness that characterized the Late Bronze Age world created systemic vulnerabilities when multiple stress points were activated simultaneously."

Conclusion: Understanding Imperial Decline

The final century of Hittite imperial history offers valuable insights into the dynamics of ancient state systems under stress. Rather than a single catastrophic event, the evidence points to a complex interplay of environmental, economic, political, and social factors that gradually undermined the foundations of imperial power.

The Hittite response to these challenges combined practical adaptations—defensive fortifications, administrative reforms, resource management—with ideological efforts to reinforce traditional sources of authority through monumental architecture, religious reorganization, and propagandistic texts. These responses proved insufficient not because they were poorly conceived, but because they addressed individual symptoms rather than the underlying structural vulnerabilities of the imperial system.

Particularly significant was the empire's dependence on agricultural surplus from a relatively limited productive core in central Anatolia, combined with resources and tribute from peripheral territories. When climate change reduced agricultural productivity while frontier pressures simultaneously increased military costs and reduced access to peripheral resources, the fundamental equation of imperial economics became unsustainable.

The Hittite case also highlights the importance of legitimacy and ideological cohesion in maintaining complex political systems. As practical authority diminished, Hittite kings increasingly emphasized religious and traditional sources of legitimacy. The elaborate monumental and textual programs of Tudḫaliya IV and Šuppiluliuma II can be understood as attempts to maintain social cohesion and elite loyalty when material incentives were becoming less reliable.

Perhaps most instructive is the recognition that imperial systems, despite their apparent power and permanence, contain inherent fragilities. The very specialization and integration that generate efficiency and power during periods of growth can become liabilities during periods of stress, as the failure of one component cascades through interconnected systems.

The Hittite Empire did not so much collapse as gradually transform, with regional continuities persisting in the Neo-Hittite states of northern Syria and southeastern Anatolia during the Early Iron Age. These successor states maintained elements of Hittite political culture, artistic traditions, and religious practices while adapting to new geopolitical realities. This pattern of continuity amid transformation reminds us that even dramatic political endings rarely represent complete cultural breaks.

As we continue to explore the archaeological and textual evidence from this crucial period, our understanding of these complex processes will undoubtedly evolve. What remains clear is that the end of the Hittite Empire was neither inevitable nor unpredictable, but rather the result of specific historical circumstances and the limits of adaptive capacity in the face of multiple, simultaneous challenges.

Chapter 14

Hittite Society and Administration

Royal Court and Aristocracy

At the apex of Hittite society stood the royal court, an institution that evolved considerably over the five centuries of Hittite history. The king (Labarna or Tabarna) and queen (Tawananna) formed the nucleus of this elite sphere, surrounded by a complex hierarchy of officials, aristocrats, and specialists. While early scholarship portrayed Hittite kingship as primarily autocratic, recent research reveals a more nuanced picture of power balanced among various institutions and elite groups.

"The Hittite king was not an absolute monarch in the modern sense," explains Theo van den Hout, "but rather operated within a web of constraints imposed by tradition, religious obligations, and the practical need to maintain aristocratic support" (van den Hout 2018: 124). This balance is evident in the role of the *panku*, an assembly of nobles that served as a judicial body in cases of royal succession disputes and high treason. While the *panku* lacked formal legislative powers, its existence demonstrates the institutionalized role of the aristocracy in governance.

The royal court centered on the palace complex, which archaeological evidence from Hattuša shows was not a single structure but rather a collection of administrative, ceremonial, and residential buildings. The most impressive remains are found in the Upper City at Büyükkale, where the royal citadel contained audience halls, administrative offices, archives, and residential quarters. Excavator Peter Neve described the complex as "designed to project royal authority while facilitating the practical administration of an empire" (Neve 1992: 15).

Court society was highly stratified, with detailed records of titles and positions preserved in administrative texts. The inner circle included the *GAL MEŠEDI* (Chief of the Royal Bodyguard), who often served as the king's most trusted military commander, and the *GAL DUMU.MEŠ.É.GAL* (Chief of the Palace Attendants), who oversaw the daily operations of the royal household. These positions were typically filled by members of the royal family or highest-ranking nobles.

A letter from the Maşat archive illustrates the close relationship between these officials and the king: "To my lord speak thus: Your servant Kassu says as follows: Concerning what my lord wrote to me: 'Are the troops ready?' Yes, my lord, they are ready. The chariots are prepared as my lord commanded" (HKM 24). This correspondence demonstrates both the formality of court communication and the personal relationships that underpinned administrative efficiency.

The aristocracy (*LÚ.MEŠ DUGUD*, "important men") comprised both hereditary nobles and appointed officials whose status derived from royal favor. Land grants documented in cuneiform texts show how the king maintained aristocratic loyalty through the distribution of agricultural estates. The "Land Donation Texts" detail precise boundaries of granted properties and stipulate service obligations in return. One such text states: "The Great King Tudhaliya has given to Šahurunuwa, the Chief of the Scribes, the town of Ištahara with all its fields, vineyards, dependents, cattle and sheep" (KBo 1.28).

Archaeological evidence from provincial centers like Kuşaklı (ancient Šarišša) reveals that aristocratic residences followed similar architectural principles throughout the empire, suggesting a shared elite culture. These buildings typically featured stone foundations, timber-frame superstructures, and distinctive ceramic assemblages that included fine drinking vessels for banqueting—a central aristocratic social practice.

The queen (Tawananna) maintained a position of remarkable authority, controlling her own household, lands, and personnel. Unlike many ancient Near Eastern royal women, the Hittite queen kept her position even after her husband's death, continuing to exercise power during her son's reign. This arrangement occasionally led to tensions, as in the case of Puduhepa, widow of Hattušili III, who maintained significant influence during her son Tudhaliya IV's reign. A letter from the Ugarit archives demonstrates her independent authority: "Thus says Puduhepa, Great Queen of Hatti, to Niqmaddu, king of Ugarit: Concerning the matter about which you wrote to me..." (RS 17.116).

Royal siblings and children occupied privileged positions at court, often serving as provincial governors, military commanders, or priests. Prince Telipinu, son of Šuppiluliuma I, became a priest before being appointed governor of Aleppo, while his brother Piyaššili (also called Šarri-Kušuh) ruled Carchemish as viceroy. This practice of appointing royal family members to key positions helped maintain imperial cohesion while providing practical training for potential successors.

The *haššannan* ceremony, documented in ritual texts, provides insight into how royal authority was publicly performed. During this festival, the king processed through the streets of Hattuša, receiving homage from nobles and foreign representatives. The ritual culminated in a ceremonial banquet where strict protocols governed seating arrangements according to rank. As Itamar Singer noted, "These elaborate ceremonies served to reaffirm the social hierarchy while providing occasions for the redistribution of resources that cemented elite loyalty" (Singer 2011: 173).

By the 13th century BCE, court society had grown increasingly complex, with specialized bureaucratic roles and elaborate protocols. Records from Tudhaliya IV's reign reveal over forty distinct court titles, from cupbearers to chariot-fighters to scribes. This bureaucratic elaboration may reflect attempts to maintain administrative control during a period of increasing external pressures.

Provincial Administration and Vassal States

The Hittite approach to territorial control was remarkably pragmatic, employing different administrative strategies based on geographic proximity, strategic importance, and local political traditions. This flexible system can be divided into three concentric zones: the core territories under direct rule, an intermediate zone of provinces governed by appointed officials, and an outer ring of vassal states bound by treaties.

In the Hittite heartland of central Anatolia, administration centered on the *BĒL MADGALTI* ("Lord of the Watchtower"), a provincial governor responsible for military security, agricultural production, and judicial oversight. Instructions to these officials provide detailed insights into governance practices:

"You shall keep watch on the fortified places. The roads shall be kept in good repair. You shall not neglect the watchtowers and beacons. When a message comes from another land, you shall promptly relay it to My Majesty... You shall ensure that the plowing and harvesting are done at the proper times. The storehouses shall be kept full." (CTH 261)

These texts reveal a governance system focused on security, communication, and resource management—the fundamental concerns of Bronze Age statecraft. Archaeological evidence from provincial centers like Maşat Höyük (ancient Tapikka) confirms this administrative footprint, with excavations uncovering storage facilities, defensive works, and archives of administrative tablets.

The Maşat letters, discovered in 1973, provide an unparalleled window into provincial administration. This archive of 97 letters documents communication between local officials and the central government, covering military matters, agricultural production, and religious observances. One letter reports: "The enemy came from Mount Kassu. They burned down Istitina and took captives. We pursued them but could not catch them. Now we have strengthened the watchtowers as my lord commanded" (HKM 46). Such correspondence demonstrates both the challenges of frontier administration and the responsiveness of the central government to local conditions.

Beyond the core territories lay provinces governed by appointed officials who often held the title *UGULA.KALAM.MA* ("Overseer of the Land"). These administrators typically came from the royal family or highest aristocracy and wielded considerable authority while remaining directly accountable to the king. Archaeological research at provincial capitals like Šapinuwa (modern Ortaköy) reveals monumental architecture, administrative archives, and defensive works comparable to those at Hattuša, suggesting substantial investment in provincial infrastructure.

The outer administrative layer consisted of vassal states bound to Hatti through elaborate treaties. Trevor Bryce characterizes this system as "an efficient means of extending imperial control with minimal administrative overhead" (Bryce 2005: 48). Vassal treaties followed a consistent format, including historical preambles, specific obligations, divine witnesses, and curses for violation. The treaty with Tarhuntašša, a secondary Hittite kingdom in southern Anatolia, illustrates this approach:

"These are the words of the Sun Tudhaliya, Great King, King of Hatti: Formerly Kurunta was a prince in Hattuša. But I, the Great King, established him as king in the land of Tarhuntašša... He shall come to the aid of the Sun with infantry and chariotry. He shall not admit into his territory any enemy of the Sun... If anyone speaks an evil word against the Sun, he shall not conceal it but shall report it to the Sun." (CTH 106)

These treaties created a web of obligations that extended Hittite influence while acknowledging local autonomy. Vassals retained their royal titles and domestic authority but surrendered control of foreign relations, paid tribute, and provided military support. Archaeological evidence from vassal capitals like Karkamiš (modern Karkamış) and Aleppo shows a blend of local traditions with Hittite imperial elements, suggesting cultural influence accompanied political control.

Administration of this complex system relied on efficient communication networks. The Hittites maintained a sophisticated road system with waystations (*É. KASKAL*) positioned at regular intervals. Tablets from Maşat Höyük document the movement of messengers, with one text noting: "The messenger arrived on the fifth day and delivered the sealed tablet from My Majesty" (HKM 52). This communication infrastructure allowed for surprisingly rapid information flow across the empire.

The provincial administrative system faced significant challenges during the 13th century BCE. Climate change reduced agricultural productivity in marginal zones, while frontier pressures from groups like the Kaška in the north and Assyrians in the east strained military resources. Administrative texts from this period show increasing concern with resource management and security, suggesting adaptation to deteriorating conditions.

Tudhaliya IV attempted to address these challenges through administrative reforms, including more detailed record-keeping and intensified extraction of resources from vassal states. The Bronze Tablet, discovered at Hattuša in 1986, records a revised treaty with Kurunta of Tarhuntašša that includes more specific obligations than earlier agreements. This trend toward bureaucratic elaboration may represent an attempt to maintain control in the face of growing systemic stress.

Legal System and the Hittite Law Code

The Hittite legal tradition represents one of the most sophisticated systems of the ancient Near East, combining elements of indigenous Anatolian practice with influences from Mesopotamian legal traditions. The Hittite Law Code, compiled around 1650-1500 BCE and revised in later periods, provides our primary window into this system.

Unlike the more famous Code of Hammurabi, the Hittite laws were not presented as divine revelation but as practical guidelines for judges and officials. As Harry Hoffner notes, "The Hittite laws lack the theological framework found in other ancient Near Eastern legal collections, focusing instead on pragmatic solutions to social problems" (Hoffner 1997: 25). This pragmatism is evident in the frequent revisions to penalties, with earlier versions prescribing more severe punishments than later revisions.

The laws address a wide range of issues, from personal injury and property damage to sexual offenses and religious violations. A distinctive feature is the predominance of compensation over corporal punishment, particularly in the revised versions. For example:

"If anyone blinds a free person or knocks out his tooth, formerly they would pay 40 shekels of silver, but now he shall pay 20 shekels of silver." (Law §7)

"If anyone steals a bull or a horse, formerly the thief would replace it thirtyfold. But now he shall replace it fifteenfold." (Law §63)

These revisions reveal an evolving legal philosophy that increasingly favored restitution over retribution, particularly for non-violent offenses. Capital punishment was reserved for serious crimes like witchcraft, certain sexual offenses, and specific forms of insubordination.

The law code shows remarkable attention to contextual factors and gradations of responsibility. Different penalties applied based on the status of perpetrator and victim, the intent behind actions, and whether an offense occurred in urban or rural settings. For instance:

"If anyone sets a house on fire, he shall rebuild the house. Whatever is lost in the fire—whether persons, cattle, or sheep—he shall replace. If the owner of the house does not accept compensation, then the arsonist must give his estate instead." (Law §98)

"If a slave commits a theft, his master shall make restitution. If the master refuses to make restitution, he shall give up the slave instead." (Law §95)

These provisions demonstrate sophisticated concepts of liability and compensation that balanced individual accountability with practical considerations of restitution.

The implementation of law occurred through a hierarchical court system. At the local level, village or town elders (*LÚ.MEŠ ŠU.GI*) handled minor disputes, while more serious cases were referred to provincial governors. The highest judicial authority was the king himself, who served as final arbiter in cases involving capital offenses or high-status individuals. A judicial protocol states: "If a case is too difficult for the provincial governor to decide, he shall send it to My Majesty. Only the king may pronounce a death sentence" (CTH 261.1).

Legal proceedings were primarily oral, though written records were kept of judgments in significant cases. The Hittite archives preserve many legal documents, including depositions, judicial decisions, and oaths. One deposition records testimony about a theft: "I saw Palla enter the storehouse at night. The next morning, two copper vessels were missing. I swear by the Storm God that this testimony is true" (KUB 13.35).

Oaths played a central role in Hittite legal procedure, with litigants and witnesses swearing by the gods to the truthfulness of their statements. Perjury was considered not only a legal offense but a religious transgression that would invite divine punishment. Trial by ordeal was occasionally used in cases lacking clear evidence, with defendants required to cross a river or undergo other tests believed to reveal divine judgment.

The Hittite conception of law extended beyond human legislation to include divine requirements. Treaties and loyalty oaths frequently invoke the gods as witnesses, with elaborate curses for violation. The Instructions for Temple Personnel state: "If anyone alters a word of this tablet, may the thousand gods of Hatti destroy him and his descendants" (CTH 264). This integration of religious and legal concepts created a comprehensive normative system that regulated both public and private behavior.

Archaeological evidence provides physical context for legal practice. The "King's Gate" structure at Hattuša likely served as a public court where the king or his representatives heard cases, while similar structures at provincial centers suggest standardized venues for legal proceedings throughout the empire.

The Hittite legal tradition influenced later Anatolian and Syrian legal practices, with elements persisting into the Neo-Hittite period after the empire's collapse. As Richard Haase observes, "The Hittite laws represent not merely a collection of regulations but a sophisticated jurisprudential tradition that balanced retribution, restitution, and social harmony" (Haase 2003: 631).

Urban and Rural Populations

Hittite society was predominantly agricultural, with an estimated 90% of the population engaged in farming, herding, and related activities. This rural majority produced the agricultural surplus that supported urban elites, craftspeople, and military forces. Archaeological survey data from central Anatolia reveals a settlement hierarchy ranging from major urban centers to small villages and isolated farmsteads.

Urban centers served as administrative, religious, and economic hubs. Hattuša, with its massive fortifications, monumental temples, and palatial complexes, represented the apex of Hittite urbanism. At its height in the 13th century BCE, the city covered approximately 180 hectares with an estimated population of 15,000-20,000 people. Other major centers included Šapinuwa, Šarišša (Kuşaklı), and Tapikka (Maşat Höyük), each serving as provincial capitals with populations of several thousand.

Urban planning followed consistent principles across the empire. Cities typically featured an upper citadel housing administrative buildings and elite residences, with lower towns occupied by craftspeople, merchants, and agricultural workers. Defensive works were particularly impressive, with Hattuša's walls incorporating postern tunnels, sally ports, and monumental gateways decorated with relief sculptures. As Jürgen Seeher notes, "Hittite urban fortifications served both practical defensive purposes and symbolic expressions of state power" (Seeher 2006: 62).

Archaeological excavations at urban sites reveal specialized craft production areas, including metalworking districts, pottery kilns, and textile workshops. At Šarišša, excavators identified a bronze workshop containing crucibles, molds, and slag, showing specialized production of tools and weapons. Urban economies thus combined administrative functions with craft production and market exchange.

The Hittite texts distinguish several urban social groups beyond the aristocracy and officials discussed earlier. These included craftspeople (*LÚ.MEŠ GIŠ-TUKUL*, literally "men of the tool"), merchants (*LÚ.MEŠ DAM.GÀR*), and various categories of dependent laborers. The Instructions for the Mayor of the City provide insights into urban governance:

"The Mayor shall ensure that the streets are kept clean. He shall inspect the city wall monthly and report any damage. He shall oversee the marketplace and ensure that weights and measures are honest. During festivals, he shall organize the processions and ensure that all citizens participate appropriately." (CTH 257)

Urban religious life centered on temples, which archaeological evidence shows were substantial structures with specialized storage facilities, workshops, and administrative areas. The Great Temple at Hattuša occupied over 20,000 square meters and housed not only religious activities but also significant economic operations, controlling agricultural lands, workshops, and storehouses.

Agricultural villages dominated the rural landscape (*URU*) of varying sizes, typically housing between 50 and 500 inhabitants. Survey data from the Hittite heartland denotes approximately one settlement per 10 square kilometers during the empire period, with higher densities in fertile river valleys. Villages typically consisted of residential compounds with associated outbuildings, storage facilities, and animal pens, often clustered around a central open area.

Agricultural production focused on cereal cultivation (primarily barley and wheat), supplemented by legumes, fruit trees, and viticulture. Zooarchaeological evidence shows animal husbandry centered on sheep, goats, cattle, and pigs, with hunting making a minor contribution to diet. The "Instructions to the LÚA-GRIG" (Storehouse Keeper) detail agricultural management practices:

"You shall ensure that the seed grain is of good quality. The plowing shall be done to the proper depth. When harvest comes, you shall oversee the reaping and threshing. The grain shall be properly cleaned before storage. One-third shall be set aside for seed, one-third for rations, and one-third as surplus for the palace." (CTH 258)

Land tenure systems included royal estates, temple lands, communal village holdings, and private property. The Hittite concept of *šaḫḫan* and *luzzi* (corvée labor and military service) obligated landholders to provide labor and military service in proportion to their holdings. One administrative text notes: "The village of Anziliya shall provide 12 men for fortress repair and 6 soldiers for the campaign" (KBo 16.83).

Archaeological and textual evidence indicates significant state investment in agricultural infrastructure. The "Inventory of DINGIR.MAḪ" describes irrigation works: "The canal that Šuppiluliuma dug from the river to the fields of Tiwanzana is three leagues long. It waters 120 fields" (KUB 42.100). Such projects increased agricultural productivity while demonstrating royal concern for economic prosperity.

Rural religious practices centered on local shrines and sacred natural features like springs, groves, and rock formations. The "Cult Inventory" texts document hundreds of such sites throughout the empire, each with specific deities, offerings, and festivals. One such text records: "In the village of Katapa there is a shrine of the Storm God. The village provides one sheep, ten loaves of bread, and one jug of wine for the spring festival" (CTH 501).

The relationship between urban and rural populations was essentially extractive, with agricultural surplus flowing to urban centers through taxation, religious offerings, and market exchange. However, evidence suggests this relationship was not purely exploitative. Royal inscriptions frequently mention concerns for agricultural prosperity and relief measures during times of famine or natural disaster.

Population mobility between rural and urban contexts appears to have been significant. Texts mention seasonal migration for agricultural work, craft apprenticeships bringing rural youth to urban centers, and military service temporarily relocating rural men. The "Palace Chronicle" describes one such movement: "When famine struck the land of Hatti, the king opened the granaries and distributed grain to the people. Many came from the villages to Hattuša seeking food" (CTH 8).

The final century of the empire saw increasing stress on this urban-rural relationship. Climate data indicates growing aridity across central Anatolia after 1250 BCE, reducing agricultural productivity precisely when military pressures required increased resource mobilization. Archaeological evidence from rural sites shows abandonment of marginal agricultural lands and concentration of population in more fertile areas, suggesting adaptive responses to environmental challenges.

Conclusion

The Hittite administrative and social systems demonstrate remarkable sophistication and adaptability across five centuries of imperial history. From the elaborate court hierarchy to the pragmatic legal tradition, from flexible provincial governance to the interdependent urban-rural relationship, Hittite institutions balanced centralized control with practical accommodation of local conditions.

What emerges from this examination is not a static imperial structure but a dynamic system that evolved in response to changing circumstances. The gradual shift from punitive to compensatory legal penalties, the development of increasingly formalized vassal relationships, and the intensification of administrative record-keeping during the empire's final century all reflect institutional adaptation to changing conditions.

The Hittite achievement lies not merely in military conquest but in creating governance structures that integrated diverse populations across vast geographic areas. As Gary Beckman observes, "The genius of Hittite imperial administration was its flexibility—different regions were governed through different mechanisms according to local conditions and strategic requirements" (Beckman 2013: 97).

The eventual collapse of this system in the early 12th century BCE resulted not from any single factor but from the compounding effects of climate change, economic disruption, and external pressure. That the imperial structure maintained cohesion for so long despite these challenges testifies to the resilience of institutions developed over centuries of practical statecraft.

Chapter 15

ECONOMY AND MATERIAL CULTURE

Agriculture, Pastoralism, and Land Tenure

The Hittite economy rested foundationally on agricultural production, with the empire's prosperity directly tied to its ability to exploit the varied landscapes of central Anatolia. Stark contrasts characterized the region's agricultural potential: fertile river valleys and plateaus capable of producing surplus grain in good years, juxtaposed with marginal lands where crop failure remained a persistent threat.

The agricultural calendar followed seasonal rhythms dictated by central Anatolia's continental climate. Plowing and planting of winter cereals occurred in autumn, with spring bringing cultivation of legumes and summer crops. Harvest seasons were occasions of intense activity and religious significance, as reflected in festival texts:

"When they have completed the harvest, they celebrate the festival of the Thunder God. The priests bring bread and libation vessels to the sacred field. The king pours a libation to the Thunder God and says: 'See, O Storm God, Lord of Hatti, the harvest is complete. Be satisfied with this offering'" (CTH 631).

Cereal cultivation formed the backbone of Hittite agriculture, with barley (*ḫalki-*) and several varieties of wheat, including emmer and einkorn, as primary crops. Paleobotanical evidence from sites like Kuşaklı (ancient Šarišša) reveals a diverse agricultural portfolio including legumes (lentils, chickpeas, bitter vetch), flax, and fruit crops. Wilma Wetterstrom's analysis of plant remains from Kaman-Kalehöyük indicates "a sophisticated agricultural system with crop rotation practices and soil management strategies that maintained productivity across centuries of occupation" (Wetterstrom 2009: 174).

Viticulture held particular economic and cultural importance. Wine production is extensively documented in texts and archaeological evidence, with specialized terminology distinguishing between varieties and qualities. The *GEŠTIN* (wine) industry supported specialized personnel, from vineyard managers to cupbearers, and formed a significant component of ritual offerings. Archaeobotanical remains from Boğazköy-Hattuša include grape pips from multiple cultivars, suggesting sophisticated viticultural knowledge.

Agricultural technology remained relatively stable throughout the Hittite period, with bronze-tipped plows, sickles, and threshing sledges forming the primary toolkit. Irrigation infrastructure, crucial for reliable production in Anatolia's semi-arid climate, received royal attention. An inscription of Muwatalli II boasts: "I dug canals where there had been none before, and brought water to fields that had been dry" (Otten 1988: 23). Archaeological surveys have identified remnants of water management systems, including dams, reservoirs, and canals, particularly in the Kızılırmak basin.

Pastoralism complemented agriculture throughout Hittite territory, with sheep and goat husbandry dominant in upland regions less suitable for cultivation. Transhumance practices are documented in texts that regulate seasonal movement between summer and winter pastures. The *"Instructions for the HAZANNU Officials"* stipulate: "When the herdsmen bring the flocks from the summer pastures, count them carefully. Ensure that the number matches what was recorded in spring. If animals are missing, the herdsman must make compensation" (CTH 261).

Livestock provided wool, dairy products, meat, and traction power. Textile production, particularly woolen textiles, constituted a major economic sector with specialized workshops in urban centers. The importance of animal husbandry is reflected in ritual texts addressing the fertility of flocks and in administrative documents recording meticulous livestock inventories.

Land tenure in the Hittite kingdom operated within a complex system that balanced royal authority with various forms of conditional ownership and use rights. The king theoretically owned all land, but in practice, several distinct categories of land tenure existed:

The Edict of Telepinu (c. 1525 BCE) references these land categories when establishing inheritance principles: "The fields, orchards, and vineyards that the king has given to a man as a gift belong to his sons after him, so long as they fulfill the service obligation" (CTH 19).

Archaeological evidence for this land tenure system comes from boundary stones (*ḫuwasi*) marking property divisions and from settlement patterns reflecting differential land use. Survey work by Roger Matthews in the Upper Kızılırmak basin revealed "a hierarchical settlement pattern with elite-controlled agricultural estates surrounded by dependent settlements" (Matthews 2011: 192).

The flexibility of this system allowed the Hittite state to adapt to changing circumstances. During periods of expansion, newly conquered territories could be incorporated through grants to loyal supporters. During crises, the crown could reassert control over service lands or intensify production on royal estates. This adaptability contributed significantly to the longevity of Hittite political structures.

Trade, Crafts, and Industrial Production

The Hittite economy integrated diverse production systems, from household crafts to specialized workshops and state-controlled industries. While primarily agrarian, the empire developed sophisticated production and exchange networks that connected local resources with distant markets.

Hittite commercial activities operated at multiple scales. Local exchange occurred at markets (*happar*) where agricultural surplus, textiles, and household goods changed hands. Regional trade networks connected specialized production centers, while long-distance commerce linked the Hittite heartland with Mesopotamia, the Levant, and the Aegean.

The state took an active role in regulating commerce. The "*Instructions for the Border Guards*" stipulate: "Merchants entering the land of Hatti must register their goods at the border station. The guard shall record the quantity and type of merchandise, and collect the appropriate tariff" (CTH 261). These regulations served both fiscal and security purposes, allowing the crown to tax commerce while monitoring movement across imperial boundaries.

Unlike their predecessors, the Old Assyrian merchants of the *kārum* period (c. 1950-1700 BCE), Hittite-era traders operated without permanent foreign trading colonies on Anatolian soil. Instead, the evidence points to state-sanctioned merchant operations and diplomatic gift exchange as primary mechanisms for international trade. Treaties with vassal states often included clauses guaranteeing safe passage for merchants and standardizing weights and measures.

Archaeological evidence for trade comes from imported goods found throughout Hittite territory. Cypriot and Mycenaean pottery appears at numerous sites, while Egyptian luxury items, Syrian glassware, and Baltic amber demonstrate the empire's integration into far-reaching exchange networks. Chemical analysis of artifacts has identified raw materials from diverse sources, including tin from Afghanistan, lapis lazuli from northeastern Afghanistan, and ivory from Syria and Egypt.

Textile production represented one of the most significant Hittite industries. Wool processing and weaving occurred at multiple scales, from household production to specialized workshops attached to palaces and temples. Texts describe elaborate textiles with specific terminology for different qualities, weaves, and decorative techniques. The *"Palace Chronicle"* mentions: "The king inspected the weaving workshops and saw fine garments of red wool with gold thread. He rewarded the master weaver with a silver cup" (CTH 8).

Archaeological evidence for textile production includes spindle whorls, loom weights, and specialized tools found throughout Hittite sites. At Kuşaklı-Šarišša, excavators identified a large building with concentrations of textile tools, suggesting an institutional workshop. Iconographic evidence, including representations on seals and relief sculptures, depicts elaborate garments with complex patterns demonstrating technical sophistication.

Ceramic production ranged from household manufacture to specialized pottery workshops. Hittite pottery shows strong regional traditions with distinctive forms and decorative styles. Technical analysis by Pamela Vandiver and Yuval Goren has demonstrated "standardized production methods and material selection strategies indicating professional specialization" (Vandiver and Goren 2004: 147).

The most distinctive Hittite ceramic innovation was the production of thin-walled, highly burnished "Hittite Red Lustrous Ware," which appears across the empire during the New Kingdom period. Production centers for this prestigious ware have been identified at Boğazköy and Ortaköy, with specialized kilns capable of maintaining the precise firing conditions required for its characteristic finish.

Glassmaking represented a high-status craft practiced under royal patronage. The *"Inventory of Manninni"* lists "ten vessels of blue glass from the royal workshop" among valuable temple offerings (CTH 504). Archaeological evidence for glass production includes crucibles with glass residue and glass ingots from Hattuša. Chemical analysis indicates that Hittite glassmakers used formulations similar to those of contemporary Egyptian and Mesopotamian producers, suggesting technological exchange.

Stone working encompassed both utilitarian production (grinding stones, architectural elements) and elite crafts (sculpture, seal carving). Hittite stone sculptures range from monumental gateway lions and sphinxes to delicate relief carvings. The technical skill demonstrated in these works indicates specialized workshops with trained artisans. Royal texts mention stone carvers among craftsmen receiving special rations and privileges.

Woodworking is less visible archaeologically due to preservation issues, but textual evidence shows its importance. The "*Building Ritual*" describes elaborate wooden architectural elements: "They shall make the roof beams of cedar, and the door frames of boxwood, carved with figures of lions" (CTH 414). Furniture production, chariot manufacture, and shipbuilding all required specialized woodworking knowledge.

Industrial-scale production is best documented for metallurgy, but other sectors also saw concentrated production. At Kuşaklı-Šarišša, excavators identified specialized facilities for oil pressing and textile processing within the city's lower town. At Hattuša, evidence for specialized production quarters includes workshops for ceramic, glass, and metal production clustered in specific neighborhoods.

The organization of craft production followed several models operating simultaneously:

Administrative texts document craftsmen of various specialties (*LÚ.MEŠG IŠTUG* or "men of the hand") organized into guilds under master craftsmen. Some specialists held hereditary positions, while others were recruited or forcibly relocated to meet state needs. Foreign craftsmen appear in texts, suggesting the deliberate import of technical expertise. The "*Palace Chronicle*" mentions: "The king brought coppersmiths from Kizzuwatna and settled them in Hattuša, granting them houses and fields" (CTH 8).

Metallurgy and Military Technology

The Hittites' reputation as masters of metallurgy is well-deserved. Their technological innovations, particularly in iron working and bronze production, provided crucial advantages in military conflicts and economic development. Hittite metallurgical expertise rested on Anatolia's abundant mineral resources, including copper, tin, silver, gold, and iron ores.

Copper mining and smelting formed the foundation of Hittite metallurgy. Major copper sources included the Pontic Mountains, the Taurus range, and deposits in central Anatolia. Archaeological evidence for copper production includes mining galleries, slag heaps, and smelting facilities. At sites like Hattuša and Kayalıpınar, excavators have identified specialized metalworking quarters with furnaces, crucibles, and molds.

Bronze production required tin, which was scarcer in Anatolia. While some tin deposits existed within Hittite territory, significant quantities were imported from distant sources. The *Instructions for the MEŠEDI Guards* mention "merchants bringing tin from beyond the Upper Sea" (CTH 262), likely referring to sources in Afghanistan or Central Asia. This dependence on imported tin made bronze production strategically vulnerable to trade disruptions.

Hittite metallurgists developed sophisticated alloying techniques to optimize bronze properties for specific applications. Metallographic analysis of artifacts by Andreas Hauptmann and Ernst Pernicka has revealed "deliberate manipulation of tin content to achieve desired hardness and durability in different categories of objects" (Hauptmann and Pernicka 2004: 43). Weapons typically contained 8-12% tin, while decorative items showed greater variability.

The most significant Hittite metallurgical achievement was their pioneering work with iron. While meteoric iron had been worked since the fourth millennium BCE, the Hittites developed techniques for smelting terrestrial iron ores. This process, far more complex than copper smelting, required higher temperatures and sophisticated furnace management to reduce iron oxide to metallic iron.

Textual evidence for Hittite iron production includes the famous letter from Hattušili III to the king of Assyria (c. 1250 BCE): "As for the good iron about which you wrote to me, good iron is not available in my storehouse in Kizzuwatna. I have written that it is an unfavorable time to produce iron. They will produce good iron, but they have not yet finished it. When they finish it, I will send it to you" (KBo 1.14).

Archaeological evidence for iron production includes bloomery furnaces, slag, and iron artifacts from Hittite contexts. The relative rarity of iron objects suggests that iron remained a prestigious material, not yet replacing bronze for everyday applications. The "iron monopoly" theory, which proposed that the Hittites maintained strict control over iron technology, has been modified by recent scholarship recognizing wider knowledge of ironworking techniques across the Near East by the late second millennium BCE.

Metallurgical expertise directly supported Hittite military technology. The empire's armies relied on high-quality bronze weapons, armor, and chariot fittings. Military equipment described in texts and depicted in art includes:

Archaeological discoveries of Hittite military equipment include the famous bronze sword from Hattuša with cuneiform inscription naming king Tudhaliya, and the Boğazköy dagger with silver and electrum inlay. These artifacts demonstrate sophisticated metallurgical techniques including casting, forging, inlay work, and gilding.

The chariot (*GIŠGIGIR*) represented the pinnacle of Hittite military technology, combining woodworking, leatherworking, and metallurgy. Hittite chariots evolved from heavier three-man vehicles in the Old Kingdom to lighter, more maneuverable two-man platforms in the Empire period. Textual evidence includes detailed instructions for chariot construction and maintenance in the "*Instructions for the KARTAPPU Officials*" (CTH 258).

Archaeological evidence for chariots includes metal fittings, harness components, and iconographic representations. Relief sculptures from Hattuša and Alaca Höyük depict standardized chariot designs with six-spoked wheels, open-sided platforms, and composite construction using bent wood techniques. The standardization evident in these representations suggests centralized production under state supervision.

Hittite military architecture integrated defensive innovations. These architectural features appear at multiple Hittite sites, suggesting standardized military engineering principles. The massive fortifications at Hattuša, with walls up to 8 meters thick and incorporating these innovative features, represent the most impressive example of Hittite defensive architecture.

Military technology development occurred within a sophisticated administrative framework. The "*Instructions for the BĒL MADGALTI*" (CTH 261) detail the responsibilities of provincial governors for maintaining weapons stockpiles, training troops, and ensuring equipment readiness. Specialized personnel including the *GIŠGIDRU* (military officers) and *LÚ.MEŠSIMUG* (smiths) supported military preparedness through production, maintenance, and training activities.

Architecture and Urban Planning

Hittite architectural traditions combined indigenous Anatolian elements with influences from Mesopotamia and the Levant, creating distinctive built environments that expressed imperial ideology while adapting to local conditions. From monumental public buildings to vernacular housing, Hittite architecture reflected practical responses to central Anatolia's challenging environment and the administrative needs of a complex state.

Urban planning in Hittite cities followed topographic contours rather than rigid geometric patterns. At Hattuša, the city expanded organically from its original settlement on the lower slopes to eventually encompass the rocky outcrop of Büyükkale (the royal acropolis) and the surrounding plateaus. Peter Neve's excavations revealed "a city layout responding intelligently to terrain constraints while incorporating sophisticated water management and defensive considerations" (Neve 1996: 92).

The fundamental Hittite urban planning principle was functional zoning. These functional zones appear clearly at Hattuša, where the Upper City contained primarily religious structures while administrative buildings concentrated on Büyükkale, and residential quarters occupied the lower slopes. Similar patterns appear at provincial centers like Kuşaklı-Sarišša and Ortaköy-Šapinuwa.

Defensive considerations profoundly influenced Hittite urban planning. Cities were typically sited in naturally defensible locations—on elevated plateaus, rocky outcrops, or protected peninsulas formed by river bends. The fortification systems surrounding these settlements represented major investments of labor and materials, with walls extending for kilometers at major centers.

The most impressive example is Hattuša's defensive system. Archaeological investigation by Jürgen Seeher has revealed that "the Upper City fortifications at Hattuša represented a single massive construction project, completed within a relatively short timeframe, suggesting centralized planning and execution" (Seeher 2006: 68).

Water management formed another crucial aspect of Hittite urban planning. The capital incorporated sophisticated systems for water collection, storage, and distribution. Similar systems appear at other Hittite centers, adapted to local hydrological conditions. At Kuşaklı-Sarišša, excavators identified a massive reservoir capable of storing 14,000 cubic meters of water sufficient to supply the city during extended dry periods.

Monumental architecture served as a primary expression of Hittite royal ideology. Palace complexes (*É.GAL* or "Great House") combined administrative, residential, and ceremonial functions. The most extensively excavated example is Building A at Büyükkale in Hattuša.

The architectural layout facilitated controlled access, with progressively restricted entry points creating a hierarchy of spaces. Similar organizational principles appear in provincial palaces at sites like Maşat Höyük and Ortaköy-Šapinuwa, suggesting standardized administrative requirements translated into architectural form.

Temple architecture represented the other major category of monumental construction. Hittite temples followed a distinctive plan with characteristic elements.

The Great Temple (Temple 1) at Hattuša exemplifies this pattern on an impressive scale, with a central cult room surrounded by storage magazines containing hundreds of vessels for offerings and ritual equipment. Excavations by Peter Neve revealed "a complex that could support elaborate state-sponsored rituals involving large numbers of participants" (Neve 1999: 143).

Beyond the capital, provincial temples followed similar patterns on reduced scales. At Kuşaklı-Šarišša, Temple C reproduced the essential elements of capital temples, demonstrating the dissemination of standardized religious architecture throughout the empire.

Building materials and construction techniques adapted to local resources while maintaining consistent architectural principles.

Construction techniques demonstrated sophisticated engineering knowledge. Stone masonry ranged from roughly dressed blocks to precisely fitted ashlar work in monumental contexts. Mud-brick walls typically rested on stone foundations to prevent moisture damage. Roof systems utilized timber beams supporting clay layers waterproofed with lime plaster.

Architectural decoration enhanced the visual impact of important structures. The Lion Gate and King's Gate at Hattuša exemplify the integration of monumental sculpture with architectural function. These imposing structures combined practical defensive features with powerful symbolic imagery communicating royal ideology to visitors and residents alike.

Residential architecture varied according to social status and urban context. Elite residences in the capital featured opulent interiors and breathtaking city panoramas. Middle-class housing typically followed a courtyard plan with fewer rooms and simpler construction. Lower-status housing consisted of simpler rectilinear structures, often sharing walls with neighboring units. Archaeological investigations at Hattuša's lower town have revealed dense residential quarters with narrow streets and small house plots suggesting "a population of artisans and service personnel supporting the administrative and religious institutions of the capital" (Schachner 2011: 79).

Rural architecture is less well documented archaeologically but appears to have centered on the extended family farmstead. Surveys in the Hittite heartland have identified numerous small settlements consisting of clusters of rectangular structures with associated agricultural installations. These rural settlements formed the productive foundation supporting urban centers and their specialized populations.

Specialized architectural types developed for specific functions.

The Hittite landscape was further shaped by extra-urban sacred architecture. The rock sanctuary of Yazılıkaya near Hattuša represents the most spectacular example, with relief sculptures depicting divine processions carved into natural limestone formations. Similar open-air sanctuaries have been identified throughout Hittite territory, suggesting a consistent approach to sacralizing the natural landscape.

Conclusion

The material foundations of Hittite civilization—its agricultural systems, craft traditions, technological innovations, and built environments—reveal a society that successfully adapted to challenging environmental conditions while developing sophisticated solutions to the practical problems of imperial administration. From the agricultural fields of central Anatolia to the workshops of Hattuša, from military technologies to monumental architecture, Hittite material culture reflected both pragmatic responses to immediate needs and ambitious expressions of imperial ideology.

What emerges from this examination is not a static or isolated culture, but a dynamic civilization engaged in constant technological exchange and adaptation. The Hittites absorbed influences from neighboring societies while developing distinctive traditions suited to their circumstances. Their achievements in metallurgy, architecture, and agricultural management demonstrate innovative problem-solving within the constraints of Bronze Age technology.

The archaeological and textual evidence reveals a society that maintained remarkable continuity in basic subsistence practices while implementing innovations in specialized production and monumental construction. This balance between tradition and innovation, between local practices and imperial standards, contributed significantly to the longevity and resilience of Hittite civilization.

The eventual collapse of this material system in the early 12th century BCE resulted from a complex interplay of factors—climate change reducing agricultural productivity, disruption of trade networks limiting access to critical resources, and external pressures overwhelming defensive capabilities. Yet the material legacy of Hittite civilization persisted, influencing subsequent Anatolian cultures and contributing to the technological and architectural traditions of the Iron Age Near East.

Chapter 16

THE THOUSAND GODS OF ḪATTI

Religious Syncretism and the Hittite Pantheon

The Hittite religious system stands as one of the most striking examples of syncretism in the ancient world. Far from imposing their own Indo-European deities on conquered territories, the Hittites demonstrated remarkable religious tolerance and adaptability, incorporating foreign gods into their pantheon through a process they themselves described as "the thousand gods of Hatti." This approach served both theological and political purposes, allowing the Hittites to harness the perceived power of local deities while facilitating the integration of diverse populations into their empire.

The resulting pantheon was extraordinarily complex, with textual evidence documenting over 1,000 divine names. As Emmanuel Laroche's comprehensive catalog of Hittite religious texts demonstrates, this theological system operated through what scholars have termed "translation equivalence," where deities from different traditions were identified with one another through explicit equations

(Laroche 1975). A prime example appears in the treaty between Šuppiluliuma I and Šattiwaza of Mitanni, which invokes "the Storm-god, lord of heaven and earth" alongside his Hurrian equivalent "Tešub, lord of heaven and earth" (CTH 51).

The foundation of the Hittite pantheon rested on indigenous Hattic deities, most prominently the Sun-goddess of Arinna and the Storm-God of Hatti. As Volkert Haas (1994) has shown, these two deities formed the divine couple at the head of the state pantheon, representing the divine counterparts to the king and queen. In a prayer of Queen Puduhepa, this relationship is made explicit:

"The Sun-goddess of Arinna, my lady, queen of all lands! In Hatti you bear the name 'Sun-goddess of Arinna,' but in the land which you made the cedar land, you bear the name 'Hepat'" (CTH 384).

This passage illustrates how the Hittites maintained theological flexibility while preserving hierarchical order within their divine world.

The Storm-God occupied a position of particular prominence as divine patron of kingship. Iconographic representations, such as those at Yazılıkaya, depict him standing on mountains, wielding lightning bolts and accompanied by his sacred bull, Šeri. His importance is underscored by the many local manifestations recorded in cult inventories—the Storm-God of Zippalanda, the Storm-God of Nerik, the Storm-God of Aleppo—each maintaining distinct cult practices while being understood as aspects of the same divine power.

Hurrian influence dramatically transformed the Hittite pantheon during the Empire period (c. 1400-1180 BCE). As Gary Beckman (2013) has demonstrated, this was not merely cultural diffusion but active appropriation, with Hurrian deities like Tešub, Hepat, and Šaušga (Ištar) achieving prominence in state cult. The rock sanctuary of Yazılıkaya near Hattuša provides the most dramatic visual representation of this syncretistic pantheon, with relief sculptures depicting a divine procession where Hurrian and Hattian-Hittite deities intermingle in hierarchical order.

Mesopotamian influences further enriched this theological tapestry. The Hittites incorporated Sumero-Akkadian deities like Ea, Ištar, and Šamaš, often preserving their Mesopotamian characteristics while integrating them into local cult structures. The "Kingship in Heaven" narrative, preserved in the Song of Kumarbi (CTH 344), reveals striking parallels with the Mesopotamian Enūma Eliš, though adapted to Hurro-Hittite theological frameworks.

Archaeological evidence supplements the textual record of this syncretistic approach. Excavations at Hattuša have uncovered temple complexes with distinct architectural features corresponding to different religious traditions. Temple 1 in the Upper City displays typical Hittite features, while Temple 5 incorporates Syrian architectural elements, suggesting the accommodation of different ritual practices within the imperial capital (Schachner 2011).

The "thousand gods" were organized into hierarchical groupings with male and female deities often paired as divine couples. This organization reflected social and political structures, with major deities having their own "households" of subordinate gods, just as human nobles maintained households of dependents. Divine hierarchies mirrored human ones, reinforcing social order through theological structures.

A distinctive feature of Hittite religion was the concept of the deity's "embodiment" (Hittite: tuekki-), which could be manifested in multiple locations simultaneously. This theological concept facilitated the integration of local cults, as it allowed for a deity to be present in multiple shrines while maintaining essential unity. As Itamar Singer (1994) notes, this concept was crucial for imperial administration, allowing conquered populations to maintain local cults while acknowledging their subordination to the central pantheon.

The Hittite approach to divine integration is perhaps best illustrated in a prayer of Muwatalli II:

"Whatever kind of god (you are), if you are a god of heaven, or if you are a god of the dark earth, or if you are a god of the mountains and rivers, or if you are a god of foreign lands...to you I, Muwatalli, Great King, am now making invocation" (CTH 381).

This inclusive approach to divinity reflected the practical needs of an empire governing diverse populations with distinct religious traditions. By acknowledging and incorporating local gods, Hittite rulers legitimized their authority while harnessing the perceived power of all available divine forces.

State Cult and Royal Religious Duties

The Hittite king occupied a unique position as intermediary between human and divine realms, bearing the title "Priest of the Sun-goddess of Arinna" alongside his political designations. This religious role was not merely symbolic but entailed specific ritual obligations that consumed a significant portion of the royal calendar. As Jörg Klinger (1996) has demonstrated through analysis of festival texts, the king's ritual duties represented a central aspect of royal legitimacy and governance.

The king's primary religious responsibility was maintaining proper relations with the gods through regular performance of prescribed rituals. A Middle Hittite text makes this obligation explicit:

"If the king does not celebrate the festivals at the appropriate time, if he alters the time, that is a matter of [divine] anger" (KBo 13.58).

This religious obligation created a theological framework for royal accountability, as the king's ritual performance directly affected the well-being of the entire kingdom.

The most extensive documentation of royal ritual duties comes from the festival texts, which describe elaborate ceremonies conducted throughout the year. The AN.TAH.ŠUM festival, spanning 38 days in spring, required the king's participation in ceremonies at multiple locations throughout the Hittite heartland. As Volkert Haas (1994) has shown, this festival integrated agricultural concerns with dynastic celebration, reinforcing the king's role as guarantor of cosmic and social order.

The nuntarriyasha festival, conducted in autumn, similarly required royal participation in ceremonies at various cult centers. These seasonal festivals connected royal authority to agricultural cycles, positioning the king as mediator between divine powers and agricultural productivity. The king's movement between cult centers during these festivals also served to reinforce political bonds with provincial elites and maintain the integration of peripheral regions into the state cult system.

The purulli festival, dedicated to the dragon-slaying myth of the Storm-god's victory over the serpent Illuyanka, carried particular significance for royal ideology. In this ritual, the king symbolically reenacted the Storm-god's primordial victory over chaos, reinforcing his identity as the god's earthly representative. As Beckman (1982) has argued, this mythic identification provided a powerful theological foundation for royal authority.

Archaeological evidence supplements textual descriptions of royal ritual performance. Excavations at Hattuša have uncovered specialized ritual spaces within the palace complex, including a throne room with adjacent cultic installations. The proximity of royal living quarters to temple precincts further underscores the integration of political and religious functions in Hittite governance.

The queen (Tawananna) also held significant religious responsibilities, particularly in relation to the Sun-goddess of Arinna. The prayers of Queen Puduhepa demonstrate her active role in state cult, including the authority to commission votive offerings and participate in major festivals. Her ritual responsibilities complemented those of the king, creating a divine-human parallel between the royal couple and the divine pair of the Storm-God and Sun-goddess.

Royal religious duties extended beyond regular festival performance to include crisis rituals performed in response to specific threats. During military campaigns, kings conducted elaborate rituals to secure divine support, as described in the Annals of Muršili II:

"When I arrived at Mount Lawasa, I performed the ritual of the oath for the Storm-God, my lord, and I spoke as follows: 'O Storm-God, my lord, you have entrusted to me the land that was in revolt. Behold, I am now going to suppress the revolt. Stand by me, O Storm-God, my lord!'" (KBo 3.4).

Such rituals positioned military action within a theological framework, presenting conquest as the fulfillment of divine will.

Perhaps the most distinctive aspect of royal religious duty was the king's obligation to maintain and expand the divine "guest-list" of the pantheon. When Hittite kings conquered new territories, they typically transported the statues of local deities to Hattuša, establishing new cults rather than destroying them. A text from the reign of Muwatalli II explicitly connects this practice to imperial policy:

"The gods whom my father and grandfather had resettled in Hattuša, I will resettle them in their places. I will not abandon their cult. The men whom I resettle in their places will continue to maintain the regular offerings just as before" (KUB 6.45).

This practice served both theological and political purposes, demonstrating respect for local traditions while physically incorporating conquered deities into the imperial center.

The king's religious duties culminated in his own deification after death. Royal funerary rituals, described in texts classified as šalliš waštaiš ("great sin"), transformed the deceased king into a god through elaborate ceremonies spanning fourteen days. As van den Hout (1994) has demonstrated, these rituals involved both purification and transformation, culminating in the declaration "The king has become a god" (LUGAL-uš DINGIR-LIM-iš kišari).

This posthumous deification created a continuous chain linking living kings to their divine ancestors and ultimately to the gods themselves. Royal ancestor worship thus reinforced dynastic legitimacy while providing theological justification for the king's mediating role between human and divine realms.

Festivals, Rituals, and Temple Organization

The Hittite ritual calendar was extraordinarily dense, with festival texts documenting more than 165 distinct ceremonies conducted throughout the year. These ranged from major state festivals spanning multiple weeks to local celebrations tied to specific deities or agricultural activities. As Alice Mouton (2016) has demonstrated through analysis of the festival corpus, these rituals served multiple functions: ensuring divine favor, marking seasonal transitions, reinforcing social hierarchies, and integrating diverse communities into a shared religious framework.

The major state festivals—AN.TAH.ŠUM in spring, nuntarriyašha in autumn, purulli at the new year, KI.LAM celebrating the storehouse deities, and hišuwa focusing on Hurrian traditions—formed the backbone of the official cult calendar. These festivals required extensive resources and planning, as documented in inventory texts recording provisions for divine and human participants:

"For the festival of the Storm-god of Zippalanda: 3 oxen, 12 sheep, 30 loaves of thick bread, 50 loaves of sweet bread, 10 jugs of wine, 5 jugs of beer..." (KBo 2.13).

Such detailed accounting demonstrates the significant economic investment in ritual performance and the administrative complexity involved in maintaining the state cult system.

The physical settings for these festivals were primarily temple complexes, which archaeological excavations have revealed as distinctive architectural forms. The typical Hittite temple followed a standard plan: an entrance leading to an antechamber, then to a main cella housing the deity's statue. Surrounding storerooms contained ritual equipment, offerings, and administrative records. Temple 1 at Hattuša exemplifies this pattern, with its central cella measuring approximately 42 by 42 feet, surrounded by storerooms containing thousands of ceramic vessels for ritual use (Seeher 2011).

Temples functioned as economic centers as well as ritual spaces, controlling substantial agricultural lands and workshop production. Administrative texts document the "houses of the gods" (É DINGIR^MEŠ) as major economic institutions receiving regular deliveries of foodstuffs, precious materials, and labor services. The temple of the Storm-God at Hattuša, for example, controlled numerous villages whose residents provided agricultural produce and labor for cult maintenance.

The personnel serving these temple complexes formed a specialized class of ritual experts. The Hittite term SANGA designated temple administrators who managed both economic and ritual aspects of cult maintenance. Below them served various specialists: the LÚ^AZU (divination experts), LÚ^HAL (exorcists), MUNUS^ŠU.GI (wise women), and LÚ^GUDU$_{12}$ (purification priests). Festival texts frequently specify the roles of these specialists in ritual performance:

"The SANGA-priest takes the silver rhyton in his right hand and the golden rhyton in his left hand. He bows to the deity and gives the rhyta to the king. The king libates before the deity..." (KUB 25.1).

Such detailed procedural instructions ensured ritual continuity across generations and locations.

A distinctive feature of Hittite ritual practice was the emphasis on purification. Many ceremonies began with elaborate cleansing procedures for participants, ritual spaces, and implements. The concept of parkui- ("pure") versus papratar ("impurity") structured ritual action, with specific procedures developed to address differing forms of contamination. As David Wright (1987) has demonstrated, these purification concerns reflected broader anxieties about boundary maintenance in both cosmic and social realms.

The mechanics of Hittite ritual often employed sympathetic or analogical principles, using physical actions to effect desired changes in reality. A ritual against military defeat illustrates this approach:

"They bring a ram. They decorate it with blue wool, red wool, yellow wool, and white wool. They drive it out to the enemy land, saying: 'Just as this ram carries the decorations to the enemy land, so let it carry the evil plague, impurity, sin, and transgression to the enemy land!'" (KUB 7.54).

Such rituals materialized abstract concerns, making them tangible and, therefore, manageable through physical manipulation.

Festival performances incorporated multiple sensory elements: visual displays through processions and decorated cult images; auditory components including music, chanting, and recitation; olfactory stimulation through incense and burnt offerings; and gustatory participation through communal feasting. This multisensory approach created immersive ritual experiences that reinforced community bonds while dramatizing cosmic order.

The spatial organization of ritual performances often followed a pattern of movement between centers and peripheries. Many festivals began at the palace or main temple in Hattuša, then proceeded to outlying shrines before returning to the center. This spatial pattern reinforced hierarchical relationships between the capital and provinces while physically enacting the integration of diverse cult traditions into a unified system.

Offering practices formed the core of most ritual activities. Textual and archaeological evidence indicates that animal sacrifice (primarily cattle, sheep, and goats) was the central offering act, accompanied by libations of wine, beer, and other liquids. The Hittite term šipant- covered both animal sacrifice and liquid offerings, suggesting conceptual unity between these practices. Material remains from temple contexts include specialized vessels for libation, altars with drainage channels for blood, and animal bones showing butchery patterns consistent with sacrificial practice (Popko 1995).

The destination of offerings followed a consistent pattern: portions allocated to the deity, portions to the king and priests, and portions to the general participants. This distribution pattern reinforced social hierarchies while creating communal bonds through shared consumption. Festival texts specify these allocations in detail:

"They sacrifice one ox and eight sheep for the Storm-god. The liver, heart, and shoulder are placed on the table for the deity. The right thigh is given to the king. The left thigh is given to the SANGA-priest..." (KUB 20.59).

Such distributions physically enacted the social order, with the deity at the apex, followed by the king and priests, and finally the general population.

A significant feature of Hittite festival practice was the prominence of dramatic performances reenacting mythic narratives. The purulli festival included a dramatic representation of the Storm-god's battle with the serpent Illuyanka, while the hašuwaš festival reenacted combat between groups representing Hatti and its enemies. These performances transformed abstract mythic narratives into tangible experiences, reinforcing cultural memory while providing theological frameworks for contemporary concerns.

The Hittite festival calendar thus constituted a complex system integrating economic, political, and theological dimensions of state organization. Through regular ritual performances, abstract concepts of divine favor and cosmic order were translated into physical experiences that reinforced social hierarchies while creating shared identities across the diverse populations of the empire.

Magic, Divination, and Popular Religion

Beyond the formal state cult, Hittite religious practice encompassed a rich tradition of magical rituals, divination techniques, and localized worship practices that scholars have termed "popular religion." These dimensions of religious life are documented in extensive text corpora, including ritual manuals, oracle reports, and dream texts, which reveal sophisticated systems for managing supernatural forces and discerning divine will.

Magical practice in Hittite society was not marginalized but fully integrated into official religious structures. The Hittite term alwanzatar, often translated as "sorcery," carried negative connotations only when directed toward harmful ends; beneficial magic was an accepted part of religious practice, often performed by specialists attached to the palace or temple. As Beckman (2011) has observed, the boundary between "religion" and "magic" in Hittite society was permeable, with both sharing fundamental assumptions about the nature of divine power and human-divine interaction.

Ritual specialists for magical practice included the MUNUS^ŠU.GI ("Old Woman"), who often specialized in rituals derived from Kizzuwatna (Cilicia), and the LÚ^AZU, who performed rituals of Mesopotamian origin. These practitioners operated within official structures while drawing on diverse cultural traditions, as indicated in colophons identifying the sources of their knowledge:

"Tablet of Tunnawi, the Old Woman. When someone is afflicted by impurity, she treats them as follows. They call this 'the ritual of drawing paths.' Finished. Written according to the dictation of Tunnawi" (KUB 7.53).

Such attributions preserved the distinct cultural origins of ritual practices while incorporating them into standardized textual formats.

Magical rituals addressed a wide range of concerns, from personal afflictions to communal crises. Therapeutic rituals treated physical and mental illnesses through combined practical and symbolic techniques. Apotropaic rituals protected against potential threats, particularly at vulnerable transition points like childbirth, construction of buildings, or military campaigns. Purification rituals removed various forms of contamination, whether physical, moral, or spiritual.

The mechanics of these rituals frequently employed the principle of transfer (Hittite: tarpalli-), whereby afflictions were removed from the patient and transferred to a substitute object or animal. A ritual against household discord illustrates this approach:

"She takes a piglet and waves it over them. She speaks as follows: 'I am taking away from you discord, anger, sin, and evil words. Just as this piglet digs in the earth with its snout, so let it dig in the earth with these evils!'" (KUB 9.28).

This transferential logic appears consistently across the ritual corpus, reflecting fundamental assumptions about the material nature of affliction and the possibility of its physical relocation.

Ritual materials often carried symbolic significance through their inherent properties or cultural associations. Red wool symbolized blood and life-force;

water from springs represented purification; cedar wood carried connotations of divine presence and durability. These materials were not arbitrary but selected for specific qualities that aligned with ritual purposes. As Wright (1987) has demonstrated, these material selections reflect sophisticated symbolic systems rather than primitive magical thinking.

Divination—the art of discerning divine will through systematic observation of signs—constituted another major dimension of Hittite religious practice. The Hittite state employed multiple divination systems, maintaining specialists in each technique and documenting their findings in detailed reports.

The most extensively documented form is extispicy, practiced by specialists trained in Mesopotamian techniques. Oracle reports record the specific features observed in sacrificial animals and their interpretations:

"We performed extispicy concerning the matter of the campaign. The 'station' was favorable. The 'path' was favorable. The 'strength' was favorable..." (KUB 5.1).

Such reports frequently addressed military decisions, administrative appointments, and responses to divine anger, providing theological authorization for royal actions.

The KIN oracle, unique to Hittite practice, involved the manipulation of symbolic tokens representing abstract concepts like "life," "well-being," or "evil." The movement of these tokens between different positions represented the transfer of qualities between cosmic entities. This indigenous divination system appears particularly in questions regarding divine anger and its resolution:

"We inquired through the KIN oracle: Is the Sun-goddess of Arinna angry because of the festival that was not performed? The KIN oracle was unfavorable" (KUB 16.28).

Such determinations led to specific ritual responses, creating a feedback system between divination and ritual performance.

Dreams represented another channel for divine communication, with specialized personnel (Hittite: tešhaniškeš) assigned to interpret royal dreams. Dream reports were taken seriously as indicators of divine will, often prompting specific ritual responses. A text from the reign of Hattušili III illustrates this practice:

"The queen saw a dream. In her dream, the goddess Ištar appeared to her and said: 'I will grant your husband many years and good health.' Therefore, we have made a golden statue for the goddess as the dream commanded" (KUB 31.69).

Such dream-prompted actions demonstrate the integration of personal religious experience into official cult practice.

Beyond these formalized systems, evidence suggests widespread practices of personal piety and localized worship. Votive offerings found in archaeological contexts indicate individual relationships with deities outside official cult settings. Small figurines, miniature vessels, and personal ornaments deposited at springs, caves, and other natural features suggest widespread practices of personal devotion not fully captured in official texts.

The Hittite term for "god" (šiunaš) could apply to various manifestations of divine power, including natural features like mountains, springs, and unusual rock formations. These localized divine presences received regular offerings from nearby communities, creating a sacred landscape that complemented the formal temple system. As Mouton (2016) has argued, this "religious landscape" connected local communities to specific territories through shared ritual practices.

Household religion made up another dimension of practice largely invisible in official texts but suggested by archaeological findings. Figurines found in domestic contexts, hearth installations with apparent ritual functions, and small-scale offering vessels indicate regular religious practices conducted at the household level. These practices likely focused on family continuity, protection from harm, and securing prosperity—concerns complementary to but distinct from state cult emphases.

Ancestor veneration formed an important component of this household practice. The ritual of "drinking the karat-vessel" involved libations to deceased family members, maintaining connections between living and dead through regular offerings. While royal ancestor worship is well-documented in texts, archaeological evidence suggests similar practices at non-elite levels, creating continuity between elite and non-elite religious experiences.

The complex interplay between official and local religious practices created a religious system remarkable for both its coherence and flexibility. The Hittite state incorporated diverse traditions while maintaining core theological principles, creating a religious framework that supported imperial integration while accommodating local variation. This approach to religious management—systematic yet adaptable—contributed significantly to the longevity of Hittite political structures and their cultural influence long after the empire's collapse.

Chapter 17

LANGUAGES, LITERATURE, AND LEARNING

Language, Literacy, and Literature

The discovery of over 30,000 clay tablet fragments at Hattuša and other Hittite sites revealed a civilization of remarkable linguistic complexity and textual sophistication. The Hittite archives, primarily preserved through the catastrophic fires that destroyed the imperial capital around 1180 BCE, provide an unparalleled window into ancient Anatolian intellectual traditions. The multilingual character of these texts, the sophisticated scribal infrastructure that produced them, and the diverse literary genres they represent collectively demonstrate that the Hittites were not merely military conquerors but custodians of a rich cultural heritage that synthesized multiple traditions while maintaining distinctive characteristics of their own.

The Multilingual Character of Hittite Civilization

The Hittite state operated as a fundamentally multilingual entity from its inception. While Hittite (Nesite) served as the primary language of administration and royal ideology, at least seven other languages enjoyed official or semi-official status within the empire. This linguistic diversity reflected both the multiethnic composition of the Hittite realm and the pragmatic approach to governance that characterized Hittite imperial administration.

Hittite itself belongs to the Anatolian branch of Indo-European languages and represents the earliest attested Indo-European language written in substantial texts. Its relationship to other Indo-European languages has been the subject of considerable scholarly debate, with some linguists arguing that Anatolian languages separated from Proto-Indo-European before other branches, potentially preserving more archaic features (Melchert 2003). The language underwent significant evolution during the roughly five centuries of textual attestation, with scholars conventionally distinguishing Old Hittite (17th-16th centuries BCE), Middle Hittite (15th century BCE), and Neo-Hittite (14th-13th centuries BCE) phases.

As Theo van den Hout (2009: 22) observes, "The Hittite language may have been the official vehicle of communication, but it was embedded in a thoroughly multilingual environment." This multilingual environment included several indigenous Anatolian languages. Hattic, the non-Indo-European language of the autochthonous population of central Anatolia, continued to be used for religious ceremonies throughout the Hittite period, particularly in rituals connected to the old Hattic deities. Although Hattic had ceased to be a spoken language by the imperial period, its preservation in ritual contexts demonstrates the Hittite commitment to maintaining religious traditions even when they required specialized linguistic knowledge.

Luwian, another Anatolian Indo-European language closely related to Hittite, was widely spoken in southern and western Anatolia. During the Empire period,

Luwian speakers constituted a significant portion of the population even in the Hittite heartland, leading to substantial Luwian influence on Late Hittite. As Ilya Yakubovich (2010: 274) notes, "The gradual Luwianization of the Hittite empire represents one of the most interesting cases of language shift in the ancient world." Luwian was written both in cuneiform and in the indigenous Anatolian hieroglyphic script, with the latter becoming increasingly prominent for monumental inscriptions during the Empire period.

Palaic, a third Anatolian Indo-European language spoken in north-central Anatolia, is more sparsely attested but similarly preserved in religious contexts. These three indigenous Anatolian languages—Hattic, Luwian, and Palaic—represent the earliest stratum of linguistic diversity in the Hittite realm.

The Hittite conquest of northern Syria brought Hurrian into the imperial linguistic repertoire. Hurrian, a non-Indo-European language related to Urartian, had a significant impact on Hittite religious and literary traditions, particularly during the Empire period. Queen Puduhepa, the influential wife of Hattušili III, promoted Hurrian cults and texts as part of her religious reforms. The famous "Song of Release" (Šarrena), preserved in a Hurrian-Hittite bilingual version, exemplifies the integration of Hurrian literary traditions into the Hittite cultural sphere.

Akkadian served as the diplomatic lingua franca throughout the ancient Near East during the Late Bronze Age. The Hittite chancery maintained scribes capable of composing and translating diplomatic correspondence in Akkadian, as evidenced by the numerous international treaties and letters found in the Hattuša archives. Significantly, while other ancient Near Eastern powers like Egypt and Babylon expected foreign correspondents to communicate in their languages, the Hittites adapted to the linguistic conventions of international diplomacy by embracing Akkadian for external communication.

Sumerian, though long extinct as a spoken language, continued to function as a scholarly and scribal language throughout the ancient Near East. Hittite scribes mastered a basic repertoire of Sumerian logograms (cuneiform signs representing whole words rather than syllabic values), which they incorporated into otherwise Hittite texts as a form of shorthand. The Hittite scribal curriculum included standard Mesopotamian lexical lists that preserved Sumerian vocabulary alongside Akkadian and sometimes Hittite equivalents.

Finally, isolated texts in Ugaritic and Egyptian found at Hattuša demonstrate the cosmopolitan character of the imperial capital and the Hittite interest in foreign literary traditions. As Mark Weeden (2011: 599) concludes, "The Hittite capital was thus a true crossroads of ancient Near Eastern written traditions, where texts and scholars from across the region contributed to a unique cultural synthesis."

This linguistic diversity necessitated sophisticated translation practices. The Hittite archives include numerous bilingual texts, particularly in religious contexts where precision in ritual language was essential. Hittite scribes developed technical terminology for translation, distinguishing between literal renderings and more interpretive approaches. The colophons of translated texts often specify the source language and occasionally name the translator, suggesting that translation was recognized as a specialized intellectual activity.

The Hittite approach to multilingualism reflects what Gary Beckman (1983: 102) has called "cultural inclusiveness"—a willingness to incorporate diverse traditions rather than imposing linguistic uniformity. This approach served practical political purposes, facilitating communication across the diverse populations of the empire while respecting local cultural traditions. It also enriched Hittite intellectual life, exposing scribes and elites to multiple literary and religious traditions that they could selectively incorporate into their own cultural synthesis.

Cuneiform Literacy and Scribal Schools

The Hittites adopted the cuneiform writing system from Mesopotamia, most likely via Syria, during the Old Kingdom period. This complex script, consisting of hundreds of signs representing syllables and logograms, required years of specialized training to master. The acquisition and adaptation of cuneiform writing represents one of the most significant Hittite cultural achievements, enabling the development of a sophisticated bureaucracy and the preservation of diverse literary traditions.

Archaeological evidence for Hittite scribal education remains limited, but textual references and comparative evidence allow us to reconstruct the basic contours of the system. Unlike Mesopotamia, where scribal schools (É.DUB.BA) operated as independent institutions, Hittite scribal training appears to have been concentrated in the temples and palace. The title "scribe of the temple" (DUB.SAR É.DINGIR-LIM) appears in several texts, suggesting institutional affiliation.

The Hittite scribal curriculum adapted Mesopotamian educational practices to local needs. Beginning students likely started with simple exercises in sign formation before progressing to copying standard lexical lists. At Hattuša, researchers found several fragments of these elementary exercises; these fragments include tablets with repeated signs, typical of beginner exercises. More advanced students copied literary texts, often adding colophons that identified them as scribal trainees (DUMU É.DUB.BA, "son of the tablet house").

The acquisition of cuneiform literacy involved mastering multiple linguistic systems simultaneously. As Theo van den Hout (2015: 79) explains, "Learning to write Hittite in cuneiform meant learning Sumerian and Akkadian at the same time, even if only in a limited way." Students memorized Sumerian logograms and their Hittite equivalents, learned the syllabic values of signs for writing Hittite phonetically, and acquired enough Akkadian to handle diplomatic correspondence and international treaties.

The complexity of this training created a distinctive class of literate specialists. Estimates suggest that no more than a few hundred individuals in the Hittite Empire possessed full cuneiform literacy at any given time, with most concentrated in the capital and major administrative centers. This scribal elite enjoyed considerable status, with some rising to high administrative positions. The most accomplished scribes added their names to the texts they produced, with formulas like "Written by the hand of PN, scribe."

Scribal specialization increased during the Empire period, with evidence for distinct groups focusing on different types of texts. Religious specialists (LÚ. MEŠ DUB.SAR.GIŠ, "scribes on wood") recorded divination results and ritual instructions on wooden tablets (later copied to clay for archival purposes), while others specialized in diplomatic correspondence or administrative documentation. The most prestigious specialization involved the creation and maintenance of royal annals and historical texts central to Hittite political ideology.

The physical process of text production involved multiple stages. Scribes typically composed drafts on wax-covered wooden writing boards (GIŠ.ḪUR) before creating the final clay tablet version. For important texts, a draft would be read aloud and checked against the original before the final version was prepared. Completed tablets were stored in dedicated archives, organized by wooden shelving and labeled with clay tags. Some tablets include archival notations indicating their storage location or relationship to other texts in a series.

Hittite scribes adapted the cuneiform system to the phonological structure of their language, creating distinctive orthographic conventions. While maintaining the basic syllabic principles of Mesopotamian cuneiform, they developed specific sign values and spelling conventions for representing Hittite phonemes. They also extensively used Sumerograms (Sumerian logograms) and Akkadograms (Akkadian words written logographically) as a form of shorthand within otherwise Hittite texts. This mixed writing system, combining syllabic spelling with logograms, created texts that appear visually similar to Mesopotamian models while encoding distinctly Hittite linguistic content.

The most distinctive Hittite innovation in writing technology was the development of the Anatolian hieroglyphic script, which evolved alongside cuneiform during the Empire period. This indigenous writing system, used primarily for Luwian, appeared first on seals and gradually expanded to monumental inscriptions and administrative documents. By the final decades of the Empire, hieroglyphic writing had become sufficiently prestigious to appear alongside cuneiform in some contexts, particularly on royal monuments. After the collapse of the Hittite Empire around 1180 BCE, the hieroglyphic script continued in use in the Neo-Hittite states of southeastern Anatolia and northern Syria, preserving aspects of Hittite literary and political traditions into the early first millennium BCE.

The Hittite investment in literacy and textual production reflects the central role of written documentation in imperial governance. As a territorial state controlling diverse populations across a wide geographic area, the Hittite Empire relied on written records to standardize administrative practices, communicate royal decisions, and preserve institutional memory. The scribal apparatus thus served as a crucial infrastructure of imperial power, enabling forms of governance that would have been impossible without written documentation.

Literary Traditions: Myths, Epics, and Historical Texts

The Hittite archives preserve a remarkable diversity of literary texts, ranging from indigenous Anatolian myths to adaptations of Mesopotamian and Hurrian literary works. These texts served multiple functions within Hittite society—religious, political, and entertainment—while collectively making up a distinctive literary tradition that synthesized diverse cultural influences.

Mythological Texts

Hittite mythological texts draw from multiple cultural traditions, with indigenous Anatolian, Hurrian, and Mesopotamian elements combined in various proportions. The most distinctive Anatolian myths focus on the disappearance and return of deities associated with agricultural fertility, reflecting the central importance of agricultural production in Hittite society.

The "Telepinu Myth" represents the most complete example of this disappearance genre. In this narrative, the god Telepinu becomes angry and disappears, taking agricultural fertility with him. His absence causes cosmic disruption:

"Mist seized the windows. Smoke seized the house. On the hearth the logs were stifled. On the altars the gods were stifled. In the fold the sheep were stifled. In the corral the cows were stifled. The sheep refused her lamb. The cow refused her calf." (KUB 17.10 i 13-17)

After failed attempts to locate him, the bee sent by the goddess Hannahanna finally finds Telepinu and stings him, leading to his return and the restoration of fertility. Similar disappearance myths feature the Storm-God, the Sun-goddess, and other deities, suggesting a common narrative pattern adapted to different divine protagonists.

The "Illuyanka Myth" recounts the Storm-god's battle with a serpent (illuyanka), incorporating elements of combat myths common throughout the ancient Near East while adding distinctive Anatolian elements. The narrative exists in two versions; both framed as etiologies for the purulli spring festival. In the first version, the serpent initially defeated the Storm-God but achieves victory through the assistance of the goddess Inara and a mortal named Hupasiya. In the second version, the Storm-god's son marries the serpent's daughter and retrieves his father's heart and eyes, which had been taken by the serpent.

Hurrian mythological traditions entered the Hittite literary corpus primarily during the Empire period, with the Kumarbi Cycle representing the most substantial example. This cycle, preserved in fragmentary form, describes a succession of divine kingship from Alalu to Anu to Kumarbi to the Storm-God Teshub. The narrative includes vivid episodes of violence and usurpation, including Kumarbi's biting off and swallowing Anu's genitals, resulting in his impregnation with several deities including Teshub. As Mary Bachvarova (2013: 107) observes, "The Kumarbi Cycle shows clear parallels with Hesiod's Theogony, suggesting either direct influence or common Indo-European mythological heritage."

The "Song of Release" (Šarrena), preserved in a Hurrian-Hittite bilingual version, combines mythological elements with social commentary. The text describes the city of Ebla, where the ruling class refuses to release debt slaves despite divine commands. This refusal leads to the city's destruction, framed as divine punishment for social injustice. The text's concern with debt slavery and social ethics distinguishes it from more purely mythological narratives.

Mesopotamian mythological traditions appear in Hittite adaptations of texts like the Gilgamesh Epic and Atrahasis. These adaptations demonstrate the Hittite scribal engagement with canonical Mesopotamian literature while showing significant modifications to suit Hittite cultural contexts. The Hittite version of Gilgamesh, for example, abbreviates certain episodes while expanding others, and sets portions of the narrative in Anatolia rather than Mesopotamia.

Historical and Historiographic Texts

Perhaps the most distinctive Hittite literary genre is historical narrative, particularly the royal annals that document the military campaigns and achievements of Hittite kings. Unlike the year-by-year administrative records found in Mesopotamia, Hittite annals represent sophisticated literary compositions that combine chronological narrative with ideological framing.

The annals of Hattušili I (CTH 4), the earliest preserved Hittite historical text, establish patterns that would characterize the genre for centuries. The text presents the king's military campaigns as responses to rebellion or external threat, emphasizing his personal courage and divine support. A distinctive feature is the direct address to the king's successor:

"Now I have given you my throne. But protect my son and my name! If he commits an offense, discipline him with a shepherd's staff, but listen to his word! If any brother, sister, in-law, or family member rebels, the one who is brought to your attention, judge him according to his offense. If it warrants death, let him die, but do not kill secretly or in anger." (KBo 10.2 iii 17-24)

This address transforms the historical narrative into a form of political testament, instructing future rulers while legitimizing the current king's actions.

The most extensive historical texts come from the reigns of Muršili II and Hattušili III. Muršili's "Comprehensive Annals" (CTH 61) provide a detailed year-by-year account of his first ten years as king, describing military campaigns, diplomatic interactions, and religious activities. The text combines precise geographic and chronological information with literary framing that emphasizes divine support for the king's actions. Muršili regularly consults oracles before military action and attributes his victories to divine intervention, particularly from the Sun-goddess of Arinna and the Storm-God of Hatti.

Hattušili III's "Apology" (CTH 81) represents a unique form of historical literature that combines biography, legal defense, and religious testimony. Composed to justify his usurpation of the throne from his nephew Urhi-Tešub, the text frames Hattušili's career as guided by the goddess Ištar/Šauška:

"The goddess, my lady, took me by the hand and led me on the path of kingship. She raised me from the sea, that is, from obscurity. The goddess, my lady, always protected me." (KUB 1.1 i 24-27)

By attributing his rise to power to divine will, Hattušili transforms a potentially illegitimate seizure of power into the fulfillment of divine purpose. The text's sophisticated rhetorical strategy has led some scholars to compare it to later Hellenistic royal propaganda.

Historical consciousness also appears in texts describing earlier periods of Hittite history. The "Palace Chronicle" (CTH 8) presents episodes from the Old Kingdom as negative examples of court behavior, using historical anecdotes for didactic purposes. The "Proclamation of Telepinu" (CTH 19) reviews the reigns of previous kings to contrast periods of unity and strength with periods of internal conflict and weakness, creating a cyclical model of history that justifies Telepinu's institutional reforms.

These historical texts collectively demonstrate what Trevor Bryce (2002: 100) calls "a highly developed historical consciousness, perhaps unparalleled in the ancient Near East." The Hittites viewed history as meaningful and instructive, preserving records of both successes and failures to guide future action. This historical consciousness contributed to institutional continuity despite periods of crisis, allowing the Hittite state to learn from experience and adapt to changing circumstances.

Literary Epics and Tales

Beyond mythology and historical narrative, the Hittite archives include various literary tales and epics that appear to have served primarily entertainment functions. These texts often feature heroic protagonists facing supernatural challenges or navigating complex social situations.

"The Story of Appu" tells of a wealthy but childless man who eventually fathers two sons named "Right" and "Wrong." The brothers quarrel over inheritance, with Wrong attempting to cheat Right but eventually facing divine judgment. The tale combines narrative entertainment with ethical instruction, affirming cosmic justice while acknowledging social conflict.

"The Hunter Kešši" describes the adventures of a hunter who encounters supernatural beings in the wilderness. Although preserved only in fragments, the text appears to explore boundaries between human and divine realms through the liminal figure of the hunter who operates at the edge of civilized space.

"The Story of Gurparanzah" recounts conflicts between the eponymous hero and various opponents, including the Sea. The fragmentary state of the text makes the complete narrative difficult to reconstruct, but surviving portions suggest a heroic adventure story with both martial and magical elements.

These literary tales demonstrate that Hittite textual production extended beyond strictly practical religious and administrative functions to include works created primarily for entertainment and ethical instruction. The tales often incorporate elements from multiple cultural traditions, reflecting the syncretic character of Hittite civilization more broadly.

Legal and Administrative Documentation

The practical functions of writing in Hittite society are most clearly visible in the extensive corpus of legal and administrative texts. These documents—including laws, treaties, land grants, inventories, and various records of economic transactions—formed the documentary infrastructure of the Hittite state, enabling complex administrative operations across the empire's diverse territories.

The Hittite Laws

The Hittite Laws (CTH 291-292) represent one of the most substantial legal compilations from the ancient Near East. Preserved in multiple copies spanning several centuries, the laws address a wide range of social situations, from property crimes and personal injury to sexual offenses and ritual pollution. Unlike the Babylonian Code of Hammurabi, which frames legal provisions within a cosmic order established by divine authority, the Hittite Laws present themselves as pragmatic responses to specific social problems.

The laws are conventionally divided into two "tablets" or collections, with the first containing more severe penalties (often death) and the second featuring more moderate penalties (typically compensation). This division may reflect chronological development, with the more severe penalties representing older traditions gradually modified toward more moderate approaches. Many provisions show revision over time, with later versions explicitly noting changes:

"If anyone blinds a free person or knocks out his tooth, formerly they would pay 40 shekels of silver, but now he pays 20 shekels of silver." (§VII, KBo 6.4 i 17-18)

This explicit acknowledgment of legal change demonstrates a sophisticated understanding of law as a human institution subject to revision rather than an unchangeable divine decree.

The Hittite Laws show particular concern with establishing fixed compensation for various injuries and offenses, creating a system that could resolve conflicts without perpetuating cycles of revenge. The laws distinguish between intentional and accidental harm, with different penalties applied based on the actor's intent. They also recognize social distinctions, with different penalties for offenses against free persons versus slaves, while still affirming the basic humanity of all subjects:

"If anyone causes a female slave to miscarry, if it is the tenth month, he shall pay 5 shekels of silver... If anyone causes a free woman to miscarry, if it is the tenth month, he shall pay 20 shekels of silver." (§§XVII-XVIII, KBo 6.3 ii 2-5)

While maintaining social hierarchy, the laws nonetheless recognize the slave's right to compensation, albeit at a lower rate than a free person.

The laws address agricultural issues extensively, with provisions concerning irrigation rights, crop damage by animals, and theft of farming implements. This agricultural focus reflects the economic foundations of Hittite society and the state's interest in maintaining productive capacity. Other provisions address commercial matters, including weights and measures, prices for common goods, and obligations of various craftsmen.

Ritual purity concerns appear in provisions prohibiting sexual contact with certain animals (notably horses and mules but not other livestock) and regulating sexual relationships between family members. These provisions blend practical governance with religious concepts of pollution and purification, demonstrating the integration of religious and legal thinking in Hittite society.

International Treaties

The Hittite archives preserve over 30 international treaties, representing the most extensive corpus of such documents from the ancient world before the Roman period. These treaties formalized relationships between the Hittite king and various vassals, allies, and peer rulers, creating a documentary framework for international relations.

Vassal treaties typically followed a standard structure: historical prologue, stipulations, divine witnesses, and curses/blessings. The historical prologue established the relationship between the Hittite king and the vassal, often emphasizing past benefits granted by the Hittite ruler. This section could be extensive, recounting multiple generations of interaction to establish the legitimacy of Hittite overlordship.

The stipulations section detailed the vassal's obligations, including military support, extradition of fugitives, regular tribute, and loyalty to the designated heir of the Hittite king. These obligations were typically asymmetrical, with the Hittite king promising protection while the vassal promised service. The divine witness section listed gods of both parties who would enforce the treaty, while the curses and blessings section described consequences for violation or adherence.

The most famous Hittite treaty—the Egyptian-Hittite peace treaty of 1259 BCE between Hattušili III and Ramesses II—represents a rare example of a parity treaty between equal powers. Unlike vassal treaties, this agreement emphasizes reciprocal obligations and mutual recognition:

"Ramesses, Great King, King of Egypt, shall be at peace with Hattušili, Great King, King of Hatti, his brother, forever. The sons of Ramesses shall be at peace with the sons of Hattušili forever." (KBo 1.7 obv. 8-10)

The treaty establishes mutual defense obligations, extradition procedures, and guarantees for royal succession, creating a framework for peaceful coexistence between former enemies. Versions were prepared in both Egyptian hieroglyphic and Akkadian cuneiform, with each party keeping copies in both languages.

Treaties served as fundamental instruments of Hittite imperial governance, creating legally binding relationships that extended Hittite authority without requiring direct administrative control. The emphasis on historical relationship and divine enforcement reflects the Hittite understanding of international relations as embedded in both human history and cosmic order.

Administrative Documents

The daily operations of the Hittite state generated thousands of administrative documents recording economic transactions, personnel assignments, inventory management, and various other practical matters. These texts, often formulaic and brief, provide crucial insights into the actual functioning of Hittite institutions beyond the ideological presentations of royal inscriptions.

Land donation texts (CTH 222) record royal grants of land to favored officials, often with tax exemptions and other privileges. These documents typically include precise boundary descriptions, statements of tax status, and prohibitions against future alienation of the property. They conclude with witness lists and curses against anyone who might violate the grant, transforming a bureaucratic transaction into a sacred commitment.

Inventory texts record palace and temple possessions, from valuable metal objects to everyday implements. These documents often include information about an object's weight, material, condition, and storage location, demonstrating sophisticated tracking systems for institutional assets. Some inventory texts record regular inspections, with notations about missing items or changes since the previous inventory.

Personnel lists document individuals assigned to various royal and temple services, sometimes with information about rations, equipment, or specific duties. These texts reveal the complex organization of labor in Hittite institutions, with specialized workers organized into units under designated supervisors. Some lists include annotations about individual workers' status changes, such as illness, reassignment, or death, showing ongoing management of the workforce.

Oracle and divination texts record questions posed to divine powers and the resulting answers, often concerning military campaigns, political appointments, or responses to natural disasters. These texts reveal the integration of religious consultation into practical governance, with divine guidance sought for significant state decisions. The detailed recording of both questions and answers created an archive of precedents that could guide future consultations.

Festival texts describe religious ceremonies in meticulous detail, specifying required offerings, participant roles, ritual actions, and even the exact words to be spoken. These texts served as operational manuals for temple personnel, ensuring correct performance of rituals believed essential to maintaining cosmic order and divine favor. The precision of these instructions demonstrates the Hittite concern with ritual efficacy and the role of written documentation in standardizing religious practice across the empire.

Collectively, these administrative documents reveal a state apparatus that relied heavily on written records to manage resources, coordinate activities, and maintain institutional memory. The Hittite bureaucracy used writing to extend control across space and time, creating systems that could function despite personnel changes and geographic dispersion. This documentary infrastructure represented a crucial component of Hittite imperial power, enabling forms of organization that would have been impossible through oral communication alone.

Conclusion

The textual corpus preserved in the Hittite archives reveals a sophisticated civilization that used writing for diverse purposes: religious, administrative, diplomatic, historical, and literary. The multilingual character of these archives reflects the multiethnic composition of the Hittite realm and the pragmatic approach to cultural difference that characterized Hittite governance. Rather than imposing linguistic uniformity, the Hittites incorporated multiple languages into their official corpus, creating a textual tradition that synthesized diverse cultural influences.

The development of a professional scribal class capable of working with this complex multilingual tradition represented a significant Hittite cultural achievement. These scribes mastered not only the technical challenges of cuneiform writing but also the conceptual frameworks of multiple literary traditions, allowing them to translate, adapt, and create texts that served Hittite institutional needs while drawing on broader ancient Near Eastern cultural resources.

The resulting textual corpus reveals a society deeply invested in documentation, from the practical record-keeping of administrative texts to the ideological statements of royal inscriptions to the cultural preservation of literary and religious works. This documentary orientation created institutional continuity across generations, allowing the Hittite state to maintain consistent governance despite periodic crises and transitions.

The Hittite textual tradition thus offers a window into one of the ancient world's most sophisticated literate cultures—a civilization that used writing not merely to record information but to organize experience, preserve memory, and create meaning across linguistic and cultural boundaries.

Chapter 18

The End of the Hittite Empire

Šuppiluliuma II and the Final Years

Šuppiluliuma II ascended to the Hittite throne around 1207 BCE during a period of mounting challenges. As the son of Tudḫaliya IV, he inherited an empire that maintained an impressive territorial extent but faced increasing internal strains and external pressures. The archaeological and textual evidence for his reign—the final chapter in Hittite imperial history—reveals a ruler making energetic efforts to address these challenges through military campaigns, diplomatic initiatives, and monumental construction projects.

The most substantial evidence for Šuppiluliuma II's activities comes from his own inscriptions, particularly those carved on the chambers of the rock sanctuary at Nişantepe near Ḫattuša. In these texts, the king boasts of military victories:

"I, Great King Šuppiluliuma, conquered the land of Tarhuntašša... I destroyed the land of Lukka that had been hostile. And when the people of Lukka repeatedly came down to attack the land of Cyprus where I was, I, Šuppiluliuma, the Great

King, went against them in battle on the ships of the land of Alašiya [Cyprus]." (SÜDBURG inscription, trans. Hawkins 1995: 56-57)

This naval engagement represents the first documented Hittite sea battle, suggesting a significant adaptation of military strategy in response to new threats. Archaeological evidence from Cyprus (ancient Alašiya) supports the Hittite presence there, with Hittite-style seals and administrative objects found at sites like Enkomi (Karageorghis 2002: 73-75).

Šuppiluliuma II also undertook ambitious building projects, including extensive renovations at Ḫattuša. The NIŞANTAŞ inscription describes his construction activities:

"I built anew this fortress of Ḫattuša which had fallen into ruin. I erected this stone monument and inscribed upon it the mighty deeds which the Storm-god, my lord, enabled me to perform." (trans. Bryce 2005: 328)

Archaeological investigations at Ḫattuša confirm substantial building activity during this period, including reinforcement of the fortification system and the construction of additional grain storage facilities (Seeher 2001: 522-524). These projects suggest preparation for potential threats, with the strengthened defenses and expanded food reserves indicating awareness of possible siege scenarios.

The king's religious activities also intensified during this period. The Chamber B inscription at Yazılıkaya records elaborate ritual activities:

"I, Šuppiluliuma, Great King, beloved of the Storm-god, performed the great festival for the gods of the underworld. I established new offerings for the ancestors and renewed the sacred rites that had fallen into neglect." (trans. Bittel et al. 1975: 248-249)

This emphasis on underworld deities and ancestral cults may reflect anxiety about the empire's future, with the king seeking supernatural assistance during a time of crisis (Bachvarova 2016: 145-147).

Despite these energetic initiatives, textual evidence from the final years of Šuppiluliuma II's reign becomes increasingly scarce. The latest securely dated document from Ḫattuša—a land donation text—dates to around 1190 BCE, suggesting the imminent abandonment of the capital (Klengel 1999: 294). The final fate of Šuppiluliuma II himself remains unknown; unlike earlier kings, we have no record of his death or burial. This textual silence speaks volumes about the abrupt nature of the Hittite collapse.

The archaeological evidence from Ḫattuša reveals a planned abandonment rather than a catastrophic destruction. While there are localized burn layers, the systematic removal of cult statues, royal insignia, and archive tablets indicates an organized withdrawal (Seeher 2001: 623-625). The Hittite elite apparently recognized the unsustainability of their position and strategically relocated, taking with them the symbols of state power and religious authority.

The Sea Peoples and the Late Bronze Age Collapse

The final decades of the 13th century BCE witnessed one of history's most dramatic systemic collapses, with nearly every major Eastern Mediterranean civilization experiencing severe disruption or destruction. This "Late Bronze Age collapse" transformed the political landscape of the region, ending the internationalized system that had characterized the preceding centuries and initiating a prolonged dark age in many areas.

The most vivid contemporary account of this tumultuous period comes from Egypt, where Ramesses III recorded his battles against the "Sea Peoples" on the walls of his mortuary temple at Medinet Habu (ca. 1175 BCE):

"The foreign countries made a conspiracy in their islands. All at once the lands were removed and scattered in the fray. No land could stand before their arms, from Hatti, Kode, Carchemish, Arzawa, and Alashiya on, being cut off at [one time]. A camp [was set up] in one place in Amurru. They desolated its people, and its land was like that which has never come into being. They were coming forward toward Egypt, while the flame was prepared before them." (trans. Redford 2018: 124-125)

This dramatic text describes a coalition of peoples—identified as Peleset (Philistines), Tjekker, Shekelesh, Denyen, and Weshesh—moving through the Eastern Mediterranean as a destructive force. The Egyptian depictions show them traveling with women, children, and possessions in oxcarts, suggesting a migration rather than simply a military expedition.

Archaeological evidence confirms widespread destruction across the Eastern Mediterranean during this period. Major sites showing destruction layers dating to approximately 1200-1180 BCE include:

The identity and origins of the "Sea Peoples" remain controversial. The Egyptian texts list several groups, some potentially identifiable with later known populations (such as the Peleset with the Philistines). Archaeological evidence from sites like Tell Tayinat, Tarsus, and various Philistine settlements shows the introduction of Aegean-style pottery, cooking practices, textile production, and architectural elements, suggesting at least some connection to the Aegean world (Yasur-Landau 2010: 216-224).

However, recent scholarship has moved away from viewing the Sea Peoples as a single coherent force. Cline (2014: 1-5) argues that they were "both the products and the agents of a complex series of events that together contributed to the end of the Late Bronze Age." Rather than a single wave of invaders, the movements of diverse groups likely represented responses to already-developing systemic failures across the interconnected Late Bronze Age world.

The relationship between the Sea Peoples and the Hittite collapse remains unclear. No Hittite text directly mentions them, though the naval battle described by Šuppiluliuma II against the people of Lukka may represent an early encounter with groups that later coalesced into the Sea Peoples coalition (Bryce 2005: 333). The Egyptian texts place the Hittites among the victims rather than the perpetrators of the upheaval, suggesting that the Hittite Empire had already collapsed before the Sea Peoples reached Egypt.

Archaeological Evidence for Destruction and Abandonment

The archaeological record provides crucial evidence for understanding the final phase of the Hittite Empire. Excavations at numerous sites across the Hittite realm reveal a pattern of destruction and abandonment occurring within a relatively narrow timeframe—approximately 1200-1180 BCE—though with important variations in the nature and intensity of these events.

At Ḫattuša itself, the archaeological evidence presents a complex picture. Contrary to earlier interpretations that envisioned a catastrophic destruction, more recent excavations indicate a planned abandonment of the capital. Jürgen Seeher, who directed excavations at the site from 1994 to 2005, observes:

"The archaeological record at Ḫattuša does not support the theory of a violent end to the city. While there are indeed burn layers in several areas, these appear localized and inconsistent. More significantly, we find evidence for the systematic removal of valuable and symbolically important items. The temples were cleared of cult statues, the archives of their most important tablets, and royal insignia are conspicuously absent." (Seeher 2001: 623)

This pattern suggests that the Hittite leadership recognized the unsustainability of maintaining Ḫattuša and orchestrated a strategic withdrawal. Supporting this interpretation is the discovery of deliberately blocked entrances to temple storerooms and the organized deposition of cult objects in pits—actions indicating ritual closure rather than panicked flight (Genz 2013: 469-471).

However, the situation differs markedly at other Hittite centers. At Kuşaklı (ancient Šarišša), excavations revealed extensive destruction by fire, with collapsed buildings containing crushed storage vessels and, in one case, a human skeleton, suggesting a violent attack with casualties (Müller-Karpe 2009: 97-99). Similarly, at Ortaköy (ancient Šapinuwa), archaeologists documented a major destruction layer containing burned wooden architectural elements and crushed artifacts (Süel 2015: 61-63).

Lower-ranking provincial centers show an even more consistent pattern of violent destruction. At Maşat Höyük (ancient Tapikka), the Level I settlement ended in a catastrophic fire that preserved numerous artifacts in situ, including clay sealings that securely date the destruction to the final phase of the empire (Özgüç 1982: 133-135). The abandonment of the site followed, lasting for several centuries.

The archaeological evidence from western Anatolia presents a striking picture of disruption. At Troy (Level VIIa), Beycesultan, and Miletus, excavators found clear destruction layers followed by significant cultural changes in the subsequent settlements. At Miletus, the appearance of new pottery styles followed the destruction of the Late Bronze Age city with clear Aegean affiliations, suggesting population movement into the region (Niemeier 2009: 15-17).

Beyond destruction evidence, settlement pattern data reveals dramatic demographic changes. Systematic survey work in central Anatolia by Ronald Gorny and others has documented a roughly 75% reduction in occupied settlement area from the 13th to the 12th century BCE (Gorny 2006: 32-35). This population collapse appears most severe in the Hittite heartland, with some peripheral regions showing greater continuity.

The material culture of the post-collapse settlements that eventually emerged differs significantly from Hittite patterns. At sites like Kaman-Kalehöyük and Porsuk, the post-destruction levels contain handmade pottery that breaks sharply with the wheel-made Hittite ceramic tradition (Matsumura 2008: 215-217). Architecture becomes simpler, with small irregular structures replacing the formal planned buildings of the Hittite period.

Importantly, the archaeological evidence also documents the survival of Hittite cultural traditions in southeastern Anatolia and northern Syria, where the so-called Neo-Hittite states emerged during the Early Iron Age. At sites like Carchemish, Malatya, and Tell Tayinat, Luwian hieroglyphic inscriptions and distinctive artistic conventions demonstrate cultural continuity despite political fragmentation (Hawkins 2009: 164-166). These Neo-Hittite polities preserved elements of Hittite religious practices, artistic styles, and political ideology into the 8th century BCE, when they were ultimately absorbed by the expanding Assyrian Empire.

Theories of Collapse: Internal vs. External Factors

The dramatic disappearance of the Hittite Empire has generated a multitude of explanatory models, with scholarly debate often framed around the relative importance of internal versus external factors. Rather than a single cause, contemporary scholarship increasingly emphasizes the interaction of multiple stressors creating a "perfect storm" that overwhelmed the Hittite state's adaptive capacity.

Climate Change and Environmental Degradation

Paleoclimatic data from multiple sources—including lake sediment cores, speleothems (cave formations), and pollen records—indicates that the last centuries of the Hittite Empire coincided with a significant shift toward more arid conditions across the Eastern Mediterranean. Drake (2012: 1862-1870) synthesized data from multiple proxy records showing a 30-50% reduction in precipitation between 1250 and 1100 BCE in central Anatolia.

Tree-ring records from juniper wood found at Gordion provide particularly precise evidence for severe drought conditions. According to Kuniholm and Newton (2001: 378):

"The dendrochronological record shows a series of extremely narrow growth rings beginning around 1200 BCE and continuing for nearly two decades, indicating sustained drought conditions unprecedented in the preceding three centuries."

This climatic deterioration would have directly impacted agricultural productivity in a state heavily dependent on grain production. The Hittite texts themselves contain evidence of food shortages during this period. A letter from the Hittite king (likely Šuppiluliuma II) to the king of Ugarit requests emergency grain shipments:

"Concerning the grain which I wrote to you about, it is a matter of life or death! Send grain in ships from your land, to keep me alive." (RS 20.212, trans. Hoffner 2009: 98)

Archaeological evidence also suggests environmental degradation resulting from centuries of intensive land use. Pollen cores from Lake Tecer show increasing erosion and soil depletion during the 13th century BCE, with declining tree cover and indicators of overgrazing (Kuzucuoğlu et al. 2011: 173-175). The combined effects of climate change and environmental degradation would have undermined the agricultural foundation of the Hittite economy, triggering cascading social and political consequences.

Political Fragmentation and Civil Conflict

Internal political instability represents another crucial factor in the Hittite collapse. The historical trajectory of the empire shows recurring succession crises, and evidence suggests these intensified during its final decades. The relationship between the main branch of the royal family and the appanage kingdom of Tarhuntašša appears particularly problematic.

After Kurunta (son of Muwatalli II) was installed as ruler of Tarhuntašša, tensions emerged with the main Hittite line. A seal impression found at Ḫattuša shows that Kurunta apparently declared himself "Great King," suggesting a period of competing claims to the throne (Hawkins 2002: 58-59). This political fragmentation likely weakened the state's ability to respond effectively to external threats.

The archaeological evidence from Ḫattuša itself reveals internal conflict. Excavations documented the deliberate destruction and burial of monuments depicting Šuppiluliuma II's cousin and rival Kurunta, suggesting internal political violence (Seeher 2001: 640-642). Such factional conflict would have divided resources and undermined central authority during a period when unity was essential for survival.

Textual evidence also points to increasing difficulties in controlling vassal states during the empire's final decades. A letter from the last known Hittite king to the prefect of Ugarit reveals desperation:

"The enemy advances against us, and there is no number. Whatever is available, look for it and send it to me." (RS 18.038, trans. Singer 1999: 726)

This progressive weakening of imperial control created a feedback loop—as central authority diminished, resources declined, further undermining the state's capacity to maintain control of its territories.

Economic Disruption and Systems Collapse

The Hittite Empire existed within an interconnected Late Bronze Age economic system that linked diverse polities through trade networks, diplomatic exchanges, and shared elite culture. The disruption of this international system played a crucial role in the Hittite collapse.

Archaeological evidence demonstrates substantial disruption of Mediterranean trade routes during the late 13th century BCE. Shipwrecks like Uluburun and Cape Gelidonya document the intensive maritime commerce that characterized the period, but such trade appears to have declined dramatically after about 1200 BCE (Monroe 2009: 270-272). The destruction of coastal centers like Ugarit severed critical links in these networks.

Susan Sherratt (2003: 39) argues that the Bronze Age economic system had developed inherent fragilities:

"The Late Bronze Age political economy had evolved into a complex, specialized system dependent on long-distance trade in prestige goods, raw materials, and specialized products. This interdependence created vulnerability—disruption in one sector could trigger cascading failures throughout the system."

For the Hittites, whose imperial economy relied on the redistribution of resources from diverse ecological zones, such systemic disruption would have been particularly devastating. The empire's location at the nexus of multiple trade routes initially provided economic advantages but ultimately created exposure to system-wide disruptions.

Evidence for economic stress appears in the archaeological record through the debasement of metals, the disappearance of luxury imports, and changes in production patterns at sites across the Hittite realm during the 13th century BCE (Divon 2008: 97-99). These indicators suggest a progressive economic contraction preceding the final collapse.

External Attacks and Population Movements

While internal factors created vulnerabilities, external pressure likely delivered the coup de grâce to the weakened Hittite state. The identity of these external threats remains debated, but several possibilities emerge from the available evidence.

The Kaška people of the Pontic region had long threatened the northern Hittite frontier. Texts from the reign of Tudḫaliya IV indicate intensified Kaška activity, with the king conducting repeated campaigns to secure the northern borders (Glatz and Matthews 2005: 49-51). Archaeological evidence confirms destruction at northern Hittite sites like Maşat Höyük that could be attributed to Kaška attacks.

From the west, population movements associated with the broader Aegean disruption may have placed pressure on Hittite territories. The appearance of new cultural elements in western Anatolia following the destruction of Late Bronze Age sites suggests population influx, possibly including groups later associated with the "Sea Peoples" (Yasur-Landau 2010: 216-224).

The Assyrian Empire under Tukulti-Ninurta I (1243-1207 BCE) presented another external threat. Assyrian texts claim victories over Hittite forces, and the disruption of eastern trade routes would have further isolated the Hittite realm (Machinist 2000: 189-191).

Synthesis: The Cascade Failure Model

Rather than privileging either internal or external factors, recent scholarship has developed more sophisticated models that emphasize the interaction between multiple stressors. Cline's (2014: 139-170) "complexity theory" approach views the Late Bronze Age collapse as a system-wide failure triggered when multiple subsystems exceeded their adaptive capacity simultaneously.

Knapp and Manning (2016: 99-120) propose a "cascade failure" model in which initial stressors (climate change, food insecurity) triggered social responses (population movement, conflict) that generated additional stressors, creating a self-reinforcing cycle of systemic failure. In this model, the Hittite collapse represents not a single event but a process unfolding over decades.

The archaeological and textual evidence supports this integrated approach. The Hittite state demonstrated remarkable resilience throughout its history, successfully adapting to numerous challenges over five centuries. Its ultimate failure came not from a single catastrophic blow but from the convergence of multiple crises that overwhelmed its adaptive capacity.

The final abandonment of Ḫattuša likely represented not the beginning of collapse but its culmination—a strategic decision by the remaining elite to salvage what they could from a failing system. Some elements of Hittite political and cultural traditions survived in the Neo-Hittite states of southeastern Anatolia and northern Syria, suggesting partial system adaptation rather than complete failure.

The end of the Hittite Empire thus offers important insights into the dynamics of complex societies under stress. As Middleton (2017: 89) observes:

"The Hittite collapse demonstrates both the vulnerability and resilience of complex political systems. While the imperial structure ultimately failed, elements of Hittite culture and identity persisted, transformed through adaptation to new circumstances. This pattern of collapse and regeneration appears repeatedly throughout human history."

Chapter 19

The Neo-Hittite Kingdoms

The Neo-Hittite Successor States

The collapse of the Hittite Empire around 1180 BCE did not represent a complete erasure of Hittite civilization. Rather, it started a process of political fragmentation and cultural transformation that would play out across southeastern Anatolia and northern Syria over the following five centuries. As the centralized imperial structure disintegrated, elements of Hittite political organization, cultural practices, and artistic traditions found new expression in a constellation of smaller polities commonly referred to as the "Neo-Hittite" or "Syro-Hittite" states.

Successor States in Syria and Southeastern Anatolia

Remarkable diversity characterized the political landscape that emerged in the wake of the Hittite collapse. Archaeological evidence from sites like Carchemish,

Malatya, Tell Tayinat, and Zincirli reveals a patchwork of small kingdoms that maintained varying degrees of connection to their Hittite imperial past. These polities filled the power vacuum left by the empire's dissolution, establishing themselves primarily in regions that had previously constituted the empire's southern and southeastern provinces.

"The transition from the Late Bronze Age to the Early Iron Age in this region was not marked by a complete break," notes Trevor Bryce in his comprehensive study *The World of the Neo-Hittite Kingdoms* (2012:56). "Rather, we observe a process of political reconfiguration, with former provincial centers and vassal states asserting their independence while maintaining elements of Hittite administrative structures and royal ideology."

The geographic distribution of these successor states was not random but followed a distinct pattern. They emerged primarily in regions where Hittite cultural influence had been most firmly established during the empire period, particularly along major trade routes and in fertile agricultural valleys. J. David Hawkins, whose work on Hieroglyphic Luwian inscriptions has revolutionized our understanding of this period, observes that "the Neo-Hittite states occupied a strategic corridor connecting Anatolia to Syria and Mesopotamia, positioning them as cultural and commercial intermediaries in the early Iron Age world" (Hawkins 2000:38).

The chronological development of these states followed a general pattern. In the immediate aftermath of the Hittite collapse (ca. 1180-1000 BCE), many of these polities maintained strong connections to Hittite imperial traditions, with rulers emphasizing their links to the former imperial dynasty. This period of direct continuity gradually gave way to more diverse cultural expressions as new population groups, particularly Aramaean and Luwian elements, gained prominence in the region.

"The distribution of Hieroglyphic Luwian inscriptions across these successor states reveals the complex ethnolinguistic landscape of the early Iron Age," notes Ilya Yakubovich (2015:35). "While Luwian appears to have been the prestige language for monumental display in many of these polities, the increasing presence of Aramaic inscriptions from the 9th century onward points to the changing demographic and cultural composition of the region."

Archaeological evidence indicates significant population movements during this transitional period, with some regions experiencing demographic decline while others saw the influx of new groups. Settlement pattern studies in the Amuq Valley, for instance, document a shift from fewer, larger settlements in the Late Bronze Age to more numerous, smaller communities in the early Iron Age (Casana 2007:199-214). This pattern suggests a more decentralized political organization, consistent with the fragmentation of imperial structures.

Continuity and Change in Political Organization

The political structures that emerged in the Neo-Hittite states represented a complex blend of continuity and innovation. In many respects, these smaller kingdoms preserved elements of Hittite imperial governance, adapting them to new circumstances and smaller territorial scales.

Royal ideology in the Neo-Hittite states displayed strong connections to Hittite imperial traditions. Rulers in kingdoms like Carchemish and Melid explicitly positioned themselves as heirs to the Hittite imperial dynasty. Kuzi-Tešub of Carchemish, for instance, styled himself "Great King, Hero, son of Talmi-Tešub, King of Carchemish, grandson of Šaḫurunuwa, Great King, Hero" (Hawkins 2000:80), employing titles and genealogical legitimation strategies directly borrowed from Hittite imperial practice.

The physical manifestations of royal power likewise demonstrated continuity with imperial traditions. Neo-Hittite rulers invested heavily in monumental architecture and public sculptural programs that visually referenced Hittite imperial precedents. The "Long Wall of Sculpture" at Carchemish, the orthostats at Malatya, and the gate lions at Tell Tayinat all employed artistic conventions and iconographic elements derived from imperial Hittite models (Gilibert 2011:76-98).

Administrative structures in the Neo-Hittite states appear to have preserved many elements of Hittite bureaucratic practice. The continued use of Hieroglyphic Luwian for official inscriptions suggests the survival of scribal traditions, while the appearance of specific official titles implies continuity in administrative hierarchies. Annick Payne's analysis of administrative terminology in Neo-Hittite inscriptions demonstrates that "many of the bureaucratic positions known from Hittite cuneiform texts reappear in the hieroglyphic corpus, suggesting institutional continuity despite the political fragmentation" (Payne 2012:65).

Religious institutions similarly maintained strong connections to Hittite traditions. Temple complexes excavated at sites like Tell Tayinat and Aleppo reveal architectural forms and ritual spaces that closely parallel those known from Hittite imperial centers. The pantheon of deities worshiped in Neo-Hittite states, as documented in inscriptions and iconography, largely corresponded to the divine world of the Hittite Empire, with particular emphasis on the Storm-God Tarhunza and the Sun-goddess Hebat (Hutter 2003:211-241).

Yet alongside these continuities, significant innovations emerged in Neo-Hittite political organization. Perhaps most notably, the scale of governance contracted dramatically. While the Hittite Empire had controlled territories stretching from western Anatolia to northern Syria, even the largest Neo-Hittite states encompassed only a fraction of this territory. This reduction in scale necessitated adaptations in administrative structures and resource mobilization strategies.

The relationship between rulers and subordinate elites appears to have shifted as well. Hieroglyphic Luwian inscriptions from various Neo-Hittite states document the increasing prominence of non-royal officials who commissioned monuments in their own names, suggesting a more distributed power structure than had characterized the highly centralized Hittite imperial system (Gilibert 2011:122-145).

International relations among the Neo-Hittite states and with neighboring powers followed distinct patterns than had prevailed during the empire period. The elaborate diplomatic system of the Late Bronze Age, with its carefully regulated interactions among "Great Kings," gave way to more fluid and often conflictual relationships. Neo-Hittite rulers engaged in shifting alliances and frequent military confrontations with one another and with emerging powers like the Aramaean states and the expanding Assyrian Empire.

"The political landscape of the early Iron Age was characterized by a dynamic equilibrium," observes Mark Weeden (2013:12). "Without the stabilizing presence of the great powers of the Late Bronze Age, smaller polities engaged in constant competition and realignment, creating a much more volatile international environment."

Military organization in the Neo-Hittite states similarly reflected both continuity and change. Iconographic evidence, particularly from reliefs at Carchemish and Malatya, indicates the continued importance of chariot warfare, a hallmark of Hittite military practice. However, the composition of armies appears to have shifted, with greater emphasis on infantry forces and the adoption of new weapons technologies, including iron weaponry (Beal 2014:583-605).

Defensive architecture represents another domain where continuity and innovation intersected. Neo-Hittite centers like Carchemish, Zincirli, and Tell Tayinat featured impressive fortification systems that built upon Hittite precedents while incorporating new elements. The elaborate gate complexes with their sculptural programs served both defensive and ideological functions, projecting royal power while protecting the urban core (Pucci 2008:75-91).

Economic organization in the Neo-Hittite states reflected adaptations to new circumstances. The collapse of the palace-centered economies of the Late Bronze Age necessitated alternative approaches to resource mobilization and distribution. Archaeological evidence suggests a greater emphasis on local production and exchange networks, though long-distance trade remained important, particularly for luxury goods and strategic resources like metals (Klengel 2000:21-35).

Cultural and Artistic Developments

The cultural and artistic traditions of the Neo-Hittite states represent one of the most distinctive and significant aspects of their legacy. In this domain, perhaps more than any other, we can trace the complex interplay between inherited Hittite traditions and innovative developments shaped by new cultural contacts and changing social conditions.

Monumental art provides the most visible expression of Neo-Hittite cultural continuity and innovation. The sculptural programs at sites like Carchemish, Malatya, Tell Halaf, and Zincirli display clear connections to Hittite imperial artistic conventions while simultaneously introducing new elements and stylistic approaches. Orthostats—stone slabs carved in relief and used to line the lower portions of monumental buildings—became the signature art form of the Neo-Hittite states, developing the limited use of this technique in the Hittite Empire into an elaborate and distinctive tradition.

"The orthostats of the Neo-Hittite kingdoms represent a remarkable artistic flowering," notes Alessandra Gilibert in her comprehensive study of Neo-Hittite monumental art (2011:37). "They transformed the relatively restrained relief tradition of the Hittite Empire into a more narrative and visually complex medium that served as a powerful vehicle for royal ideology and cultural memory."

Thematically, Neo-Hittite relief sculpture maintained many subjects familiar from imperial Hittite art, including royal hunt scenes, military processions, and divine imagery. However, these traditional themes were executed with greater narrative complexity and visual detail. The "Long Wall of Sculpture" at Carchemish, for instance, presents an elaborate sequence of mythological scenes, ritual activities, and royal imagery that far exceeds the narrative scope of imperial Hittite relief carving (Woolley and Barnett 1952:157-180).

Stylistically, Neo-Hittite sculpture displays a distinctive visual language that combines Hittite elements with new approaches. Figures are typically rendered in profile with frontal eyes, following Hittite convention, but with greater attention to anatomical detail and more dynamic compositional arrangements. The treatment of clothing and regalia similarly builds upon Hittite precedents while introducing more elaborate patterning and decorative elements (Orthmann 1971:147-162).

Iconographic innovations are evident in the representation of royal power. Neo-Hittite rulers developed new visual strategies to assert their legitimacy and authority, combining traditional Hittite royal imagery with new symbolic elements. The motif of the ruler seated before a table laden with offerings, for example, became a standard component of Neo-Hittite royal iconography, appearing at sites throughout the region (Bonatz 2000:89-114).

Religious iconography in Neo-Hittite art maintained strong connections to Hittite traditions while introducing new elements. Representations of deities like the Storm-God Tarhunza and the Sun-goddess Hebat followed established iconographic conventions, but often with elaborated attributes and more complex compositional settings. The famous "God on the Stag" relief from Malatya exemplifies this combination of continuity and innovation, depicting a traditional Hittite deity with new stylistic elements (Hawkins 2000:Plate 110).

Hieroglyphic Luwian writing represents another domain where cultural continuity exists. This script, developed during the Hittite Empire period as a monumental writing system complementary to cuneiform, became the primary medium for official inscriptions in most Neo-Hittite states. The continued use and further development of Hieroglyphic Luwian points to the survival of scribal traditions and educational institutions through the period of imperial collapse.

"The flourishing of Hieroglyphic Luwian in the Neo-Hittite states represents a remarkable case of cultural resilience," observes Annick Payne (2012:12). "Not only did the script survive the collapse of the political system that had fostered its development, but it actually expanded in its use and formal complexity during the early Iron Age."

The content of Hieroglyphic Luwian inscriptions reveals much about the cultural values and historical consciousness of Neo-Hittite elites. Royal inscriptions frequently reference the distant Hittite imperial past, positioning contemporary rulers within a historical continuum stretching back to the great kings of Hattuša. The inscription of King Yariri of Carchemish, for instance, claims connections to "the house of Kubaba and the house of the Great King," explicitly linking the ruler to both local and imperial traditions of legitimacy (Hawkins 2000:124-125).

Architectural traditions in the Neo-Hittite states similarly demonstrate the complex interplay of continuity and innovation. Temple complexes at sites like 'Ain Dara, Tell Tayinat, and Aleppo preserve fundamental elements of Hittite sacred architecture, including distinctive ground plans and ritual installations. However, these traditional elements were often combined with new architectural features and construction techniques (Novák 2012:43-64).

Domestic architecture and urban planning in Neo-Hittite centers reveal adaptations to new social and political circumstances. The bit-hilani, a distinctive architectural form featuring a columned portico leading to a main hall, became characteristic of elite residences in many Neo-Hittite cities. This architectural type, while having antecedents in Late Bronze Age Syria, developed into a distinctive status marker for Neo-Hittite elites (Pucci 2008:173-191).

Material culture at a broader level reflects both continuity with Hittite traditions and the incorporation of new elements. Ceramic assemblages from Neo-Hittite sites typically show gradual transformation rather than abrupt change, with many vessel forms and production techniques persisting from the Late Bronze Age into the early Iron Age. However, new decorative styles and functional types were introduced over time, reflecting changing consumption practices and cultural influences (Mazzoni 2000:31-59).

Burial practices in the Neo-Hittite states demonstrate significant continuity with Hittite traditions. Cremation, which had been the predominant funerary practice in the Hittite Empire, remained common in many Neo-Hittite regions. Archaeological investigations at sites like Hama and Tell Tayinat have documented cremation cemeteries with burial assemblages that combine traditional elements with new grave goods (Riis 1948:27-58).

Language use in the Neo-Hittite states presents a complex picture of continuity and change. While Hieroglyphic Luwian remained the primary language of monumental display in most Neo-Hittite polities through the 9th and 8th centuries BCE, Aramaic gradually gained prominence, particularly in more southerly regions. By the late 8th century, bilingual inscriptions in Luwian and Aramaic appear at several sites, reflecting the changing linguistic landscape of the region (Younger 2016:107-127).

Religious practices in the Neo-Hittite states maintained many elements of Hittite tradition while incorporating new cultic elements. The storm god, under the name Tarhunza, remained the principal deity in most Neo-Hittite pantheons, as he had been during the empire period. However, local manifestations of deities gained greater prominence, and new divine figures entered the pantheon through cultural contact with neighboring regions (Hutter 2003:224-231).

Relations with Assyria and Gradual Incorporation

Their interaction with the resurgent Assyrian Empire profoundly shaped the historical trajectory of the Neo-Hittite states. From the late 10th century BCE onward, Assyrian military campaigns increasingly penetrated the territories of the Neo-Hittite kingdoms, starting a protracted process of confrontation, accommodation, and eventual incorporation that would ultimately bring an end to Neo-Hittite political independence.

The initial phase of Assyrian-Neo-Hittite interaction, roughly spanning the 10th and early 9th centuries BCE, was characterized by intermittent military confrontation without permanent territorial conquest. Assyrian kings like Ashurnasirpal II (883-859 BCE) conducted campaigns into Neo-Hittite territories, extracting tribute and demonstrating Assyrian military power but not attempting to establish direct administrative control.

"Early Assyrian interaction with the Neo-Hittite states followed the traditional pattern of Assyrian imperial expansion," notes Mario Liverani (2014:434). "Military campaigns served primarily to extract resources and establish Assyrian prestige rather than to incorporate territories directly into the imperial system."

Assyrian royal inscriptions from this period frequently mention campaigns against Neo-Hittite states, typically emphasizing the submission of local rulers and the collection of tribute. Ashurnasirpal II's inscriptions, for instance, record that "the kings of the land Hatti came down to me and seized my feet. I received tribute from them" (Grayson 1991:216). Such formulations present Neo-Hittite rulers as acknowledging Assyrian supremacy while maintaining their local authority.

Archaeological evidence from Neo-Hittite centers corroborates this pattern of initial accommodation. Sites like Tell Tayinat and Carchemish show continuous occupation and ongoing monumental construction programs through the 9th century BCE, suggesting that early Assyrian pressure did not fundamentally disrupt Neo-Hittite political structures or cultural practices (Harrison 2009:187-190).

The dynamics of Assyrian-Neo-Hittite relations shifted dramatically during the reign of Shalmaneser III (858-824 BCE), who pursued a more systematic policy of expansion into Syria and southeastern Anatolia. His campaigns faced coordinated resistance from coalitions of Neo-Hittite and Aramaean states, most notably at the Battle of Qarqar in 853 BCE, where a coalition including Carchemish, Patina, and Sam'al temporarily checked Assyrian expansion (Yamada 2000:143-163).

The Assyrian response to this resistance was increasingly punitive. Royal inscriptions and palace reliefs from the mid-9th century onward depict more violent treatment of Neo-Hittite cities and rulers who resisted Assyrian demands. The famous Black Obelisk of Shalmaneser III, for instance, depicts the ruler of Patina/Unqi prostrating himself before the Assyrian king, visually representing the increasingly unequal power relationship (Shafer 2007:133-159).

By the late 9th century BCE, some Neo-Hittite states began to be transformed into Assyrian provinces, losing their political autonomy entirely. This process accelerated under Tiglath-pileser III (745-727 BCE), who implemented comprehensive administrative reforms that standardized provincial governance across the empire. His inscriptions record the conversion of several Neo-Hittite kingdoms, including Unqi/Patina and Gurgum, into directly administered Assyrian provinces (Tadmor and Yamada 2011:46-52).

The archaeological record documents this transition in material terms. At sites like Tell Tayinat, which became the center of the Assyrian province of Unqi/Patina, excavations have revealed the construction of distinctively Assyrian administrative buildings alongside or replacing earlier Neo-Hittite structures. The material culture assemblage similarly shows increasing Assyrianization, with the appearance of characteristic Assyrian ceramic types and other artifacts (Harrison 2016:252-266).

Not all Neo-Hittite states were incorporated simultaneously or in the same manner. Some, like Carchemish, maintained their formal independence as vassal kingdoms well into the 8th century BCE, with local dynasties continuing to rule under Assyrian suzerainty. These vassal rulers walked a precarious political line, balancing the demands of their Assyrian overlords with the need to maintain legitimacy among their own populations.

"The differential treatment of Neo-Hittite polities reflected Assyrian imperial strategy," observes Bradley Parker (2001:85). "Direct provincial administration was imposed where resistance had been strongest or where strategic considerations demanded tight control, while vassal arrangements were maintained elsewhere to reduce administrative costs and leverage local governing structures."

The final phase of Neo-Hittite political existence came during the reigns of Sargon II (721-705 BCE) and Sennacherib (704-681 BCE), who completed the process of provincial incorporation. Carchemish, the last major independent Neo-Hittite kingdom, was finally annexed as a province in 717 BCE following an alleged conspiracy by its ruler, Pisiri, against Assyrian interests (Radner 2006:42-67).

With the loss of political independence, Neo-Hittite cultural traditions entered a new phase of transformation. While local cultural elements persisted within the Assyrian provincial system, they increasingly blended with Assyrian imperial forms. Monumental art production in the Neo-Hittite style largely ceased, replaced by standardized Assyrian artistic conventions in official contexts. Hieroglyphic Luwian fell out of use for administrative purposes, though it may have continued in religious contexts for some time (Hawkins 2009:164-173).

Yet even as political structures were transformed, elements of Neo-Hittite cultural identity persisted at local levels. Archaeological investigations at provincial centers like Tell Tayinat and Zincirli document the continuation of local ceramic traditions and other aspects of material culture alongside newly introduced Assyrian elements. This pattern suggests that while political elites rapidly adopted Assyrian cultural markers, broader population groups maintained connections to pre-Assyrian traditions (Osborne 2017:97-120).

Religious practices appear to have been an area of particular cultural resilience. Assyrian imperial policy generally accommodated local cultic traditions, and evidence suggests that Neo-Hittite deities continued to be worshipped within the provincial system. At Carchemish, for instance, the cult of Kubaba, a goddess with deep roots in local tradition, persisted through the period of Assyrian control and beyond (Hawkins 2000:592-614).

The legacy of Neo-Hittite culture extended well beyond the period of political independence. Certain artistic and architectural traditions that developed in the Neo-Hittite states influenced neighboring cultures, particularly in North Syria, Phoenicia, and the emerging kingdoms of Phrygia and Lydia in western Anatolia. The bit-hilani architectural form, for instance, was adopted in various contexts across the region and even influenced Assyrian palatial architecture (Pucci 2008:188-191).

"The cultural impact of the Neo-Hittite states far exceeded their political significance," notes Gunnar Lehmann (2008:137). "They served as crucial transmitters of artistic, architectural, and religious traditions from the Late Bronze Age into the Iron Age world, creating a cultural bridge that helped shape the diverse civilizations of the first millennium BCE."

The Neo-Hittite legacy may have extended even further afield. Scholars have identified potential connections between Neo-Hittite artistic conventions and early Greek art, suggesting possible channels of cultural transmission through intermediate regions like Phrygia and Lydia (Burkert 1992:9-25). While the precise mechanisms of such influence remain debated, the formal similarities in certain artistic motifs and compositional approaches suggest at least indirect connections.

By the late 7th century BCE, with the collapse of the Assyrian Empire and the rise of new imperial powers in the form of Babylon and Persia, the distinctive political and cultural identity of the Neo-Hittite regions had largely been subsumed within broader regional patterns. Yet elements of this tradition persisted in local practices and cultural memory, forming one strand in the complex tapestry of Near Eastern civilization.

Conclusion

The Neo-Hittite states represent a fascinating case study in cultural resilience and adaptation in the face of imperial collapse. Rising from the ashes of the Hittite Empire, these smaller polities preserved elements of Hittite political organization, cultural practices, and artistic traditions while developing innovative responses to new challenges and opportunities. Their gradual incorporation into the Assyrian Empire brought an end to their political independence but not to their cultural legacy, which continued to influence the broader Near Eastern world in subtle but significant ways.

The archaeological and textual evidence from the Neo-Hittite period challenges simplistic models of cultural collapse and replacement. Instead, it reveals a complex process of transformation, in which traditions were not simply preserved intact or wholly abandoned, but rather selectively maintained, adapted, and combined with new elements to create distinctive cultural expressions suited to changed circumstances.

This pattern of continuity and innovation offers valuable insights into broader questions of cultural resilience and the dynamics of imperial collapse. The Neo-Hittite experience suggests that even dramatic political ruptures need not result in complete cultural discontinuity. Under appropriate conditions, cultural traditions can demonstrate remarkable persistence, finding new expressions in changed political and social contexts.

As our understanding of the Neo-Hittite states continues to develop through ongoing archaeological investigations and textual studies, their significance as a crucial link between the Bronze Age and Iron Age worlds becomes increasingly apparent. In their political structures, artistic expressions, and cultural practices, these fascinating polities embodied both the enduring legacy of the Hittite imperial tradition and the creative adaptations that would help shape the diverse civilizations of the first millennium BCE.

Chapter 20

REDISCOVERY AND MODERN SCHOLARSHIP

Early Modern Encounters with Hittite Monuments

The journey toward rediscovering the Hittites began long before scholars recognized what they were seeing. Throughout the Ottoman period, European travelers occasionally documented strange monuments and inscriptions across Anatolia without understanding their significance. These early encounters represent the first tentative steps toward recovering a lost civilization.

In 1812, the Swiss explorer Johann Ludwig Burckhardt became one of the first Europeans to document the impressive rock reliefs at Yazılıkaya near Boğazköy, though he lacked any framework for interpreting them. "Strange figures carved upon the living rock," he wrote in his journal, "of a character wholly unfamiliar to me, yet executed with considerable skill." Burckhardt's observations, while perceptive, could not connect these monuments to any known historical context.

The French traveler Charles Texier made more systematic observations during his 1834 expedition through central Anatolia. At Boğazköy, Texier documented massive fortification walls, monumental gateways, and curious hieroglyphic inscriptions. His published drawings in *Description de l'Asie Mineure* (1839) introduced European scholars to these monuments, though he mistakenly attributed them to a late Greco-Roman period. "The style appears to be of considerable antiquity," Texier noted, "yet bears no clear relation to the known artistic traditions of the region."

British explorer William Hamilton visited the same sites in 1836, publishing his findings in *Researches in Asia Minor, Pontus and Armenia* (1842). Hamilton recognized that the ruins at Boğazköy were far more ancient than Texier had supposed, suggesting they might belong to "some great capital of an early people about whom we know nothing." This prescient observation came closer to the truth, yet still could not identify the builders of these impressive structures.

The Scottish explorer William John Hamilton documented the Karabel rock relief near Izmir in 1842, which features a warrior figure accompanied by hieroglyphic inscriptions. Hamilton connected this monument to similar reliefs he had seen in central Anatolia, suggesting they belonged to the same cultural tradition. Though he could not identify this tradition, his observation of a consistent artistic style across wide geographical areas was an important insight.

By the mid-nineteenth century, explorers had documented numerous monuments across Anatolia featuring similar artistic styles and inscriptions. In 1872, the British archaeologist Archibald Henry Sayce made a crucial connection, linking these monuments to references in Egyptian texts to a people called the "Kheta" and to biblical mentions of "Hittites." In a landmark paper delivered to the Society of Biblical Archaeology, Sayce proposed that these monuments were the work of "a great empire that rivaled Egypt and Assyria, yet has been completely forgotten."

"We are confronted with the remarkable fact," Sayce wrote, "that a great empire has passed away from the memory of man, and that the vast ruins and monuments which it has left behind have been referred by us to the wrong people." This insight marked a pivotal moment in Hittite studies, establishing for the first time that these scattered monuments belonged to a single, significant civilization.

The Irish missionary William Wright further developed this connection in his 1884 book *The Empire of the Hittites*, compiling evidence from Egyptian, Assyrian, and biblical sources alongside documentation of monuments across Anatolia and northern Syria. Wright's work helped establish the term "Hittite" in scholarly discourse, though many questions remained about the chronology, language, and political organization of this rediscovered civilization.

French archaeologist Ernest Chantre conducted the first systematic excavations at Boğazköy between 1893-1894, uncovering many clay tablets inscribed with cuneiform. Though Chantre could not read these texts, his discovery suggested that Boğazköy had been an important administrative center. "The abundance of written documents," Chantre observed, "indicates a highly organized state with sophisticated bureaucratic practices."

These early encounters and explorations laid essential groundwork for the systematic archaeological investigations that would follow. As archaeologist Trevor Bryce (2019:12) notes: "The rediscovery of the Hittites proceeded through a series of chance encounters, misidentifications, and gradual realizations, before culminating in the definitive archaeological and philological breakthroughs of the early twentieth century."

The Decipherment of Hittite Cuneiform

The turning point in Hittite studies came through the combined efforts of archaeological excavation and philological analysis. In 1906, the German archaeologist Hugo Winckler began systematic excavations at Boğazköy, quickly uncovering an extensive archive of clay tablets. Over several seasons of work, Winckler's team recovered approximately 10,000 tablet fragments, constituting one of the largest archives discovered in the ancient Near East.

Winckler immediately recognized the significance of these findings. "We have discovered the central archive of the Hittite Empire," he wrote to colleagues in 1907. "These documents will revolutionize our understanding of ancient Anatolia and its relations with neighboring civilizations." Working with the Assyriologist Friedrich Delitzsch, Winckler identified several languages in the archive, including Akkadian, the diplomatic lingua franca of the Late Bronze Age.

Among the most significant discoveries was a cuneiform copy of the famous peace treaty between the Hittite king Ḫattušili III and the Egyptian pharaoh Ramesses II, previously known only from the Egyptian version carved on temple walls at Karnak and Abu Simbel. This bilingual text provided crucial evidence connecting Boğazköy with the Hittite capital Hattuša mentioned in Egyptian and Assyrian sources.

While Akkadian texts could be read immediately, most tablets were written in an unknown language using cuneiform script. Winckler tentatively identified this as "the language of Hatti" or "Arzawa," but could not determine its linguistic affiliation. The outbreak of World War I in 1914 interrupted archaeological work at Boğazköy and delayed publication of many findings, but scholarly work on the texts continued.

The breakthrough came in 1915 when the Czech linguist Bedřich Hrozný, working with published tablets in Vienna, recognized that the unknown language of the Boğazköy archives was Indo-European in structure. Examining a passage about eating and drinking, Hrozný noticed the phrase: *nu NINDA-an ezzatteni watar-ma ekutteni*. He recognized that *ezzatteni* resembled the German *essen* (to eat) and Latin *edo*, while *ekutteni* resembled Latin *aqua* (water).

In his groundbreaking paper "Die Lösung des hethitischen Problems" (The Solution to the Hittite Problem), published in 1915, Hrozný declared: "The language of the Hittites is Indo-European." This announcement astonished the scholarly world, as no one had expected to find an Indo-European language in Anatolia at such an early date. Previous theories had placed the entry of Indo-European languages into Anatolia much later, during the classical period.

Hrozný continued his decipherment work through the difficult years of World War I, publishing his comprehensive grammar *Die Sprache der Hethiter* (The Language of the Hittites) in 1917. His analysis established that Hittite was not only Indo-European but represented the earliest attested Indo-European language, predating classical Greek and Sanskrit by nearly a millennium.

"The decipherment of Hittite," notes linguist Craig Melchert (2003:7), "forced a fundamental reconsideration of Indo-European linguistics and prehistoric migrations. The presence of an Indo-European language in central Anatolia by the second millennium BCE could not be reconciled with existing models of Indo-European origins and dispersal."

Following Hrozný's breakthrough, a generation of scholars including Emil Forrer, Johannes Friedrich, and Albrecht Götze refined the grammatical analysis of Hittite and began the systematic translation of the vast textual corpus. Their work revealed the sophisticated literary, historical, and legal traditions of the Hittite civilization, transforming understanding of Late Bronze Age geopolitics.

The decipherment process continued with related languages found in the archives. In the 1930s, scholars recognized that many religious texts were written in Hattic, a non-Indo-European language that had been spoken in central Anatolia before the arrival of Indo-European speakers. Emil Forrer and Hans Ehelolf identified passages in Hurrian, a language spoken across northern Mesopotamia and eastern Anatolia, while other texts contained Luwian, a language related to Hittite but distinct from it.

Parallel to the decipherment of cuneiform texts, scholars worked to understand the hieroglyphic inscriptions found on monuments throughout Anatolia and northern Syria. Initially termed "Hittite hieroglyphs," these inscriptions proved challenging to decipher due to their limited number and the absence of bilingual texts. In 1934, Emil Forrer and Ignace Gelb independently recognized that these hieroglyphs actually recorded the Luwian language rather than Hittite proper.

The definitive breakthrough in deciphering Luwian hieroglyphs came in 1947 when Helmuth Theodor Bossert discovered the bilingual Phoenician-Hieroglyphic Luwian inscription of Karatepe in southeastern Turkey. This text allowed for significant advances in reading the hieroglyphic script, though complete decipherment would require decades of additional work by scholars including Emmanuel Laroche, David Hawkins, and Anna Morpurgo Davies.

"The decipherment of Hittite cuneiform and Luwian hieroglyphs," observes Theo van den Hout (2020:45), "represents one of the great intellectual achievements of twentieth-century philology. These breakthroughs not only recovered lost languages but opened windows into the political, religious, and social worlds of Bronze Age Anatolia."

Major Archaeological Discoveries and Ongoing Excavations

The archaeological exploration of Hittite civilization has proceeded continuously since Winckler's pioneering excavations, though with interruptions caused by world wars and regional conflicts. Each generation of archaeologists has brought new techniques and perspectives to the investigation of Hittite sites, gradually building a more comprehensive understanding of this civilization's material culture and historical development.

After World War I, excavations at Boğazköy (ancient Hattuša) resumed under the direction of Kurt Bittel, who would lead work at the site from 1931 until 1977. Bittel's methodical approach emphasized understanding the city's complex urban development, defensive systems, and monumental architecture. His work established the basic chronological framework for Hittite archaeology, identifying distinctive ceramic sequences and architectural phases.

Bittel's excavations revealed the impressive scale of Hattuša's fortifications, including the massive stone walls with postern tunnels and elaborately carved gateways featuring lions, sphinxes, and warrior figures. The famous Lion Gate and King's Gate, with their monumental sculptures, were carefully documented and partially reconstructed under Bittel's supervision. "These gateways," Bittel wrote in 1970, "were not merely defensive structures but powerful statements of royal ideology and divine protection."

One of the most significant discoveries came in 1966 with the identification of the Great Temple in the Lower City of Hattuša. This massive structure, covering over 20,000 square meters, represented the religious heart of the Hittite capital. Excavations revealed elaborate storage facilities containing ritual vessels, suggesting the temple's central role in state religious ceremonies. Bronze tablets discovered in a side chamber documented land grants and treaties, confirming the temple's administrative functions.

Bittel's team thoroughly documented the nearby rock sanctuary of Yazılıkaya, with its remarkable relief sculptures depicting Hittite deities. The careful analysis of these reliefs, combined with textual evidence, allowed for the identification of major figures in the Hittite pantheon and clarified understanding of religious syncretism in the Hittite Empire. Bittel's interpretation of Yazılıkaya as a site for the royal ancestor cult and New Year ceremonies remains influential, though debated.

Since 1978, excavations at Hattuša have continued under the direction of Peter Neve and subsequently Jürgen Seeher and Andreas Schachner of the German Archaeological Institute. These more recent investigations have employed advanced technologies including geophysical prospection, digital mapping, and archaeometric analysis of materials, revealing new dimensions of the ancient capital.

Particularly significant was the 1986 discovery of the "Südburg" (Southern Fortress) complex with its mysterious underground chambers and water installations. Neve's excavations also uncovered the remains of Hattuša's oldest settlement on Büyükkale (the acropolis), providing crucial evidence for the city's early development in the Old Kingdom period.

In 1991, excavators made a sensational discovery in Chamber 31 of the Great Temple: a collection of bronze tablets including the only known example of a Hittite royal seal. The most significant of these, measuring 35 × 45 cm, contains a treaty between the Hittite king Tudhaliya IV and his cousin Kurunta of Tarhuntassa. "This remarkable document," notes Trevor Bryce (2005:296), "provides unprecedented insight into the complex political relationships within the Hittite royal family during the final decades of the empire."

Recent work at Hattuša has focused on understanding the city's water management systems, agricultural hinterland, and eventual abandonment. Jürgen Seeher's excavations of massive grain silos near the southern fortifications demonstrated Hattuša's capacity to withstand extended sieges, while environmental sampling has provided evidence for climate change during the final decades of the Hittite Empire.

While Hattuša remains the most extensively investigated Hittite site, archaeological work has expanded to numerous other locations across Turkey and northern Syria. At Alaca Höyük, excavations begun in 1935 by the Turkish Historical Society uncovered remarkable royal tombs predating the Hittite period, providing crucial evidence for cultural developments in central Anatolia during the Early Bronze Age. The site's monumental gateway with sphinx sculptures and orthostats depicting ceremonial scenes demonstrates its importance during the Empire period.

At Carchemish on the Syrian-Turkish border, excavations initiated by the British Museum in 1911-1914 with Leonard Woolley and T.E. Lawrence were resumed in 2011 by a Turkish-Italian team. These investigations have clarified the site's development from a Hittite viceregal center to one of the most important Neo-Hittite kingdoms of the Early Iron Age. The extensive relief sculptures and hieroglyphic inscriptions from Carchemish provide crucial evidence for cultural continuity following the collapse of the Hittite Empire.

The site of Tell Atchana (ancient Alalakh) in Turkey's Hatay province, excavated by Leonard Woolley in the 1930s-40s and more recently by K. Aslıhan Yener since 2000, has yielded important evidence for Hittite imperial administration in northern Syria. Tablets discovered at the site document complex interactions between Hittite overlords and local rulers, illuminating the empire's flexible approach to governing diverse territories.

At Ortaköy (ancient Sapinuwa), excavations led by Aygül Süel since 1990 have uncovered a major Hittite administrative center with extensive tablet archives. These texts include unique compositions not found at Hattuša, suggesting regional variations in scribal traditions and religious practices. The site's sudden destruction by fire around 1400 BCE preserved numerous artifacts in their original contexts, providing rare insights into Hittite material culture.

The most dramatic recent discovery came at Kayalıpınar (ancient Samuha) in Sivas province, where excavations led by Andreas Müller-Karpe since 2005 have uncovered a significant Hittite settlement. In 2019, archaeologists discovered a spectacular bronze sword with gold and silver inlay, bearing a hieroglyphic inscription identifying it as belonging to king Tudhaliya III. "This weapon," Müller-Karpe stated, "represents one of the finest examples of Hittite metalwork ever discovered and provides tangible evidence of royal presence at the site."

Archaeological investigations have increasingly extended beyond major centers to understand rural settlement patterns and resource exploitation. Survey work in the Hittite heartland by Roger Matthews and Claudia Glatz has documented changing settlement hierarchies throughout the Bronze Age, while paleoenvironmental research has clarified the agricultural systems that sustained the empire.

The application of scientific techniques has transformed understanding of Hittite material culture. Metallurgical analysis of Hittite artifacts has revealed sophisticated alloying practices and distinctive workshop traditions, while residue analysis of ceramic vessels has provided evidence for ancient brewing and cooking practices. Ancient DNA studies have begun to illuminate population movements and biological relationships, though such research remains in its early stages for Anatolian populations.

"Contemporary Hittite archaeology," observes Claudia Glatz (2017:143), "has moved beyond the monument-focused approaches of earlier generations to embrace a more holistic understanding of ancient landscapes, technologies, and everyday practices. These diverse approaches are revealing a more textured and complex picture of Hittite society than was previously possible."

Current Debates and Future Research Directions

Modern Hittite studies represent a vibrant, interdisciplinary field encompassing archaeology, philology, historical geography, and environmental science. Several key debates animate current research, reflecting both long-standing questions and new perspectives emerging from recent discoveries.

The chronology of Indo-European arrival in Anatolia remains perhaps the most fundamental question in Hittite studies, with significant implications for broader understanding of Indo-European dispersal. The traditional model, based on linguistic evidence, suggests that Indo-European speakers entered Anatolia around 2300-2000 BCE, shortly before the earliest attestation of Hittite personal names in Assyrian merchant texts from Kanesh.

However, this model has been challenged by the "Anatolian hypothesis" advanced by Colin Renfrew and supported by some historical linguists, which places the arrival of Indo-European speakers in Anatolia much earlier, during the Neolithic period (c. 7000-6000 BCE). This hypothesis suggests that Indo-European languages spread with early farming rather than through later migrations or invasions.

Recent archaeogenetic studies have contributed important additional evidence to this debate. A 2019 study by Damgaard et al. analyzed ancient DNA from Bronze Age Anatolian populations, finding evidence for only limited genetic input from Steppe populations associated with Indo-European expansions elsewhere. "These results," the researchers concluded, "suggest that the early spread of Indo-European languages into Anatolia was not associated with a large-scale migration or population replacement."

The interpretation of these genetic findings remains contested. Archaeologist David Anthony argues that "elite dominance" models can reconcile the linguistic evidence for Indo-European presence with the genetic evidence for population continuity: "A relatively small number of Indo-European speakers could have established themselves as a ruling elite, imposing their language while contributing minimally to the genetic makeup of the broader population."

The nature of Hittite state formation presents another area of active research. Traditional narratives emphasized the role of Ḫattušili I as the founder of a unified Hittite state around 1650 BCE. However, recent scholarship has highlighted the importance of earlier political developments, particularly under kings Pithana and Anitta of Kanesh in the 18th century BCE.

The discovery and publication of new texts from Ortaköy/Sapinuwa and Kayalıpınar/Samuha has forced reconsideration of Hittite political geography. These provincial archives reveal more complex administrative structures than previously recognized, with evidence for regional scribal traditions and religious practices distinct from those at Hattuša. As Theo van den Hout (2018:76) observes, "The Hittite state was less centralized and more heterogeneous than earlier models suggested, with significant regional autonomy persisting throughout the imperial period."

The collapse of the Hittite Empire around 1180 BCE continues to generate scholarly debate. Traditional explanations emphasized external factors, particularly invasions by the mysterious "Sea Peoples" mentioned in Egyptian texts. More recent approaches favor systemic models that consider multiple interacting factors including climate change, political fragmentation, economic disruption, and population movements.

Paleoclimatic data from lake sediments, speleothems, and dendrochronology has provided evidence for severe drought conditions across the Eastern Mediterranean during the late 13th and early 12th centuries BCE. A 2022 study by Manning et al. using tree-ring data from juniper timbers at Porsuk demonstrated "unprecedented drought conditions coinciding with the final decades of the Hittite Empire," supporting climate change as a significant stress factor.

Archaeological evidence from Hattuša indicates that the Hittite capital was not destroyed in a violent conflagration but rather abandoned in an organized manner, with valuable items removed and archives secured. This pattern suggests a planned withdrawal rather than sudden catastrophe, raising questions about political decisions during the empire's final years.

The relationship between the Hittite Empire and its Neo-Hittite successors presents another area of ongoing research. Traditional scholarship emphasized discontinuity, with the Neo-Hittite states seen as largely new political formations that merely appropriated elements of Hittite imperial ideology. Recent work has highlighted evidence for greater continuity in administrative practices, artistic traditions, and religious institutions.

Particularly significant is the growing recognition of Carchemish's role as a center of political and cultural continuity. As a viceregal seat during the Empire period and subsequently an independent kingdom, Carchemish maintained Hittite scribal traditions and artistic conventions well into the Iron Age. David Hawkins (2009:164) characterizes Carchemish as "the legitimate successor state to the Hittite Empire," noting that its rulers continued to use imperial titles and maintained diplomatic relations with other regional powers.

The nature of Hittite religion continues to generate significant scholarly discussion. Earlier approaches tended to emphasize the syncretistic character of Hittite religion, with its incorporation of Hattic, Hurrian, and Mesopotamian elements. More recent work has focused on identifying specifically Hittite contributions to this religious synthesis and understanding how religious practices functioned in political and social contexts.

The interpretation of Yazılıkaya, the rock sanctuary near Hattuša with its remarkable divine processions carved in relief, exemplifies evolving approaches to Hittite religion. While Kurt Bittel interpreted the site primarily in terms of the royal ancestor cult and New Year celebrations, recent research by Eberhard Zangger and Rita Gautschy has proposed that the relief program incorporates sophisticated astronomical knowledge, potentially functioning as a lunar-solar calendar.

This astronomical interpretation remains controversial, with critics questioning whether the specific arrangement of divine figures supports such functional claims. The debate illustrates broader methodological questions about how to interpret religious iconography and the relationship between textual and archaeological evidence in understanding ancient belief systems.

Future research directions in Hittite studies will likely emphasize several key areas. The application of scientific techniques including ancient DNA analysis, isotope studies, and materials science promises to provide new insights into population movements, trade networks, and technological practices. Ongoing excavations at provincial centers like Ortaköy/Sapinuwa and Kayalıpınar/Samuha will continue to illuminate regional variations within the Hittite state.

Digital humanities approaches are transforming access to Hittite textual materials. The Hethitologie Portal Mainz and the electronic Chicago Hittite Dictionary project are creating comprehensive digital resources for textual study, while 3D scanning and photogrammetry are documenting monuments and artifacts with unprecedented precision. These digital resources are making Hittite materials accessible to broader scholarly communities and enabling new forms of analysis.

Environmental archaeology will likely play an increasingly important role in understanding the Hittite world. As Ulf Schoop (2020:218) notes, "The integration of paleoclimatic data, archaeobotanical studies, and settlement survey is essential for understanding how Hittite communities adapted to environmental challenges and how climate change may have contributed to the empire's ultimate collapse."

Comparative approaches placing Hittite civilization in broader context continue to yield important insights. Studies examining Hittite diplomatic practices in relation to other contemporary powers or comparing Hittite imperial strategies with those of other ancient empires, help illuminate both unique aspects of Hittite civilization and shared patterns across ancient complex societies.

"The field of Hittite studies stands at an exciting juncture," observes Petra Goedegebuure (2021:12). "The combination of new archaeological discoveries, scientific techniques, and digital approaches to texts and artifacts is enabling us to ask new questions and revisit old debates with fresh evidence. While history once forgot the Hittites, they now stand revealed as a crucial component in understanding the complex interconnections of the ancient Near Eastern world."

From those early encounters with mysterious monuments to today's sophisticated multidisciplinary investigations, the rediscovery of the Hittites represents one of the great achievements of modern historical scholarship. This process has not merely recovered a lost civilization but has transformed understanding of ancient Anatolia, Indo-European linguistics, and the geopolitics of the Late Bronze Age. As research continues, the Hittites will undoubtedly continue to yield new insights into the dynamics of ancient states and the rich cultural heritage of Anatolia.

Chapter 21

The Hittite Achievement in Historical Perspective

The Hittites' Contribution to Ancient Near Eastern Civilization

The Hittite Empire, while often overshadowed by its contemporaries in Egypt and Mesopotamia, made distinctive and lasting contributions to the ancient Near Eastern world. Perhaps their most significant impact came through their innovative approach to statecraft and international relations, which transformed the political landscape of the Late Bronze Age.

"The Hittite diplomatic revolution," writes Trevor Bryce (2019:156), "fundamentally altered how ancient states interacted with one another. By developing a system of vassal treaties with clear obligations and protections, the Hittites created a framework for managing imperial relationships that influenced political practice throughout the region."

This treaty system represented a sophisticated approach to managing conquered territories. Rather than imposing direct rule through governors, the Hittites typically allowed local rulers to maintain their positions, binding them through carefully crafted agreements that specified mutual obligations. The vassal was required to provide military support, pay tribute, and maintain loyalty to the Hittite king, while the Hittite sovereign promised protection and support against external threats.

The Hittite treaty with Ulmi-Tešub of Tarhuntašša exemplifies this approach:

"If an enemy arises against the Sun [the Hittite king] and the Sun goes to battle, if you, Ulmi-Tešub, do not come promptly with infantry and chariotry and fight wholeheartedly against my enemy—if you send only your son or brother with a token force, you will transgress the oath."

These treaties served as practical instruments of governance, allowing the Hittites to maintain control over diverse territories with relatively limited administrative resources. The detailed nature of these agreements—specifying everything from military obligations to procedures for handling fugitives—demonstrates the Hittites' pragmatic approach to imperial management.

Beyond their innovations in international relations, the Hittites made significant contributions to ancient legal traditions. The Hittite Law Code, dating from the Old Kingdom period (c. 1650-1500 BCE), stands as one of the earliest and most comprehensive legal compilations from the ancient world. Unlike the contemporary Code of Hammurabi, which frequently prescribed severe punishments including death, the Hittite laws emphasized compensation and restitution.

Itamar Singer (2011:87) observes that "the Hittite legal system reflected a remarkably pragmatic approach to justice, focusing on restoring social harmony rather than exacting retribution." This emphasis on compensation is evident in numerous provisions:

"If anyone blinds a free person or knocks out his tooth, formerly they would pay 40 shekels of silver, but now he shall pay 20 shekels of silver."

This reduction in penalties over time suggests a conscious effort to make the legal system more equitable and practical. The Hittite laws also displayed unusual concern for social welfare, with provisions protecting agricultural workers, regulating prices, and establishing fair wages.

In the technological sphere, the Hittites are often credited with pioneering iron metallurgy. While this traditional view has been nuanced by recent scholarship—the transition from bronze to iron was more gradual than once thought—the Hittites certainly played a crucial role in developing metallurgical techniques. Archaeological evidence from sites like Kaman-Kalehöyük demonstrates sophisticated metalworking practices, with specialized workshops producing high-quality bronze implements while gradually incorporating iron technology.

James Muhly (2011:232) argues that "the Hittites' contribution lay not in 'inventing' iron metallurgy, but in systematically developing and applying ironworking techniques within a state-sponsored framework." Hittite texts refer to iron as "black metal" (AN.BAR GE$_6$) and suggest it was initially valued for its ritual properties rather than practical applications. By the late 13th century BCE, however, iron was increasingly used for tools and weapons, setting the stage for the Iron Age that would follow the Bronze Age collapse.

The Hittites also made notable contributions to ancient architectural practices. Their capital at Hattuša represents one of the most impressive urban achievements of the Late Bronze Age. The city's massive fortification system—with walls up to 8 meters thick, postern tunnels, and monumental gateways adorned with sculptural lions and sphinxes—demonstrated sophisticated military engineering. The distinctive bent-axis design of Hittite temples, with their sequence of courtyards leading to inner sanctuaries, influenced religious architecture throughout Anatolia and northern Syria.

Archaeologist Jürgen Seeher (2017:119) notes that "Hittite architects developed distinctive solutions to the challenges of building in Anatolia's varied terrain, creating monumental structures that effectively communicated royal power while addressing practical needs for defense and administration."

In the religious sphere, the Hittites developed a remarkably inclusive theological system that incorporated deities from multiple cultural traditions. This "thousand gods of Hatti" approach allowed the Hittites to integrate conquered populations by embracing their religious traditions rather than suppressing them. Hittite religious texts document elaborate festival cycles, ritual procedures, and mythological narratives that drew from Hattic, Hurrian, and Mesopotamian traditions while developing distinctive theological concepts.

Particularly significant was the Hittite practice of "evocation rituals" (mugawar), in which angry or absent deities were called back to their temples through elaborate ceremonies. These rituals reflect a sophisticated understanding of divine-human relations, with the gods conceived as powerful but not entirely beyond human influence.

Billie Jean Collins (2007:175) observes that "the Hittite religious system's capacity to incorporate diverse traditions while maintaining coherent theological frameworks provided a model for religious syncretism that would influence later Anatolian and Near Eastern religious developments."

Indo-European Expansion and Cultural Synthesis

The Hittite civilization provides our earliest extensive documentation of an Indo-European language and culture, offering crucial insights into the processes of Indo-European expansion and cultural interaction across Eurasia. The Hittites' experience in Anatolia exemplifies a pattern of cultural synthesis rather than simple replacement, challenging older models of Indo-European spread.

When Indo-European speakers first entered Anatolia—likely during the third millennium BCE—they encountered well-established indigenous cultures, particularly the Hattians in central Anatolia. Rather than imposing their language and customs through conquest, the archaeological and textual evidence suggests a complex process of interaction and gradual cultural transformation.

"The Hittite case demonstrates that language shift need not involve population replacement," argues archaeogeneticist David Reich (2018:96). "Ancient DNA from Anatolian sites shows relatively modest genetic input from steppe populations, suggesting that Indo-European languages spread through elite dominance rather than mass migration in this region."

This pattern differs from the Indo-European expansion into Europe, where genetic evidence indicates substantial population movement. The Anatolian experience thus represents an important variant in Indo-European dispersal, highlighting the diverse mechanisms through which these languages spread across Eurasia.

The Hittites' cultural synthesis is evident in their religious practices. While maintaining Indo-European theological concepts—such as the storm god as divine sovereign—they thoroughly incorporated Hattic deities, rituals, and religious personnel. The Sun-goddess of Arinna, a Hattic deity, became the supreme goddess of the Hittite state pantheon. Hattic ritual specialists continued to perform ceremonies in their native language even after it had ceased to be spoken in daily life.

This religious integration served important political functions. Maciej Popko (2013:45) observes that "by embracing indigenous religious traditions rather than suppressing them, Hittite rulers legitimized their authority among the native population while positioning themselves as proper stewards of ancient sacred traditions."

The Hittites similarly incorporated Hurrian cultural elements as their empire expanded southward. During the Empire period (c. 1400-1180 BCE), Hurrian deities, myths, and ritual practices were systematically integrated into Hittite state religion. The rock sanctuary at Yazılıkaya, with its processions of gods carved in relief, represents a magnificent synthesis of Hittite and Hurrian religious iconography.

Linguistic evidence also demonstrates this pattern of cultural synthesis. The Hittite language, while clearly Indo-European in its grammatical structure, incorporated extensive loanwords from Hattic and Hurrian. Administrative and religious terminology often derived from indigenous languages, reflecting the Hittites' pragmatic adoption of local institutional frameworks.

Gary Beckman (2016:78) argues that "the Hittites' capacity for cultural integration represents their most distinctive characteristic as an Indo-European people. Rather than imposing a rigid cultural identity, they created a flexible, syncretic civilization that drew strength from its diverse components."

This pattern of cultural synthesis extended to material culture as well. Hittite art and architecture combined Indo-European elements with Anatolian, Syrian, and Mesopotamian influences. The distinctive orthostats (carved stone slabs) that adorned Hittite buildings incorporated motifs from multiple traditions. Ceramic styles show continuity with earlier Anatolian forms while incorporating new elements.

The Hittite experience offers important lessons for understanding other instances of Indo-European expansion. Rather than envisioning this process as simple conquest and replacement, the Anatolian case suggests we should look for complex patterns of interaction, with language shift potentially occurring through elite dominance mechanisms rather than population replacement.

"The Hittite model of Indo-European expansion," writes J.P. Mallory (2018:213), "emphasizes cultural synthesis over conflict, gradual transformation over abrupt change, and the importance of local adaptations to specific environmental and social contexts."

As we continue to integrate linguistic, archaeological, and genetic evidence, the Hittite example reminds us that cultural and linguistic spread involves complex social processes that can follow multiple pathways in different regions.

Lessons from Hittite Statecraft and Diplomacy

The Hittite approach to statecraft and diplomacy offers striking insights for understanding how ancient empires functioned and how they managed relationships with neighbors and subjects. Perhaps most remarkable was the Hittites' pragmatic flexibility, which allowed them to adapt their governance strategies to diverse circumstances while maintaining core imperial principles.

This pragmatism is evident in the Hittites' approach to conquered territories. Unlike the Assyrians, who frequently engaged in mass deportations and imposed standardized administrative structures, the Hittites typically preserved local institutions and elites while binding them to the imperial center through treaties and oaths. This approach reduced administrative costs while acknowledging the practical challenges of controlling diverse regions from a single center.

"The Hittite imperial system," observes Mario Liverani (2014:291), "represents a sophisticated response to the geographical and cultural diversity of Anatolia and northern Syria. By allowing significant local autonomy within a framework of imperial sovereignty, the Hittites created a flexible structure that could accommodate regional differences while maintaining central control over essential resources and strategic locations."

This flexibility extended to the Hittites' religious policies. When incorporating new territories, they typically embraced local cults rather than suppressing them. The famous statement "the thousand gods of Hatti" reflects this inclusive approach, which served both theological and political purposes. By respecting local religious traditions, the Hittites reduced resistance to their rule while positioning the king as the proper intermediary between humans and the divine pantheon.

The Hittite treaty system represents one of their most significant contributions to ancient statecraft. These carefully crafted documents specified mutual obligations in remarkable detail, creating a legal framework for interstate relations. The Hittite-Egyptian peace treaty of 1259 BCE—copies of which were displayed in both capitals—stands as the earliest known international peace agreement, establishing principles that would influence diplomatic practice for centuries.

Trevor Bryce (2006:312) notes that "the Hittite treaty system established fundamental principles that continue to resonate in international relations: reciprocity, specified obligations, dispute resolution mechanisms, and divine sanctions for violations."

The treaty with Ramesses II exemplifies these principles:

"Ramesses, Great King, King of Egypt, shall be at peace with Hattušili, Great King, King of Hatti, his brother, forever. The children of Ramesses, Great King, King of Egypt, shall be at peace with the children of Hattušili, Great King, King of Hatti, forever."

This emphasis on perpetual peace extending to future generations reflects a sophisticated understanding of interstate relations as ongoing processes rather than temporary arrangements.

The Hittites also developed innovative approaches to royal succession, learning from earlier periods of instability. The Telepinu Proclamation (c. 1525 BCE) established clear principles for royal succession, attempting to prevent the destructive power struggles that had weakened the kingdom. While these principles were not always followed in practice, they represented an important effort to institutionalize peaceful transitions of power.

The Hittite diplomatic correspondence found at sites like Amarna in Egypt and Ugarit in Syria reveals sophisticated diplomatic protocols. Hittite kings addressed other "Great Kings" as brothers, exchanged elaborate gifts, and maintained resident ambassadors at foreign courts. They employed professional translators and scribes skilled in multiple languages and writing systems, facilitating communication across cultural boundaries.

"The Hittite diplomatic system," writes Amanda Podany (2012:187), "created frameworks for managing interstate relations that balanced competition with cooperation. By establishing shared expectations about appropriate behavior, these diplomatic practices helped stabilize the international system despite underlying tensions."

Perhaps most striking was the Hittites' capacity for adaptation over time. When faced with the rising power of Assyria in the 13th century BCE, they adjusted their diplomatic strategies accordingly. When climate challenges threatened agricultural productivity, they developed new water management systems and storage facilities. This adaptive capacity allowed the Hittite state to endure for over five centuries despite many challenges.

The Hittite experience offers valuable insights for understanding how ancient states navigated complex geopolitical landscapes. Their emphasis on flexible governance structures, formalized interstate relations, and cultural integration provides a sophisticated model of imperial management that contrasts with more coercive approaches employed by other ancient empires.

The Hittite Legacy in Modern Turkey and International Scholarship

The legacy of the Hittites extends far beyond their historical impact on the ancient Near East. In modern Turkey, Hittite heritage has become an important element of national identity and cultural tourism, while international scholarship continues to explore this remarkable civilization from diverse disciplinary perspectives.

When the Turkish Republic was established in 1923, its founders sought historical narratives that emphasized Anatolia's pre-Islamic heritage. The Hittites, as an indigenous Anatolian civilization predating Greek and Roman presence, offered an attractive reference point. Mustafa Kemal Atatürk, the republic's founder, took personal interest in archaeological excavations at Hittite sites and promoted public awareness of this ancient civilization.

"The Turkish embrace of Hittite heritage," notes Wendy Shaw (2007:168), "represented part of a broader effort to construct a national identity rooted in Anatolia's diverse historical experiences rather than exclusively in Ottoman or Islamic traditions."

The Hittite sun disk's adoption as a national emblem, featured on Turkish coins and official buildings, symbolized this connection between modern Turkish identity and ancient Anatolian civilizations. The Museum of Anatolian Civilizations in Ankara, opened in 1943, prominently features Hittite artifacts, positioning them as part of Turkey's national heritage.

Today, Hittite sites constitute major destinations in Turkey's cultural tourism sector. Hattuša, designated a UNESCO World Heritage Site in 1986, attracts thousands of visitors annually. The site's impressive fortifications, monumental gateways, and the nearby rock sanctuary at Yazılıkaya offer tangible connections to this ancient civilization. Other Hittite sites, including Alacahöyük, Karatepe, and Arslantepe, have been developed for tourism with museums, interpretive centers, and infrastructure improvements.

Eberhard Zangger, director of Luwian Studies Foundation, observes that "Hittite heritage has become an important economic resource for regions of central Turkey, creating employment opportunities and supporting local development through cultural tourism" (personal communication, 2022).

The Turkish government has also supported international exhibitions highlighting Hittite civilization. The 2016 exhibition "The Hittites: An Anatolian Empire" at the Louvre Museum in Paris featured hundreds of artifacts from Turkish museums, introducing this ancient culture to broader audiences. Similar exhibitions in Berlin, New York, and Tokyo have raised global awareness of Hittite achievements.

In international scholarship, Hittite studies has developed into a vibrant interdisciplinary field. The decipherment of Hittite in 1915 by Bedřich Hrozný revolutionized understanding of Indo-European linguistics, providing crucial evidence for reconstructing Proto-Indo-European and establishing the Anatolian branch as the earliest attested Indo-European language family.

Craig Melchert (2018:53) notes that "Hittite continues to play a central role in Indo-European linguistics, challenging earlier reconstructions and providing essential evidence for understanding how these languages evolved and diversified."

Archaeological research at Hittite sites has similarly transformed understanding of ancient Anatolia. Excavations at Hattuša, conducted by the German Archaeological Institute since 1931, have revealed the sophisticated urban planning, defensive systems, and monumental architecture of the Hittite capital. Recent work at provincial centers like Ortaköy/Šapinuwa and Kuşaklı/Šarišša has provided new perspectives on regional administration and daily life beyond the capital.

Technological advances have revolutionized Hittite archaeology in recent decades. Remote sensing techniques, including ground-penetrating radar and satellite imagery analysis, have identified previously unknown settlements and landscape features. Three-dimensional scanning and photogrammetry have documented monuments and artifacts with unprecedented precision, creating digital archives that facilitate research and conservation efforts.

Textual studies remain central to Hittite scholarship. The systematic publication of texts from the Boğazköy archives, begun in the early 20th century, continues today with new tablets and fragments regularly published. Digital humanities approaches, including the electronic Chicago Hittite Dictionary project and the Hethitologie Portal Mainz, have transformed access to these materials, making them available to researchers worldwide.

Petra Goedegebuure, editor of the Chicago Hittite Dictionary, emphasizes that "digital approaches have democratized access to Hittite texts, allowing scholars from diverse institutions to engage with primary sources that were previously accessible only to specialists at a few research centers" (interview, 2023).

Interdisciplinary approaches increasingly characterize Hittite studies. Archaeogenetic research has provided new insights into population movements and biological relationships in ancient Anatolia. Paleoclimatic studies have illuminated the environmental challenges faced by the Hittite state, particularly during its final century. Comparative approaches examining Hittite institutions in relation to other ancient societies have contextualized their achievements within broader patterns of state formation and imperial development.

The Hittite legacy extends beyond academic research to broader cultural awareness. References to Hittites appear in novels, films, and video games, introducing this ancient civilization to popular audiences. While these representations often simplify or romanticize Hittite society, they nonetheless contribute to public awareness of this once-forgotten empire.

Perhaps the most profound aspect of the Hittite legacy lies in what their rediscovery reveals about historical knowledge itself. The fact that a major Bronze Age empire could disappear from historical memory for millennia, only to be rediscovered through archaeological and philological research, reminds us of the contingent nature of historical awareness. As Carlo Zaccagnini (2017:412) observes, "The Hittite case demonstrates how even powerful states can fade from collective memory, their achievements preserved only in the material traces they leave behind."

Conclusion: The Enduring Significance of Hittite Civilization

The study of Hittite civilization offers more than fascinating insights into a particular ancient society. It provides a compelling case study in how complex states emerge, function, and ultimately collapse. The Hittite experience of cultural synthesis, imperial management, and adaptation to environmental challenges resonates with issues that continue to shape human societies.

Their approach to cultural integration—incorporating diverse traditions rather than suppressing them—offers a sophisticated model for managing multicultural polities. Their diplomatic innovations, particularly the formalized treaty system, established principles that would influence international relations for millennia. Their legal traditions, emphasizing compensation over punishment, demonstrate how ancient societies developed pragmatic approaches to maintaining social order.

The Hittite collapse around 1180 BCE similarly offers valuable perspectives on systemic failure. The combination of climate change, economic disruption, political fragmentation, and external pressures that contributed to the empire's end has parallels in other historical cases of state collapse. Understanding how these factors interacted in the Hittite case provides insights into the vulnerabilities of complex social systems.

"The Hittite civilization," writes Theo van den Hout (2021:314), "represents a remarkable chapter in human history—a society that developed sophisticated political, religious, and cultural institutions while maintaining remarkable adaptability in the face of changing circumstances. Their achievements and ultimate collapse offer valuable lessons about the dynamics of ancient states and the challenges they faced."

As archaeological research continues at Hittite sites across Turkey and Syria, as textual studies further illuminate their literature and historical records, and as scientific analyses provide new insights into their environment and material culture, our understanding of this remarkable civilization continues to deepen and evolve.

The Hittites—once forgotten by history, their monuments mis-attributed, their language unknown—now stand revealed as a crucial component of the ancient Near Eastern world. Their rediscovery represents one of the great achievements of modern historical scholarship, transforming understanding of ancient Anatolia, Indo-European linguistics, and Bronze Age geopolitics.

Perhaps most importantly, the Hittite story reminds us that history contains many such gaps—civilizations whose achievements have faded from memory, whose contributions await rediscovery. As Itamar Singer (2011:327) eloquently concluded in his final work on Hittite prayers: "The voices of the ancient Hittites, silenced for three millennia, speak to us again through their texts and monuments. They remind us that behind the grand narratives of empires and kings stood individual human beings, grappling with challenges not entirely unlike our own—seeking security in an uncertain world, meaning in the face of suffering, and connection across the boundaries of language and culture."

In recovering and studying the Hittite past, we not only illuminate an ancient civilization but also gain perspective on our own historical moment—its challenges, possibilities, and place in the long continuum of human experience.

APPENDIX A: CHRONOLOGICAL DATA

Chronological Frameworks

The reconstruction of Hittite chronology represents one of the most challenging aspects of Anatolian studies. As Trevor Bryce (2005:375) notes, "The establishment of a reliable chronological framework for Hittite history has been a complex and contentious undertaking." Unlike Egypt with its detailed king lists or Mesopotamia with its year-by-year limmu officials, Hittite texts rarely provide absolute chronological markers. Instead, scholars have constructed chronologies through a combination of synchronisms with better-dated neighboring cultures, internal textual evidence, and archaeological correlations.

King List and Reign Lengths

The following represents the current scholarly consensus regarding the Hittite king list, though debate continues regarding several problematic transitions:

Old Kingdom (ca. 1650 – 1500 BCE)

- Labarna I: c. 1680 – 1650 BC

- Ḥattušili I: c. 1650 – 1620 BC

- Muršili I: c. 1620 – 1590 BC

- Ḫantili I: c. 1590 – 1560 BC

- Zidanta I: c. 1560 – 1550 BC

- Ammuna: c. 1550 – 1530 BC

- Ḫuzziya I: c. 1530 – 1525 BC

- Telipinu: c. 1560 – 1500 BC (or c. 1550 – 1530 BC)

Middle Kingdom (ca. 1500 – 1400 BCE)

- Alluwamna: c. 1500 BC – ?

- Ḫantili II: c. ? – ? BC

- Taḫurwaili: c. ? – ? BC

- Zidanta II: c. ? – ? BC

- Ḫuzziya II: c. ? – ? BC

- Muwatalli I: c. ? – 1430/1400 BC

New Kingdom (Empire Period, ca. 1400 – 1180 BCE)

- Tudḫaliya I: c. 1430/1420 – 1410/1400 BC

- Ḫattušili II: c. 1410/1400 – 1400/1390 BC

- Tudḫaliya II: c. 1400/1390 – 1390/1370 BC

- Arnuwanda I: c. 1390/1370 – 1380/1355 BC

- Tudḫaliya III: c. 1380/1355 – 1370/1344 BC

- Šuppiluliuma I: c. 1370/1344 – 1330/1322 BC

- Arnuwanda II: c. 1330/1322 – 1330/1321 BC

- Muršili II: c. 1330/1321 – 1295 BC

- Muwatalli II: c. 1295 – 1282/1272 BC

- Muršili III (Urḫi-Tešub): c. 1282/1272 – 1275/1264 BC

- Ḫattušili III: c. 1275/1264 – 1245/1239 BC

- Tudḫaliya IV: c. 1245/1239 – 1215/1209 BC

- Arnuwanda III: c. 1215/1209 – 1210/1205 BC

- Šuppiluliuma II: c. 1215/1205 – ? BC

As Gary Beckman (2000:19) observes, "The Middle Kingdom sequence remains particularly problematic, with significant disagreements regarding both the order of kings and their reign lengths." The placement of Tahurwaili, for example, continues to generate scholarly debate, with some placing him as a contemporary of Telipinu rather than his successor.

Synchronisms with Other Ancient Chronologies

The establishment of a reliable Hittite chronology depends heavily on synchronisms with neighboring regions. As Jörg Klinger (2015:90) explains, "Absolute dates for Hittite history derive primarily from correlations with Egyptian, Assyrian, and Babylonian chronologies, each with their own margins of error."

The most secure synchronism comes from the Egyptian-Hittite peace treaty of 1259 BCE, precisely dated in Egyptian records to year 21 of Ramesses II. Other key synchronisms include:

"These synchronisms," writes Kenneth Kitchen (2009:163), "provide essential anchors for Hittite chronology, though interpretive challenges remain, particularly for the earlier periods where direct correlations are scarce."

The Amarna letters (14th century BCE) offer another valuable chronological reference point, documenting correspondence between Amenhotep III/Akhenaten and Hittite kings. As William Moran (1992:xxiv) notes, "The Amarna correspondence provides crucial evidence for international relations during the early Empire period, helping to establish temporal relationships between Hittite and Egyptian rulers."

Archaeological Period Correlations

Archaeological evidence provides an independent line of chronological evidence, though correlating ceramic phases with historical events remains challenging. The following sequence represents the current understanding of archaeological periods in central Anatolia:

As Roger Matthews (2011:51) observes, "Ceramic sequences from stratified contexts at Hattuša, Kuşaklı, and other sites provide essential chronological frameworks, though connecting these material sequences with specific historical events remains problematic."

Radiocarbon dating has increasingly refined these archaeological chronologies. Recent studies at Hattuša have provided more precise dating for destruction layers and building phases. According to Hermann Genz (2017:129), "New AMS radiocarbon dates from short-lived samples at Hattuša largely confirm the conventional chronology, though suggesting some compression of the Middle Kingdom period."

Dendrochronological studies have provided additional precision. Timber elements from Hittite buildings at Kuşaklı and Sarissa have yielded cutting dates that correlate with construction activities mentioned in texts. Peter Kuniholm's (1996:327) pioneering work demonstrated that "tree-ring sequences from Anatolian sites can provide absolute dates accurate to a single year, offering unprecedented chronological precision for the Late Bronze Age."

The challenge of reconciling textual and archaeological evidence remains significant. As Theo van den Hout (2018:42) concludes, "Despite advances in scientific dating methods, the integration of archaeological and historical chronologies continues to present interpretive challenges. The Hittite chronological framework remains a work in progress, with ongoing refinements as new evidence emerges."

This chronological framework, despite its remaining uncertainties, provides the essential temporal structure for understanding the development, flourishing, and ultimate collapse of Hittite civilization. As archaeological research continues and new texts are discovered and interpreted, our understanding of Hittite chronology will undoubtedly continue to evolve, offering increasingly refined insights into the timing and sequence of this remarkable civilization's achievements.

Appendix B: Translation Excerpts

Key Hittite Texts and Documents

The remarkable survival of Hittite written records offers us an unparalleled window into the political, religious, and cultural life of this Bronze Age civilization. Unlike many ancient societies known primarily through archaeological remains, the Hittites left behind a vast corpus of texts—over 30,000 clay tablet fragments recovered from the archives at Hattuša alone. These documents, written primarily in cuneiform script, span nearly five centuries and encompass multiple genres and languages. This appendix provides an overview of the major textual categories that form the foundation of our understanding of Hittite civilization.

Historical Texts

The Hittites demonstrated a sophisticated historical consciousness, producing detailed accounts of royal achievements that rank among the earliest examples of historical writing. These texts not only documented events but also served ideological purposes, legitimizing royal authority and establishing precedents for governance.

Royal Annals

The Annals tradition, begun under Hattušili I (ca. 1650-1620 BCE), represents one of the most significant Hittite contributions to ancient historiography. Unlike the static, timeless royal inscriptions of many contemporary civilizations, Hittite annals presented year-by-year accounts of royal military campaigns and administrative activities.

The "Annals of Muršili II" exemplify the genre's maturity. Covering the first ten years of his reign (ca. 1321-1311 BCE), they describe in remarkable detail his campaigns against Arzawa, Kaska, and other enemies:

"In my third year, I marched against the land of Arzawa. When I reached the Astarpa River, the people of Arzawa came and engaged me in battle. I defeated them, and they fled before me. I crossed the river and entered the land of Arzawa. I crossed Mount Lawasa and reached the city of Apasa, the royal residence of Uhha-ziti."

These annals combine straightforward military narrative with religious elements, attributing victories to divine support and defeats to divine anger. They reflect a complex understanding of causality in history, balancing human agency with divine intervention.

Apologetic Texts

A uniquely Hittite historical genre, apologetic texts defended controversial royal actions, particularly usurpations. The most famous example, Hattušili III's "Apology" (ca. 1267-1237 BCE), justifies his overthrow of his nephew Urhi-Tešub. This remarkable document combines biography, legal defense, and religious testimony:

"When my brother Muwatalli went to his fate [died], by the command of the gods, I did not do any evil to Urhi-Tešub, the son of my brother. I bowed to him and raised him to the kingship... But he began to wrong me. He took from me the cities of my lordship which my brother had given me."

Hattušili frames his usurpation as divinely sanctioned, emphasizing his devotion to the goddess Ištar/Šauška, who "held me by the hand" throughout his career. This sophisticated political apologia represents an early example of autobiography used for political legitimation.

The Telepinu Proclamation

Perhaps the most significant Hittite historical text, the Telepinu Proclamation (ca. 1525 BCE) combines historical narrative with constitutional reform. After recounting the bloody succession struggles following Muršili I's assassination, Telepinu establishes clear succession principles:

"Let only a prince of the first rank, a son, become king. If there is no first-rank prince, let a son of the second rank take kingship. If there is no prince, let them take the husband of a first-rank daughter as king."

The text's historical section provides our primary source for the "dark age" period, while its legal provisions established a framework for orderly succession that, though imperfectly followed, influenced later Hittite governance. The proclamation demonstrates the Hittites' ability to learn from historical experience and codify political reforms.

Diplomatic Texts

The Hittite archives preserve the most extensive corpus of international diplomatic documents from the ancient world, offering unprecedented insight into the functioning of the Late Bronze Age international system.

Treaties

The Hittites developed international treaties to an unprecedented level of sophistication. Over forty treaty texts survive, spanning the entire imperial period and revealing evolving diplomatic practices. Early treaties under Hattušili I were brief and focused primarily on military matters, while later treaties became increasingly comprehensive.

The Egyptian-Hittite peace treaty of 1259 BCE between Hattušili III and Ramesses II represents the pinnacle of this tradition. Remarkably, versions survive in both Hittite and Egyptian, allowing comparison of diplomatic perspectives. The treaty established "good peace and good brotherhood" between the former enemies, including provisions for mutual defense, extradition of fugitives, and amnesty for refugees:

"If an enemy comes against the land of Hatti, and Hattušili, king of Hatti, sends to me saying: 'Come to me to help me against him,' then Ramesses, the great king, king of Egypt, shall send his troops and his chariots to kill this enemy and to satisfy the desire of Hatti."

Vassal treaties followed a standard structure including historical prologue, stipulations, divine witnesses, and curses for violation. The treaty with Alaksandu of Wilusa (possibly Troy) from the reign of Muwatalli II illustrates how the Hittites balanced imperial control with recognition of local autonomy:

"If someone revolts against My Majesty, and you, Alaksandu, hear of it, march forth with your infantry and chariotry... If you cannot march forth yourself, send your infantry and chariotry with a trusted commander."

These texts reveal sophisticated understanding of international relations, balancing power politics with legal principles in a manner that foreshadows much later developments in international law.

Diplomatic Correspondence

The Amarna letters (14th century BCE) and Hittite archives preserve extensive diplomatic correspondence between the "Great Kings" of the Late Bronze Age. These letters followed strict protocols reflecting relative status. Equal rulers addressed each other as "brother," while subordinate kings were "sons" of the Great King.

A letter from Hattušili III to Kadashman-Enlil II of Babylon demonstrates the formal, sometimes prickly nature of this correspondence:

"Why, my brother, have you written to me saying: 'You did not write to me about your well-being, and you did not send your messenger to me'? For many days I had been ill, my brother, and for this reason I did not write to you about my well-being."

The correspondence covers topics from marriage negotiations to trade disputes, revealing the complex interdependence of Bronze Age kingdoms. A particularly dramatic example comes from the "Tawagalawa Letter" (possibly written by Hattušili III to the king of Ahhiyawa), which discusses tensions over the frontier region of western Anatolia and a troublesome rebel named Piyamaradu:

"Concerning Piyamaradu—he has been a fugitive from the land of Hatti for twenty years... Now he has taken refuge with you. If you wish to maintain good relations with me, either hand him over to me, or expel him from your land."

These letters reveal the day-to-day management of international relations, showing how formal diplomatic structures operated in practice.

Religious Texts

Religious texts constitute the largest category of Hittite documents, reflecting the central importance of proper ritual practice in maintaining cosmic order and divine favor.

Festival Texts

Detailed instructions for religious festivals account for nearly half the surviving Hittite texts. These documents prescribed every aspect of ceremonies that could last from one day to several months, specifying offerings, participants, movements, and recitations. The AN.TAH.ŠUM spring festival, lasting 38 days, required the king's presence at multiple locations:

"On the fifth day they prepare the road to Arinna. The king goes to Arinna and performs the great assembly. They set up the throne of the Storm-God and the throne of the Sun-goddess of Arinna... The king offers bread and libates wine to the Storm-God and the Sun-goddess."

These texts reveal a religious system focused on precise ritual performance rather than theological speculation. They also document the Hittite practice of incorporating deities from conquered regions into state worship, creating what scholars call the "thousand gods of Hatti."

Prayers and Hymns

Hittite prayers often addressed specific crises, particularly plagues and military defeats interpreted as divine punishment. The "Plague Prayers of Muršili II" represent some of the most moving examples, composed during a devastating epidemic that followed his father's violation of a treaty oath:

"What is this that you have done, O gods? A plague you have let into the land of Hatti, and the land of Hatti has been badly oppressed by the plague. For twenty years now people have been dying in my father's time and in my brother's time and in mine... The matter of the plague weighs heavily upon me."

These prayers combine formal invocation with personal appeals, revealing the emotional dimension of Hittite religious practice. They also demonstrate sophisticated theological reflection, wrestling with questions of divine justice and human responsibility.

Mythological Texts

Hittite scribes recorded myths from multiple cultural traditions, creating a valuable corpus of ancient Near Eastern mythology. The "Disappearance of Telipinu" exemplifies indigenous Anatolian mythology, describing how the anger of the vegetation god Telipinu causes cosmic disruption:

"Mist seized the windows. Smoke seized the house. On the hearth the logs were stifled. On the altars the gods were stifled. In the fold the sheep were stifled. In the corral the cows were stifled. The sheep refused her lamb. The cow refused her calf."

The myth concludes with elaborate rituals to soothe Telipinu's anger and restore natural and social order. Other myths show Mesopotamian or Hurrian influence, including the Kumarbi Cycle, which describes divine succession and cosmic conflict in ways that parallel the later Greek Theogony of Hesiod.

Ritual Texts

Practical ritual texts address specific problems through magical procedures. The ritual of Tunnawi for patients suffering from impurity prescribes elaborate symbolic actions:

"She takes a dog, a puppy, and a small pig. She waves them over the patient and speaks as follows: 'Whatever evil Tongue has been set against this person, now I have taken it away. I have taken the dog to track it down, I have taken the puppy to dig it up, I have taken the pig to root it out.'"

These texts reveal how ordinary Hittites sought to manage misfortune through ritual specialists, complementing the state religious system with more immediate, practical approaches to supernatural power.

Legal and Administrative Texts

The Hittite archives include extensive documentation of legal principles and administrative practices that governed daily life throughout the empire.

The Hittite Laws

The Hittite law code, compiled in the Old Kingdom and periodically revised, addresses criminal and civil matters with remarkable sophistication. Unlike the contemporary Code of Hammurabi, which frequently prescribed death for property crimes, Hittite law emphasized compensation over retribution:

"If anyone blinds a free person or knocks out his tooth, formerly they would pay 40 shekels of silver, but now he shall pay 20 shekels of silver."

The laws show particular concern for agricultural matters, with detailed provisions regarding field boundaries, irrigation, and livestock theft. They also reveal changing social values, as the phrase "but now" indicates legal reforms reducing penalties over time.

Land Grants

The Hittite kings controlled vast territories which they allocated to supporters through formal land grants inscribed on metal tablets. These documents specified boundaries, tax obligations, and inheritance provisions:

"The Great King Tudhaliya has given to Šahurunuwa, son of Šarpa, the city of Ištalubba with its territory, fields, meadows, vineyards, threshing floors, and personnel... It is exempt from the corvée obligation, from the military service obligation, and from the messenger service."

These texts reveal how the Hittite state managed resources and rewarded loyalty, creating networks of obligation that bound elites to the crown.

Inventories and Administrative Records

Day-to-day administration generated thousands of inventory lists, personnel records, and resource allocations. Though less dramatic than historical or religious texts, these documents provide crucial information about economic organization and administrative practices:

"5 garments of fine quality, 10 garments of standard quality, 3 copper vessels, 2 silver cups, 10 sheep, 5 measures of wine: tribute from the city of Hurma."

Such texts reveal the extensive bureaucratic apparatus that supported the Hittite state, tracking resources across the empire and documenting the flow of goods through the palace economy.

Literary and Wisdom Texts

Though primarily concerned with practical matters of governance and ritual, Hittite scribes also preserved works that might be considered literary or wisdom literature.

The "Song of Release"

This Hurro-Hittite composition combines narrative, dialogue, and ethical reflection in a complex text addressing themes of debt, freedom, and social justice. Set in the Syrian city of Ebla, it describes a conflict between the king and city assembly over debt amnesty:

"If you do not release the people of Ebla, I shall release them myself... I shall break open the storehouses. I shall split open the sealed granaries of the palace."

Though fragmentary, this text represents a rare example of social criticism in ancient Near Eastern literature, suggesting tensions between royal authority and community values.

Wisdom Literature

Hittite wisdom texts include proverb collections and instructional literature similar to those found in other ancient cultures. A collection of Hittite proverbs includes observations on human-nature and social relations:

"The contented person does not see his own abundance. The hungry person does not see his own emaciation."

These texts reflect the practical wisdom and ethical values that guided Hittite society beyond formal legal and religious prescriptions.

Conclusion

The textual legacy of the Hittites provides an extraordinarily rich resource for understanding not only this particular civilization but the broader cultural and political world of the Late Bronze Age Near East. From grand diplomatic treaties to humble administrative receipts, from elaborate ritual instructions to moving personal prayers, these texts reveal a complex society negotiating the challenges of imperial governance, international relations, and religious obligation.

The careful preservation of these documents by Hittite scribes, and their remarkable survival for over three millennia, allows us to hear authentic voices from this long-vanished civilization. As archaeological research continues and new texts are discovered and deciphered, our understanding of the Hittites continues to deepen, revealing an increasingly nuanced picture of one of antiquity's most significant yet long-forgotten empires.

BIBLIOGRAPHY

Primary Sources

Cuneiform Texts and Translations

Beckman, Gary. 1999. *Hittite Diplomatic Texts*. Second edition. Society of Biblical Literature Writings from the Ancient World Series 7. Atlanta: Scholars Press.

Beckman, Gary, Trevor Bryce, and Eric Cline. 2011. *The Ahhiyawa Texts*. Society of Biblical Literature Writings from the Ancient World Series 28. Atlanta: Society of Biblical Literature.

Collins, Billie Jean. 2003. *Hittite Ritual: A Catalog*. Society of Biblical Literature Resources for Biblical Study 49. Atlanta: Society of Biblical Literature.

Goedegebuure, Petra. 2014. *The Hittite Demonstratives: Studies in Deixis, Topics and Focus*. Studien zu den Boğazköy-Texten 55. Wiesbaden: Harrassowitz.

Güterbock, Hans G., and Theo P.J. van den Hout. 1991-2014. *The Hittite Dictionary of the Oriental Institute of the University of Chicago (CHD)*. Chicago: The Oriental Institute of the University of Chicago.

Hoffner, Harry A., Jr. 1997. *The Laws of the Hittites: A Critical Edition*. Documenta et Monumenta Orientis Antiqui 23. Leiden: Brill.

Hoffner, Harry A., Jr. 1998. *Hittite Myths*. Second edition. Society of Biblical Literature Writings from the Ancient World Series 2. Atlanta: Scholars Press.

Hoffner, Harry A., Jr. 2009. *Letters from the Hittite Kingdom*. Society of Biblical Literature Writings from the Ancient World Series 15. Atlanta: Society of Biblical Literature.

Laroche, Emmanuel. 1971. *Catalogue des textes hittites*. Paris: Klincksieck.

Miller, Jared L. 2013. *Royal Hittite Instructions and Related Administrative Texts*. Society of Biblical Literature Writings from the Ancient World Series 31. Atlanta: Society of Biblical Literature.

Mouton, Alice. 2007. *Rêves hittites: Contribution à une histoire et une anthropologie du rêve en Anatolie ancienne*. Leiden: Brill.

Puhvel, Jaan. 1984-2013. *Hittite Etymological Dictionary*. 10 vols. Berlin: Mouton de Gruyter.

Singer, Itamar. 2002. *Hittite Prayers*. Society of Biblical Literature Writings from the Ancient World Series 11. Atlanta: Society of Biblical Literature.

Ünal, Ahmet. 2007. *Multilinguales Handwörterbuch des Hethitischen / A Concise Multilingual Hittite Dictionary / Hititçe Çok Dilli El Sözlüğü*. Hamburg: Kovač.

Archaeological Reports

Bachhuber, Christoph, and R. Gareth Roberts, eds. 2009. *Forces of Transformation: The End of the Bronze Age in the Mediterranean*. Oxford: Oxbow Books.

Bittel, Kurt. 1970. *Hattusha: The Capital of the Hittites*. Oxford: Oxford University Press.

Bittel, Kurt, Hans G. Güterbock, Hans Hauptmann, and Harald Kühne. 1975-1989. *Das hethitische Felsheiligtum Yazılıkaya*. Berlin: Mann.

Genz, Hermann, and Dirk Paul Mielke, eds. 2011. *Insights into Hittite History and Archaeology*. Colloquia Antiqua 2. Leuven: Peeters.

Hawkins, J. David. 2000. *Corpus of Hieroglyphic Luwian Inscriptions, Volume I: Inscriptions of the Iron Age*. Berlin: Walter de Gruyter.

Herbordt, Suzanne. 2005. *Die Prinzen- und Beamtensiegel der hethitischen Grossreichszeit auf Tonbullen aus dem Nişantepe-Archiv in Hattuša*. Boğazköy-Hattuša 19. Mainz: Philipp von Zabern.

Mielke, Dirk Paul, Ulf-Dietrich Schoop, and Jürgen Seeher, eds. 2006. *Strukturierung und Datierung in der hethitischen Archäologie / Structuring and Dating in Hittite Archaeology*. Byzas 4. Istanbul: Ege Yayınları.

Neve, Peter. 1993. *Ḫattuša – Stadt der Götter und Tempel: Neue Ausgrabungen in der Hauptstadt der Hethiter*. Mainz: Philipp von Zabern.

Ökse, A. Tuba. 2011. *Open-Air Sanctuaries of the Hittites: An Archaeological and Philological Study*. BAR International Series 2308. Oxford: Archaeopress.

Özgüç, Tahsin. 2003. *Kültepe Kaniš/Neša: The Earliest International Trade Center and the Oldest Capital City of the Hittites*. Istanbul: Middle Eastern Culture Center in Japan.

Schachner, Andreas. 2011-2019. *Die Ausgrabungen in Boğazköy-Hattuša*. Archäologischer Anzeiger. Berlin: Deutsches Archäologisches Institut.

Seeher, Jürgen. 2006. *Gods Carved in Stone: The Hittite Rock Sanctuary of Yazılıkaya*. Istanbul: Ege Yayınları.

Seeher, Jürgen. 2011. *The Plateau: The City of Hattuša – Hittite Capital*. Istanbul: Ege Yayınları.

Summers, Geoffrey D. 1993. *Tille Höyük 3: The Iron Age*. British Institute of Archaeology at Ankara Monograph 15. London: British Institute of Archaeology at Ankara.

Secondary Scholarship

Monographs

Alparslan, Metin, ed. 2017. *Places and Spaces in Hittite Anatolia I: Hatti and the East*. Istanbul: Türk Eskiçağ Bilimleri Enstitüsü.

Beckman, Gary. 1983. *Hittite Birth Rituals*. Second revised edition. Studien zu den Boğazköy-Texten 29. Wiesbaden: Harrassowitz.

Beckman, Gary. 1989. *The Religion of the Hittites*. Biblical Archaeologist 52/2-3: 98-108.

Beal, Richard H. 1992. *The Organisation of the Hittite Military*. Texte der Hethiter 20. Heidelberg: Winter.

Beckman, Gary, Richard Beal, and Gregory McMahon, eds. 2003. *Hittite Studies in Honor of Harry A. Hoffner Jr. on the Occasion of His 65th Birthday*. Winona Lake, IN: Eisenbrauns.

Bryce, Trevor. 2002. *Life and Society in the Hittite World*. Oxford: Oxford University Press.

Bryce, Trevor. 2005. *The Kingdom of the Hittites*. New edition. Oxford: Oxford University Press.

Bryce, Trevor. 2012. *The World of the Neo-Hittite Kingdoms: A Political and Military History*. Oxford: Oxford University Press.

Burney, Charles. 2004. *Historical Dictionary of the Hittites*. Lanham, MD: Scarecrow Press.

Collins, Billie Jean. 2007. *The Hittites and Their World*. Archaeology and Biblical Studies 7. Atlanta: Society of Biblical Literature.

de Martino, Stefano. 2016. *Da Kussara a Karkemish: storia del regno ittita*. Torino: Università degli studi di Torino.

Dinçol, Ali M., and Belkıs Dinçol. 2008. *Die Prinzen- und Beamtensiegel aus der Oberstadt von Boğazköy-Hattuša vom 16. Jahrhundert bis zum Ende der Grossreichszeit*. Boğazköy-Hattuša 22. Mainz: Philipp von Zabern.

Durnford, Stephen P.B., and Jonathan D. Akeroyd. 2005. *Anatolian Weather Gods and Ancient Chronology: A Reconsideration*. Anatolian Studies 55: 1-16.

Gilan, Amir. 2015. *Formen und Inhalte althethitischer historischer Literatur*. Texte der Hethiter 29. Heidelberg: Winter.

Giorgieri, Mauro, and Clelia Mora. 2010. *Aspetti della regalità ittita nel XIII secolo a.C.* Como: New Press.

Glatz, Claudia. 2009. *Empire as Network: Spheres of Material Interaction in Late Bronze Age Anatolia*. Journal of Anthropological Archaeology 28/2: 127-141.

Goedegebuure, Petra. 2008. *Central Anatolian Languages and Language Communities in the Colony Period: A Luwian-Hattian Symbiosis and the Independent Hittites*. In Anatolia and the Jazira during the Old Assyrian Period, edited by J.G. Dercksen, 137-180. Leiden: Nederlands Instituut voor het Nabije Oosten.

Gordin, Shai. 2015. *Hittite Scribal Circles: Scholarly Tradition and Writing Habits*. Studien zu den Boğazköy-Texten 59. Wiesbaden: Harrassowitz.

Haas, Volkert. 1994. *Geschichte der hethitischen Religion*. Handbuch der Orientalistik I/15. Leiden: Brill.

Hawkins, J. David. 2002. *Anatolia: The End of the Hittite Empire and After*. In Die nahöstlichen Kulturen und Griechenland an der Wende vom 2. zum 1. Jahrtausend v. Chr., edited by E.A. Braun-Holzinger and H. Matthäus, 143-151. Möhnesee: Bibliopolis.

Hoffner, Harry A., Jr. 2001. *Some Thoughts on Merchants and Trade in the Hittite Kingdom*. In Kulturgeschichten: Altorientalistische Studien für Volkert Haas zum 65. Geburtstag, edited by T. Richter, D. Prechel, and J. Klinger, 179-189. Saarbrücken: Saarbrücker Druckerei und Verlag.

Hoffner, Harry A., Jr., and H. Craig Melchert. 2008. *A Grammar of the Hittite Language*. Winona Lake, IN: Eisenbrauns.

Hout, Theo van den. 2011. *The Elements of Hittite*. Cambridge: Cambridge University Press.

Klengel, Horst. 1999. *Geschichte des hethitischen Reiches*. Handbuch der Orientalistik I/34. Leiden: Brill.

Klinger, Jörg. 2005. *Die Hethiter*. Munich: C.H. Beck.

Košak, Silvin. 1982. *Hittite Inventory Texts (CTH 241-250)*. Texte der Hethiter 10. Heidelberg: Winter.

Larsen, Mogens Trolle. 2015. *Ancient Kanesh: A Merchant Colony in Bronze Age Anatolia*. Cambridge: Cambridge University Press.

Lehmann, Johannes. 2016. *The Hittites: People of a Thousand Gods*. London: Reaktion Books.

Liverani, Mario. 2014. *The Ancient Near East: History, Society and Economy*. London: Routledge.

Macqueen, James G. 1986. *The Hittites and Their Contemporaries in Asia Minor*. Revised edition. London: Thames and Hudson.

Marazzi, Massimiliano. 1990. *Il geroglifico anatolico: problemi di analisi e prospettive di ricerca*. Rome: Università degli Studi "La Sapienza".

McMahon, Gregory. 1991. *The Hittite State Cult of the Tutelary Deities*. Assyriological Studies 25. Chicago: The Oriental Institute of the University of Chicago.

Melchert, H. Craig, ed. 2003. *The Luwians*. Handbuch der Orientalistik I/68. Leiden: Brill.

Mora, Clelia. 1987. *La glittica anatolica del II millennio A.C.: classificazione tipologica*. Pavia: Gianni Iuculano.

Mouton, Alice, Ian Rutherford, and Ilya Yakubovich, eds. 2013. *Luwian Identities: Culture, Language and Religion Between Anatolia and the Aegean*. Leiden: Brill.

Neu, Erich. 1974. *Der Anitta-Text*. Studien zu den Boğazköy-Texten 18. Wiesbaden: Harrassowitz.

Otten, Heinrich. 1988. *Die Bronzetafel aus Boğazköy: Ein Staatsvertrag Tuthalijas IV*. Studien zu den Boğazköy-Texten Beiheft 1. Wiesbaden: Harrassowitz.

Rieken, Elisabeth. 1999. *Untersuchungen zur nominalen Stammbildung des Hethitischen*. Studien zu den Boğazköy-Texten 44. Wiesbaden: Harrassowitz.

Schachner, Andreas. 2011. *Hattuscha: Auf der Suche nach dem sagenhaften Großreich der Hethiter*. Munich: C.H. Beck.

Schoop, Ulf-Dietrich. 2003. *Pottery Traditions of the Later Hittite Empire: Problems of Definition*. In Identifying Changes: The Transition from Bronze to Iron Ages in Anatolia and its Neighbouring Regions, edited by B. Fischer, H. Genz, É. Jean, and K. Köroğlu, 167-178. Istanbul: Türk Eskiçağ Bilimleri Enstitüsü.

Singer, Itamar. 1996. *Muwatalli's Prayer to the Assembly of Gods Through the Storm-God of Lightning*. Atlanta: Scholars Press.

Singer, Itamar. 2011. *The Calm before the Storm: Selected Writings of Itamar Singer on the Late Bronze Age in Anatolia and the Levant*. Atlanta: Society of Biblical Literature.

Soysal, Oğuz. 2004. *Hattischer Wortschatz in hethitischer Textüberlieferung*. Handbuch der Orientalistik I/74. Leiden: Brill.

Taracha, Piotr. 2009. *Religions of Second Millennium Anatolia*. Wiesbaden: Harrassowitz.

Tischler, Johann. 1977-2016. *Hethitisches Etymologisches Glossar*. Innsbruck: Institut für Sprachen und Literaturen der Universität Innsbruck.

Weeden, Mark. 2011. *Hittite Logograms and Hittite Scholarship*. Studien zu den Boğazköy-Texten 54. Wiesbaden: Harrassowitz.

Yakubovich, Ilya. 2010. *Sociolinguistics of the Luvian Language*. Leiden: Brill.

Yener, K. Aslıhan. 2005. *The Amuq Valley Regional Projects, Volume 1: Surveys in the Plain of Antioch and Orontes Delta, Turkey, 1995-2002*. Chicago: Oriental Institute of the University of Chicago.

Articles and Book Chapters

Alparslan, Metin. 2011. "The History of the Hittite Alphabet: Current Status of Research." In *Hittite Studies in Honor of Harry A. Hoffner Jr. on the Occasion of His 65th Birthday*, edited by G. Beckman, R. Beal, and G. McMahon, 21-29. Winona Lake, IN: Eisenbrauns.

Archi, Alfonso. 2010. "When Did the Hittites Begin to Write in Hittite?" In *Pax Hethitica: Studies on the Hittites and Their Neighbours in Honour of Itamar Singer*, edited by Y. Cohen, A. Gilan, and J.L. Miller, 37-46. Wiesbaden: Harrassowitz.

Bachhuber, Christoph. 2013. "James Mellaart and the Luwians: A Culture-(Pre)history." In *Luwian Identities: Culture, Language and Religion Between Anatolia and the Aegean*, edited by A. Mouton, I. Rutherford, and I. Yakubovich, 279-304. Leiden: Brill.

Balza, Maria Elena. 2012. "Sealed Tablets from Hattuša." In *Organization, Representation, and Symbols of Power in the Ancient Near East*, edited by G. Wilhelm, 451-463. Winona Lake, IN: Eisenbrauns.

Beal, Richard H. 2011. "Hittite Anatolia: A Political History." In *The Oxford Handbook of Ancient Anatolia*, edited by S.R. Steadman and G. McMahon, 579-603. Oxford: Oxford University Press.

Beckman, Gary. 1982. "The Hittite Assembly." Journal of the American Oriental Society 102/3: 435-442.

Beckman, Gary. 1995. "Royal Ideology and State Administration in Hittite Anatolia." In *Civilizations of the Ancient Near East*, edited by J.M. Sasson, 529-543. New York: Scribner.

Beckman, Gary. 2003. "International Law in the Second Millennium: Late Bronze Age." In *A History of Ancient Near Eastern Law*, edited by R. Westbrook, 753-774. Leiden: Brill.

Bryce, Trevor. 2003. "History." In *The Luwians*, edited by H.C. Melchert, 27-127. Leiden: Brill.

Bryce, Trevor. 2007. "The Secession of Tarhuntašša." In *Tabularia Hethaeorum: Hethitologische Beiträge Silvin Košak zum 65. Geburtstag*, edited by D. Groddek and M. Zorman, 119-129. Wiesbaden: Harrassowitz.

Cammarosano, Michele. 2013. "Hittite Cult Inventories—Part Two: The Dating of the Texts and the Alleged 'Cult Reorganization' of Tudhaliya IV." Altorientalische Forschungen 40/2: 195-219.

Cohen, Yoram. 2009. *The Scribes and Scholars of the City of Emar in the Late Bronze Age*. Harvard Semitic Studies 59. Winona Lake, IN: Eisenbrauns.

Collins, Billie Jean. 2005. "A Statue for the Deity: Cult Images in Hittite Anatolia." In *Cult Image and Divine Representation in the Ancient Near East*, edited by N.H. Walls, 13-42. Boston: American Schools of Oriental Research.

d'Alfonso, Lorenzo. 2010. "Geo-Archaeological Survey in Northern Tyanitis and the Ancient History of Southern Cappadocia." In *Proceedings of the 6th International Congress of Hittitology*, edited by A. Süel, 219-232. Ankara: Çorum Valiliği.

Dardano, Paola. 2002. "La main est coupable, le sang devient abondant: sur quelques expressions avec des noms de parties et d'éléments du corps humain dans la littérature juridico-politique de l'Ancien et du Moyen Royaume hittite." Orientalia 71/4: 333-392.

de Martino, Stefano. 2010. "Symbols of Power in the Late Hittite Kingdom." In *Pax Hethitica: Studies on the Hittites and Their Neighbours in Honour of Itamar Singer*, edited by Y. Cohen, A. Gilan, and J.L. Miller, 87-98. Wiesbaden: Harrassowitz.

Doğan-Alparslan, Meltem, and Metin Alparslan. 2011. "Wohnsitze und Hauptstädte der hethitischen Könige." Istanbuler Mitteilungen 61: 85-103.

Forlanini, Massimo. 2008. "The Historical Geography of Anatolia and the Transition from the Kārum-Period to the Early Hittite Empire." In *Anatolia and the Jazira during the Old Assyrian Period*, edited by J.G. Dercksen, 57-86. Leiden: Nederlands Instituut voor het Nabije Oosten.

Genz, Hermann. 2006. "Imports and Their Distribution in Early Hittite Anatolia." In *Strukturierung und Datierung in der hethitischen Archäologie*, edited by D.P. Mielke, U.-D. Schoop, and J. Seeher, 185-199. Istanbul: Ege Yayınları.

Gilan, Amir. 2011. "Hittite Religious Rituals and the Ideology of Kingship." Religion Compass 5/7: 276-285.

Glatz, Claudia, and Roger Matthews. 2005. "Anthropology of a Frontier Zone: Hittite-Kaska Relations in Late Bronze Age North-Central Anatolia." Bulletin of the American Schools of Oriental Research 339: 47-65.

Gordin, Shai. 2010. "The Tablet and its Scribe: Between Archival and Scribal Spaces in Late Empire Period Hattuša." Altorientalische Forschungen 37/2: 285-305.

Güterbock, Hans G. 1983. "Hittite Historiography: A Survey." In *History, Historiography and Interpretation: Studies in Biblical and Cuneiform Literatures*, edited by H. Tadmor and M. Weinfeld, 21-35. Jerusalem: Magnes Press.

Haas, Volkert. 2006. "Die hethitische Literatur: Texte, Stilistik, Motive." Berlin: Walter de Gruyter.

Harmanşah, Ömür. 2015. "Stone Worlds: Technologies of Rock Carving and Place-Making in Anatolian Landscapes." In *The Cambridge Prehistory of the Bronze and Iron Age Mediterranean*, edited by A.B. Knapp and P. van Dommelen, 379-393. Cambridge: Cambridge University Press.

Hawkins, J. David. 1995. "The Hieroglyphic Inscription of the Sacred Pool Complex at Hattuša (SÜDBURG)." Studien zu den Boğazköy-Texten Beiheft 3. Wiesbaden: Harrassowitz.

Hawkins, J. David. 1998. "Tarkasnawa King of Mira: 'Tarkondemos', Boğazköy Sealings and Karabel." Anatolian Studies 48: 1-31.

Hoffner, Harry A., Jr. 1997. "Perspectives on Hittite Civilization: Selected Writings of Hans Gustav Güterbock." Assyriological Studies 26. Chicago: The Oriental Institute of the University of Chicago.

Houwink ten Cate, Philo H.J. 1995-1996. "The Genealogy of Mursilis II: The Difference between a Legalistic and a Genealogical Approach to the Descent of Suppuliumas I." Jaarbericht Ex Oriente Lux 34: 51-72.

Imparati, Fiorella. 1995. "Private Life Among the Hittites." In *Civilizations of the Ancient Near East*, edited by J.M. Sasson, 571-586. New York: Scribner.

Klinger, Jörg. 2005. "Herrschaftsideologie und politische Geschichte im Aleppo-Vertrag (CTH 75)." In *Motivation und Mechanismen des Kulturkontaktes in der späten Bronzezeit*, edited by D. Prechel, 183-196. Florence: LoGisma.

Košak, Silvin. 1995. "The Palace Library 'Building A' on Büyükkale." In *Studio historiae ardens: Ancient Near Eastern Studies Presented to Philo H.J. Houwink ten Cate*, edited by T.P.J. van den Hout and J. de Roos, 173-179. Leiden: Nederlands Instituut voor het Nabije Oosten.

Kryszeń, Adam. 2016. "A Historical Geography of the Hittite Heartland." Alter Orient und Altes Testament 437. Münster: Ugarit-Verlag.

Laroche, Emmanuel. 1966. "Les noms des Hittites." Paris: Klincksieck.

Matessi, Alvise. 2016. "The Making of Hittite Imperial Landscapes: Territoriality and Balance of Power in South-Central Anatolia during the Late Bronze Age." Journal of Ancient Near Eastern History 3/2: 117-162.

Melchert, H. Craig. 2011. "Hittite *huek-zi* 'slaughters' vs. hunikzi 'batters': Lexical Differentiation and the Development of the Neo-Hittite Hieroglyphic Writing System." Aramazd: Armenian Journal of Near Eastern Studies 6/1: 25-34.

Miller, Jared L. 2004. "Studies in the Origins, Development and Interpretation of the Kizzuwatna Rituals." Studien zu den Boğazköy-Texten 46. Wiesbaden: Harrassowitz.

Mora, Clelia. 2004. "Sigilli e sigillature di Karkemiš in età imperiale ittita." In *Cingano-Ghezzi*, edited by E. Acquaro and P. Callieri, 27-43. Rome: L'Erma di Bretschneider.

Moran, William L. 1992. *The Amarna Letters*. Baltimore: Johns Hopkins University Press.

Mouton, Alice. 2007. "Anatomie animale: le festin carné des dieux d'après les textes hittites I. Les membres antérieurs." Colloquium Anatolicum 6: 131-154.

Müller-Karpe, Andreas. 2009. "Recent Research on Hittite Archaeology in the 'Upper Land'." In *Central-North Anatolia in the Hittite Period: New Perspectives in Light of Recent Research*, edited by F. Pecchioli Daddi, G. Torri, and C. Corti, 109-117. Rome: Herder.

Otten, Heinrich. 1981. *Die Apologie Ḫattušilis III: Das Bild der Überlieferung*. Studien zu den Boğazköy-Texten 24. Wiesbaden: Harrassowitz.

Puhvel, Jaan. 1991. "Names and Numbers of the Pleiad in Hittite and Luwian." Zeitschrift für vergleichende Sprachforschung 104/1: 81-89.

Rieken, Elisabeth. 2009. "Die Tontafelfunde aus Kayalıpınar." In *Central-North Anatolia in the Hittite Period: New Perspectives in Light of Recent Research*, edited by F. Pecchioli Daddi, G. Torri, and C. Corti, 119-143. Rome: Herder.

Rutherford, Ian. 2001. "The Song of the Sea (ŠA A.AB.BA SÌR): Thoughts on KUB 45.63." In *Akten des IV. Internationalen Kongresses für Hethitologie*, edited by G. Wilhelm, 598-609. Wiesbaden: Harrassowitz.

Schachner, Andreas. 2017. "Hattusha: A Cult Center for the Hittite Storm-God and a City Sacred to the Sun-Goddess of Arinna." In *Sacred Landscapes of Hittites and Luwians*, edited by A. Mouton, 93-112. Oxford: Archaeopress.

Singer, Itamar. 1984. "The AGRIG in the Hittite Texts." Anatolian Studies 34: 97-127.

Singer, Itamar. 2006. "Ships Bound for Lukka: A New Interpretation of the Companion Letters RS 94.2530 and RS 94.2523." Altorientalische Forschungen 33/2: 242-262.

Soysal, Oğuz. 2005. "On the Origin of the Royal Title Tabarna / labarna." Anatolica 31: 189-209.

Starke, Frank. 1996. "Zur 'Regierung' des hethitischen Staates." Zeitschrift für Altorientalische und Biblische Rechtsgeschichte 2: 140-182.

Summers, Geoffrey D., and Erol Özen. 2012. "The Hittite Stone and Sculpture Quarry at Karakız Kasabası and Hapis Boğazı in the District of Sorgun, Yozgat, Central Anatolia." American Journal of Archaeology 116/3: 507-519.

Süel, Aygül. 2009. "Another Capital of the Hittite State: Šapinuwa." In *Central-North Anatolia in the Hittite Period: New Perspectives in Light of Recent Research*, edited by F. Pecchioli Daddi, G. Torri, and C. Corti, 193-205. Rome: Herder.

Taracha, Piotr. 2008. "The Capital Hattuša and Other Residential Cities of Hittite Great Kings." In *Proceedings of the 51st Rencontre Assyriologique Internationale*, edited by R.J. van der Spek, 555-564. Leiden: Nederlands Instituut voor het Nabije Oosten.

Ünal, Ahmet. 1988. "'You Should Build for Eternity': New Light on the Hittite Architects and their Work." Journal of Cuneiform Studies 40/1: 97-106.

van den Hout, Theo P.J. 2002. "Tombs and Memorials: The (Divine) Stone-House and Hegur Reconsidered." In *Recent Developments in Hittite Archaeology and History: Papers in Memory of Hans G. Güterbock*, edited by K.A. Yener and H.A. Hoffner Jr., 73-91. Winona Lake, IN: Eisenbrauns.

van den Hout, Theo P.J. 2007. "Institutions, Vernaculars, Publics: The Case of Second-Millennium Anatolia." In *Ancient Near Eastern Studies in Memory of H.I.J. Vanstiphout*, edited by R. de Boer and J.G. Dercksen, 217-256. Leiden: Nederlands Instituut voor het Nabije Oosten.

Weeden, Mark. 2013. "After the Hittites: The Kingdoms of Karkamish and Palistin in Northern Syria." Bulletin of the Institute of Classical Studies 56/2: 1-20.

Wilhelm, Gernot. 2004. "Generation Count in Hittite Chronology." In *Mesopotamian Dark Age Revisited*, edited by H. Hunger and R. Pruzsinszky, 71-79. Vienna: Verlag der Österreichischen Akademie der Wissenschaften.

COMING SOON...

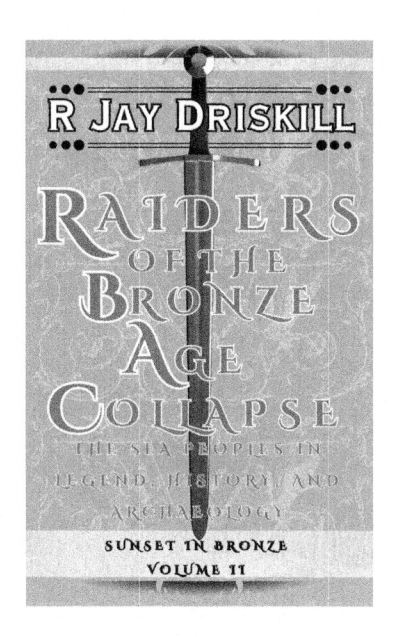

Sunset in Bronze Volume II
Raiders of the Bronze Age Collapse: The Sea Peoples in Legend, History, and Archaeology

Around 1200 BCE, the ancient world erupted in chaos. Mighty empires that had dominated the Mediterranean for centuries—the Hittites, Mycenaeans, and others—suddenly vanished from history. Cities burned, trade networks collapsed, and entire civilizations crumbled into dust. At the center of this apocalyptic transformation were the mysterious Sea Peoples, maritime raiders whose very identity remains one of archaeology's greatest puzzles.

Who were these enigmatic invaders? Where did they come from, and what drove them to unleash such devastating destruction across the ancient Mediterranean? Archaeological evidence paints a picture of coordinated attacks, mass migrations, and technological warfare that forever changed the course of human history.

Drawing on cutting-edge archaeological discoveries and ancient texts, archaeologist R Jay Driskill reconstructs this pivotal moment when the Bronze Age world died and the Iron Age was born. From the burning ruins of Ugarit to the desperate hieroglyphic accounts of Egyptian pharaohs, *Raiders of the Bronze Age Collapse* reveals how these phantom warriors triggered the first "dark age" and reshaped civilization itself.

Prepare to witness the catastrophic end of the ancient world—and discover why the Sea Peoples' legacy still echoes through history today.

R Jay Driskill is an archaeologist and an ardent explorer of history's deepest mysteries, bringing ancient worlds to life through compelling non-fiction and fiction. With a background rooted at the University of Florida, Driskill meticulously researches each story, blending scholarly insight with thrilling narratives that transport readers across millennia.

Whether you're fascinated by ancient civilizations, historical fiction, or thrilling archaeological mysteries, R Jay Driskill offers meticulously crafted stories that entertain, educate, and keep you turning pages late into the night.

Explore his books today and embark on an adventure through time!

Read more at https://rjaydriskill.com/

If you enjoyed Kings of Stone, please review at your vendor of choice.

Printed in Dunstable, United Kingdom